BURMESE HAZE

US POLICY AND MYANMAR'S
OPENING—AND CLOSING

BURMESE HAZE

US POLICY AND MYANMAR'S OPENING—AND CLOSING

Erin Murphy

Published by the Association for Asian Studies
Asia Shorts, Number 12
www.asianstudies.org

The Association for Asian Studies (AAS)

Formed in 1941, the Association for Asian Studies (AAS)—the largest society of its kind, with approximately 6,000 members worldwide—is a scholarly, non-political, non-profit professional association open to all persons interested in Asia. For further information, please visit www.asianstudies.org.

Published by Association for Asian Studies, 825 Victors Way, Suite 310, Ann Arbor, MI 48108 USA

Cover image: "Perserverance" by Sue Htet Aung (2017).

Cataloging-in-Publication Data is available from the Library of Congress.

ASIA
SHORTS

"ASIA SHORTS" offers concise, engagingly-written titles written by highly-qualified authors on topics of significance in Asian studies. Topics are intended to be substantive, generate discussion and debate within the field, and attract interest beyond it.

The AAS is exploring new ways of making rigorous, timely, and accessible work by scholars in the field available to a wide audience of informed readers. This new series complements and leverages the success of the pedagogically-oriented AAS series, "Key Issues in Asian Studies," and is designed to engage broad audiences with up-to-date scholarship on important topics in Asian studies.

"Asia Shorts" books:

- Have a clear point of view, a well-defined, and even provocative, argument rooted in a strong base of evidence and current scholarship.

- Are written in an accessible, jargon-free style suitable for non-specialist audiences.

- Are written by a single author or a small group of authors (scholars, journalists, or policymakers).

- Are rigorously peer reviewed.

For further information, visit the AAS website: www.asianstudies.org.

AAS books are distributed by Columbia University Press.

For orders or inquiries, please visit https://cup.columbia.edu

COLUMBIA
UNIVERSITY
PRESS

To acronyms

*We walk about under a load of memories which we long
to share and somehow never can.*

— George Orwell, *Burmese Days*

This is Burma, and it will be quite unlike any land you know about.

— Rudyard Kipling, *From Sea to Sea and
Other Sketches: Letters of Travel*

CONTENTS

GLOSSARY OF TERMS

Bo	military officer
Bogyoke	major general
Dacoit	bandit belonging to armed gang
Daw	means "aunt," commonly used as an honorific for older or more senior ethnic Bamar female
Hluttaw	parliament
Kyat	Myanmar currency
Nai	form of address for ethnic Mon male
Naw	form of address for ethnic Karen female
Ma	form of address for younger ethnic Bamar female
Maung	form of address for younger ethnic Bamar male
Sai	form of address for young ethnic Shan male
Sangha	Buddhist order of monks
Saw	form of address for ethnic Karen male
Sawbwa (Saopha)	hereditary prince in Shan State
Saya	teacher, honorific for respected figure or professional
Sayadaw	Buddhist abbott
Tatmadaw	Myanmar military
Thakin	means "master," title used by nationalists
Thura	means "bravery," military title awarded for valor
U	means "uncle," honorific for older or more senior ethnic Bamar males

LIST OF ACRONYMS AND ABBREVIATIONS

AA	Arakan Army
ARSA	Arakan Rohingya Salvation Army
A/S	Assistant Secretary
ASEAN	Association for Southeast Asian Nations
BSPP	Burma Socialist Programme Party
CDM	Civil Disobedience Movement
CIA	Central Intelligence Agency
CPB	Communist Party of Burma
CSO	Civil Society Organization
DAS	Deputy Assistant Secretary
DEA	Drug Enforcement Administration
DKBA	Democratic Karen Buddhist Army
DRL	Democracy, Human Rights, and Labor Bureau (State Department)
EAO	Ethnic Armed Organization
EAP	East Asian and Pacific Affairs Bureau (State Department)
EO	Executive Order
EU	European Union
GSP	Generalized System of Preferences
KIA	Kachin Independence Army
KMT	Kuomintang
KNLA	Karen National Liberation Army
KNU	Karen National Union
LDC	Least Developed Country
LID	Light Infantry Division
MEC	Myanmar Economic Corporation

MI	Military Intelligence
MNDAA	Myanmar National Democratic Alliance Army
MPC	Myanmar Peace Center
NCA	Nationwide Ceasefire Accord
NDAA	National Democratic Alliance Army
NGO	Nongovernment Organization
NLD	National League for Democracy
NUG	National Unity Government
NUP	National Unity Party
OFAC	Office of Foreign Assets Control
PRC	People's Republic of China
SAC	State Administration Council
SDN List	Specially Designated and Blocked Nationals List
SEZ	Special Economic Zone
SLORC	State Law and Order Restoration Council
SNLD	Shan Nationalities League for Democracy
SOE	State Owned Enterprise
SPDC	State Peace and Development Council
SSA-N	Shan State Army-North
TNLA	Ta-ang National Liberation Army
UMEHL	Union of Myanmar Economic Holdings Limited
UN	United Nations
UNDP	United Nations Development Program
UNGA	United Nations General Assembly
UNHCR	United Nations High Commissioner for Refugees
UNHRC	United Nations Human Rights Commission
UNSC	United Nations Security Council
USAID	United States Agency for International Development
USD	US Dollar
USDA	Union Solidarity Development Association
USDP	Union Solidarity Development Party
UWSA	United Wa State Army

TIMELINE

1824–1826	First Anglo-Burmese War, Burma loses Manipur, Assam, Arakan, and Tenasserim to the British Empire
1852	Second Anglo-Burmese War, the British Empire annexes Lower Burma
1885	Third Anglo-Burmese War, the British Empire annexes Upper Burma
1942–1945	Japanese occupation of Burma, World War II
January 1947	General Aung San signs the Aung San-Attlee Agreement, paving the way for Burmese independence from the British Empire
July 1947	Independence leader Aung San and several cabinet members assassinated
January 1948	Burma officially becomes an independent republic
1958	General Ne Win takes power in a military coup from the democratically elected U Nu government and establishes a caretaker government
1962	General Ne Win once again takes control of the government in a coup
March–September 1988	Hundreds of thousands of students, monks, and soldiers join what becomes known as the 88 Uprising to protest Burma's economic woes and to push for democracy

July–September 1988	Ne Win steps down from power; after a series of coups, the State Law and Order Restoration Council (SLORC) assumes control
September 1988	Reagan administration suspends all US aid, counternarcotics programs, and arms sales to Burma
1989	George H. W. Bush administration suspends Generalized System of Preferences program for Burma
1989	The SLORC changes the official name of the country from "Burma" to "Myanmar"
1990	The SLORC holds a general election and the National League for a Democracy (NLD) wins in a landslide. The SLORC does not recognize the results, jails protesters, and later announces it will start the process anew under a "Seven Step Roadmap to a Disciplined Flourishing Democracy"
1997	The SLORC changes its name to the State Peace and Development Council (SPDC)
1997	The Clinton administration bans new investment in Myanmar
2003	Congress passes the Burma Freedom and Democracy Act, enacting visa and travel restrictions and an import ban of Myanmar goods
August–September 2007	Hundreds of thousands of monks and activists protest removal of fuel subsidies and political oppression in what becomes known as the Saffron Uprising
May 2008	Cyclone Nargis strikes southern Myanmar
May 2008	Myanmar constitutional referendum
2008	Congress passes the JADE Act, enacting a visa ban and creating the Special Representative and Policy Coordinator for Burma position

February–September 2009	US Burma policy review
November 2010	Myanmar general election
November 2011	Secretary Hillary Clinton travels to Myanmar
January 2012	Myanmar President Thein Sein releases hundreds of political prisoners and signs a cease-fire, ending one of the world's longest running insurgencies
July 2012	Ambassador Derek Mitchell confirmed as first US ambassador to Myanmar in two decades, USAID office opens, initial easing of US sanctions begins
November 2012	President Barack Obama travels to Myanmar
November 2015	Myanmar general election, NLD wins in a landslide
October 2016	US's Burma sanctions program is fully lifted
August 2017	In response to an attack by a Rohingya organization, the Myanmar military undertakes clearance operations that eventually led to more than 700,000 people fleeing to Bangladesh
November 2020	Myanmar general election, NLD wins again in a landslide
February 2021	The Myanmar military, under the command of Senior General Min Aung Hlaing, launches a coup and seizes control of national and local governments

Map of Myanmar

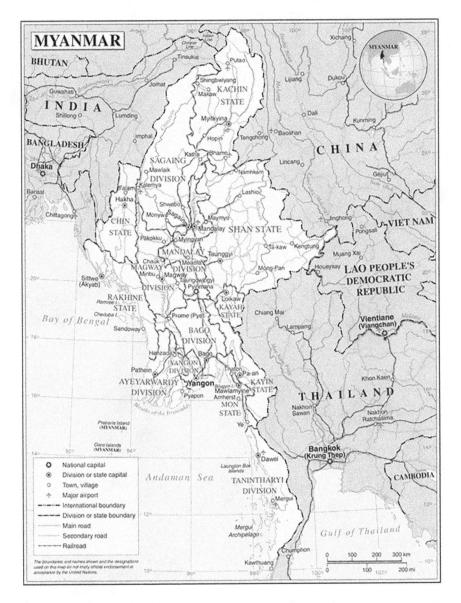

Preliminary Notes

All opinions, analyses, and assessments in this book are my own and do not reflect official US government positions or policy unless gleaned from interviews with policymakers, quotes, or official documents.

Names

This book reflects the Myanmar usage of names and titles. People do not have surnames; children's names may incorporate their parents' name or be based on recommendations from monks or astrologers. For example, Aung San Suu Kyi's name includes both her father's name, Aung San, and her mother's, Kyi. Her given name is Suu. Sometimes you will see and hear her referred to as "Daw Suu" or "Aung San Suu Kyi." Any reference to call her Suu Kyi or other iterations would be incorrect. Same with the name of the former president, Thein Sein. You would not refer to him as President Sein; it was President Thein Sein.

Names are normally preceded by an honorific to denote a person's age or station in life. The most common in this book are the ethnic Bamar "U," meaning "uncle," and "Daw," meaning "aunt." I've also used the ethnic Shan "Sai" and Karen "Saw." For example: U Thein Sein, Daw Aung San Suu Kyi, Sai Mauk Kham (former vice president and an ethnic Shan), and Saw Ba U Gyi (first president of the Karen National Union and an ethnic Karen). When discussing ethnicities, I use the term "Bamar" or "Shan" or whichever is the appropriate ethnic designation. When discussing the country's citizens as a whole, I use "Burmese" or "the Myanmar."

Burma/Myanmar

In this book, both "Burma" and "Myanmar" are used; "Burma" is used for the period before 1988 and "Myanmar" for the time after, unless they appear in a quote. In 1989, the military-led State Law and Order Restoration Council changed the country's name, as well as the names of cities, rivers, and ethnicities. "Burma" and "Myanmar" mean the same thing and one is derived from the other. "Burmah," its nineteenth-century spelling, is a local corruption of the word "Myanmar." To the junta, the renaming brought more accuracy to the actual pronunciation of these locations and places before the British colonizers romanized the country's names. Additionally, "Myanmar" was meant as a unifying name for the country's ethnic groups, as "Burma" only reflected the largest ethnic group, the Bamar.[1 and 2] Most ethnic groups disagreed.

The US and UK, and a variety of Myanmar watchers, junta opposition groups, and members and supporters of Aung San Suu Kyi's National League for Democracy (NLD) party, used and continue to use "Burma," as the junta grabbed power by illegitimate means and therefore had no legal authority to change anything. The use of the name "Burma" represents for many a solidarity with the prodemocracy and human rights activists in the country and because it was believed to be prodemocracy icon Aung San Suu Kyi's preference. It is true that Aung San Suu Kyi preferred the name Burma. When the NLD formed the government in March 2016, she noted her preference but then said both names were acceptable.[3]

The name issue remains controversial, and the use of "Myanmar" versus "Burma" may imply that you are for or against something. For example, if I say "Myanmar," it must imply I am pro-military or that I am against, or ignorant of, the prodemocracy movement that still views the junta and the military's role in government as illegitimate. Nothing could be further from the truth. I very much understand the emotion behind the argument and do not take it lightly.

PROLOGUE

THE END OF THE BEGINNING

During one of my last trips to Myanmar in 2019, I was riding with Ko Thura, a friend and my driver when I was in country.[1] He was a student activist and a former political prisoner, imprisoned three times for a total of fourteen years. He has been tortured, beaten, and starved. I had known Ko Thura for more than five years at this point; I had only heard bits and pieces of his story, giving him the space to share when he felt comfortable.

He was released in January 2012 in a general amnesty; the Myanmar government would occasionally grant amnesties for prisoners of all stripes on Buddhist holidays. Soon after, Ko Thura felt safe enough to start his life and got married and had a son. He was active in the former political prisoner network, meeting with former prisoners monthly and collecting money to either donate to a charity or help a colleague who was having a rough time. He started speaking about his experiences, and I got to learn more about what it was like for him as an activist and prisoner.

He was first imprisoned in the notorious Insein prison (pronounced "insane") after the 1988 prodemocracy uprising, along with other student activists who formed what came to be known as the 88 Generation Students. He was released a few years later but joined political protests in the mid-1990s and found himself in jail again. This time was the worst; he was punched hard enough to knock out his teeth and had so little food that he was on the brink of starvation. His final imprisonment came on the heels of the 2007 protests, known as the Saffron Uprising, where he shared a cell with his former captors from Military Intelligence (MI). Khin Nyunt, former member of the State Law and Order Restoration Council (SLORC) and its successor, State Peace and Development Council (SPDC), and MI chief, was arrested in 2004. MI was disbanded, and many of its officers were arrested. The MI folks were now jailed with the very people they put there. But Ko

Thura also said this was the closest that Myanmar might come to reconciliation; he and his cellmate had years to discuss their own perspectives and experiences, and they came to an imperfect understanding of one another's motivations and values.

When he wasn't driving, he often gave tours of sites of importance to Myanmar's political history. I had some time to spare, and Ko Thura stopped at a small park next to Inya Lake in central Yangon, picked up some snacks, and gave me an impromptu tour. Ko Thura pointed to a little white fence and said, "This was where the White Bridge Massacre happened." He talked about how during the 1988 uprising, his friends were forced into the water at that landmark and drowned. Some of his other friends had been loaded into vans and driven around the city, where several suffocated to death. Ko Thura was hoping that money could be raised to put up a memorial, but he knew that even if he was able to raise the funds, the government would never permit such a memorial. He was worried that the young people of today would begin to forget what happened and the sacrifices so many made to bring democracy and freedom to Myanmar.

He didn't have to worry about anyone forgetting. A new generation has now walked through the fire of defending democracy and the freedoms that were suddenly lost when the military seized control of the government on February 1, 2021. There are now new massacres to memorialize, new political prisoner names for whom to seek justice, and new nightmares to haunt their waking life.

It didn't take a lot for many of us to remember the dark days because they are back.

* * *

Burma, also known as Myanmar, is not a country that lacks whimsy or the eccentric. It is a place that trades in rumors and astrological predictions but also remains rooted in a deeply complex and sobering history. Tired of its bustling capital of Yangon (also known as Rangoon), the despotic and secretive generals that had ruled the country for more than five decades would uproot and move the capital overnight—a decision rumored to be informed by an astrologer specializing in auspiciousness and in line with past kings and rulers who did similar things in centuries past—to a location in the middle of nowhere, naming it Nay Pyi Taw, or "Abode of Kings." One journalist described the place "like a David Lynch film on location in North Korea."[2]

It is a wealthy country in every sense of the word: history, people, natural resources, and culture. But it is mired in poverty. It was the scene of decisive World War II battles and home to one of the most powerful Asian empires, whose rule extended from Cambodia to Yunnan to Manipur. The country produced a UN Secretary-General and a Nobel laureate. It also produced some of the world's most notorious drug kingpins.

Myanmar is home to the world's most precious natural resources. Its gem and mineral belts are embedded with rubies, sapphires, topaz, quartz, spinel, moonstone, amethyst, peridot, garnet, imperial jadeite, gold, silver, tin, tungsten, lead, and copper. The northernmost area of the country sits atop a wealth of amber, most of it infused with well-preserved fossils, including a tail of a ninety-nine-million-year-old dinosaur that proved dinosaurs had feathers.[3] These riches have also brought death and destruction in the form of landslides, environmental catastrophe, and exploitation.

Its farmlands produce rice, beans, pulses, fruits, vegetables, spices, tea, and coffee. Myanmar has potentially significant deposits of gas, its countryside is filled with teak forests, and it sits between China and India, connecting South, Southwest, Southeast, and Northeast Asia. Airlines such as Pan-Am, Air France, and KLM once used Rangoon as their Asia hub. In the 1950s and 1960s, Burma was the bright spot of Asia, with one of the region's most distinguished universities, an erudite population, the best health care, and a booming film scene. Now the country ranks among the least developed countries and has one of the worst health and education systems in the world.

The country is rich with diversity, counting dozens of ethnicities, each with their own languages, customs, and culture, including the majority Bamar people, long-necked Padaung women, the facial-tattooed Chin women, the linguistically diverse Naga people, the Shan princelings and princesses, and the wild Wa, the once-renowned headhunters (they gave up ritual beheadings in 1976)[4] whose armed group is now one of the world's largest narco-armies. But decades of civil wars and broken promises on autonomy and peace threaten to tear the fragile nation apart.

The country's successive military regimes, beginning after General Ne Win's bloody second coup in 1962, committed gross human rights abuses and drove a wealthy nation into the ground, transforming it into a least developed country under a pile of global sanctions. Once leading the United Nations, by 2008, it could only find diplomatic and economic shelter with Belarus, Russia, China, and North Korea.

It is also a country that grips people and never lets go. It seeps into the imagination, terrorizes immune systems, challenges assumptions, influences views, and makes one question one's role in the world. Myanmar has had this effect on an untold number of people from all walks of life, including actors and musicians, US presidents, US congresspersons, global leaders, donors, philanthropists, Nobel laureates, authors, poets, white saviors, and misguided fantasists.

Without even knowing it, Myanmar may have seeped into your own life, through crisp garlic or citrusy splashes from a Burmese kitchen, travelogues, references in your favorite shows or movies, Rudyard Kipling or Pablo Neruda's poetry, Bono's lyrics, or Eric Blair's dystopian visions. Eric Blair, who is better known by his pseudonym, George Orwell, was born in British India and later spent five years in Burma as a policeman during the colonial era and was deeply influenced by his time in the country. In Emma Larkin's book, *Finding George Orwell in Burma*, she traces his experiences working in the most violent corner of Britain's Indian empire, gathering intelligence on roving dacoits while getting to know ethnic communities and growing ever critical about the colonial yoke under which Burma had to live. His experiences would go on to inform his novel *Burmese Days* and his essay "Shooting an Elephant," though those that Larkin met would argue that the "prophet" Orwell would predict Burma's future miseries under successive juntas that sought to install ethnic Bamar supremacy, censor news, and insist that war was peace and ignorance was strength in his *Animal Farm* and *1984*. Even after returning to the UK, Burma never left Orwell. His experiences informed his writing and his views on governance and global engagement.

I would soon get swept up in Myanmar as well. I began to study the country at what would become a pivotal time, when one of the worst natural disasters in the region, Cyclone Nargis, struck the country. The cyclone would test the junta and its relationship with the United States, putting cracks in the walls that had been built between the two for decades.

Burma/Myanmar is unique in a myriad of ways. As someone who has spent more than a decade working in and around Burma, it is difficult for me to believe that the country is not at the center of everyone's universe. I'm here to tell you it should be at the center of yours, as its story would appeal to history buffs, foreign policy and national security wonks, conflict and military analysts, drama and intrigue lovers, and astrology and gossip fans. In a sense, it is so damn interesting. But above all, it's an important story because its inherent struggles on race, ethnicity, and democracy mirror American, and now global, struggles.

1

Aid and Assistance

The Calm before the Storm

A Tempest on the Horizon

On May 2, 2008, a Friday, the winds picked up on Myanmar's southern Ayeyarwady Delta. The winds eventually spun into a 130-mph monster, and its winds pushed a deadly storm surge measuring fifteen feet in height and up to twenty-four miles inland across the low-lying plains in the night's darkest hours, washing away villagers, animals, trees, and buildings.

The storm lurched eastward toward Myanmar's largest city of Yangon. The storm's proximity to the Andaman Sea helped Cyclone Nargis maintain its strength, and on May 3, Yangon was hit by 80-mph winds for more than twelve hours, ripping up ancient banyan trees from their roots and tossing roofs off houses. From there, it quickly weakened after approaching the Myanmar-Thailand border. After deteriorating to minimal tropical storm status, the Joint Typhoon Warning Center issued its last advisory on Nargis.

Cyclone Nargis was the deadliest natural disaster on record in Myanmar's history. Offers of international aid came pouring into Myanmar's military regime, including from the US.

But the junta said no.

A New Chapter

In June 2007, I joined the Central Intelligence Agency (CIA) as a political analyst covering Asia issues. I had spent most of my academic and scant professional life preparing for a government job focused on foreign policy. I studied international relations (IR) at Tufts University, a school renowned for such programs, and found my way to Japan after college to spend two years teaching English with the Japan Exchange and Teaching (JET) Program in rural Saga Prefecture. I spent time traveling around North and Southeast Asia and got the bug to build a career working on Asia issues. I returned to the US, got a master's in Japan Studies at the Johns Hopkins School of Advanced International Studies, a Washington, DC, policymaker factory, and joined the CIA upon graduation.

My initial analytic portfolio was very low on the national security priority list, limiting opportunities to cut my analytic chops. I asked my manager to consider me for assignments that would test and strengthen my skills and was soon rewarded for my pestering.

Myanmar was having its first vote since 1990 on May 10, 2008, to approve a controversial constitution. Given that violence often accompanied political events in Myanmar, I was to closely monitor developments on electioneering and violence against prodemocracy activists. President George W. Bush and First Lady Laura Bush were especially interested in Myanmar and were concerned about the vote and aftermath; Laura Bush was a longtime advocate for the country's democracy leader, Aung San Suu Kyi. President Bush's cousin, Elsie Walker Kilborne, had introduced the First Lady to Aung San Suu Kyi's plight, and Laura Bush became a quiet supporter, sending supplies and necessities to the Nobel laureate and promoting her cause through her husband's work while he was president.[1 and 2]

For me as an analyst, Myanmar was exciting: a military junta, a world-famous prodemocracy activist, insurgencies and anti-government armed groups, political intrigue, narcotics, and geopolitical maneuverings. I started reading up on the country's history with the few academic treatments that were available, and I delved into historical accounts, journals, and a sparse library of novels, poems, memoirs, and biographies.

Current information was hard to come by, however. Domestic news outlets, such as the *New Light of Myanmar* (NLOM) and MRTV, were state-run and censored, and global and exile press often relied on imperfect witnesses, gossipy "tea shop talk," or coded messages stuffed in objects spirited out of the country. Data was questionable; development specialists made guesstimates on extrapolated data from the 1930s (the last time any real surveys were done) on standards of living and demographics.[3]

Thanks to a series of bloody crackdowns, antidemocratic campaigns, and gross human rights violations, the bilateral relationship between the US and Myanmar was at a nadir in 2008, so information coming from official sources was sparse too. The US maintained a fully operating embassy in the country, though diplomatic ties were downgraded from full ambassador to chargé d'affaires in 1990. Years of sanctions and condemnatory statements elicited no desire from the Myanmar side to engage with US diplomats. To add to the communication woes, the State Peace and Development Council (SPDC), the official name of the military junta, unexpectedly moved its capital roughly two hundred miles north of Yangon to Nay Pyi Taw in 2005, leaving only a fax number with which to contact officials.[4 and 5]

Fighting for Survival

The brewing maelstrom worried us in Washington, and in the US embassy in Yangon, officials had an inkling as to how strong Nargis would become. Samantha Carl-Yoder, the US embassy's economic officer, said there was no mechanism to provide an early warning to Myanmar citizens or the junta; all national-level government officials were up in Nay Pyi Taw and cut off from day-to-day communications with diplomats, businesses, and citizens in Yangon. US officials went through all possible channels to get information out, including UN offices and any other diplomatic missions that might have a shot at reaching the junta.[6]

On Friday evening, May 2, I saw the storm reach the Ayeyarwady Delta. Rarely had Myanmar suffered major casualties and property damage from past storms. The most serious cyclones to hit land were in 1967 and 1968; the former destroyed 90 percent of the houses in Rakhine State, the latter killed more than 1,000 people.[7]

The next day, however, it became very clear that Cyclone Nargis was a catastrophic storm, and survivors would need food, shelter, and medical aid as soon as possible. The storm had stalled over Yangon for nearly twelve hours, and buildings' windows had blown in, spraying frightened families with glass, rain, and debris. Two days later, NASA published a shocking before and after photo that made clear what had happened in the south: the delta had been completely erased.[8]

The US embassy team sprang into action, checking in on colleagues and neighbors, implementing an action plan to provide emergency assistance, enacting small recovery programs that would fly under the junta's radar, getting visas for USAID and US military teams to deploy aid and assistance, selling the narrative that US military planes were only going to deliver supplies and not overthrow the government, and making sure any supplies brought in by donors and foreign governments reached those in need and not military families or the black market.[9]

On May 6, US President George W. Bush offered to shift US Navy assets involved in Cobra Gold military exercises[10] to Myanmar to provide assistance, search-and-rescue missions, and aid. In addition to US Navy assistance, the US had loaded C-130 cargo planes with emergency aid supplies that could leave from Thailand. Unfortunately, Bush at the same time had participated in a signing ceremony for legislation awarding the SPDC's nemesis, prodemocracy icon Aung San Suu Kyi, the Congressional Gold Medal,[11] and days earlier had expanded sanctions through Executive Order (EO) 13464, adding three state-owned enterprises to the Specially Designated and Blocked Nationals (SDN) List, the US Department of the Treasury's list of individuals and businesses off-limits to Americans.[12] The Senate would pass Senate Resolution 554, expressing "deep sympathy to and strong support for the people of Burma" and support for the Bush Administration's EO. The House would follow suit on May 13.[13]

The junta only saw the punishment and not the prize. How could the US offer aid and flog them at the same time? The SPDC only had to look at the US invasions of Afghanistan and Iraq to see what could happen to them, particularly as it had been labeled an "outpost of tyranny" by Secretary of State Condoleezza Rice and subjected to countless sanctions programs and condemnations. They researched the capabilities of the US Navy ships being offered and quickly came to the conclusion that these were warships equipped with Tomahawks and other long-range missiles. The French and US ships had half of Myanmar's fighting capabilities alone, floating out at sea. SPDC leader, Senior General Than Shwe, wanted no further discussion on the issue, and the number two in the SPDC, Vice Senior General Maung Aye, banned ships from docking.[14 and 15]

The SPDC moved three light infantry divisions, two tank divisions, and helicopters to prepare for a ground war, according to retired Myanmar military officials. Than Shwe knew his military did not have the capabilities to repel US forces. The SPDC wasn't going to allow in any aid-and-assistance Trojan horse to Myanmar when the country was at its weakest.[16 and 17]

UN agencies also had planes filled with supplies, but a few were turned away. International aid and emergency workers equipped with strategies, plans, and supplies were denied visas. Security forces also prevented movement within the country; most foreigners who were allowed in were prevented from traveling outside of Yangon. Heads of state and global leaders implored the junta to let aid in. UN Secretary-General Ban Ki-moon's calls went unanswered.[18]

Samantha and a handful of embassy and NGO officials managed to sneak down to the delta to assess the damage and deliver much-needed supplies. It was total devastation. Debris from straw huts and buildings, torn clothing, and animal and human body parts were strewn everywhere. Plastic tarps dotted the landscape, protecting survivors from the seasonal monsoon rains. The team was greeted by villagers who welcomed aid and any news. It surprised them how much people outside of Myanmar cared. The team heard stories of devastation, survival, and trauma. One of the villagers pointed to a tree in the middle of a field, completely stripped of its bark. The man said he had held on to what was once a leafy tree the entire night while waves washed over his head. He lost his entire family—wife, children, parents—and was left with a series of thick scars on the inside of his arms and legs from holding on to the tree for hours. Despite their losses, the villagers never lost their sense of generosity and hospitality, looking to host the visiting delegation and sharing their stories as heavy rain tapped the tarps.[19 and 20]

Finally, after nearly two weeks, SPDC member Lieutenant General Shwe Mann authorized the US to conduct daily C-130 flights to bring in supplies, with the stipulation that no one on board could leave the airport and the junta would deliver the supplies.[21] The commander in chief of the Navy, Vice Admiral Soe Thane, would go and monitor the landings.[22] Embassy staff effectively took over control of the airport, organizing the off-loading and pushing supplies to NGOs for delivery. World Vision, CARE, Save the Children, PSI, and other international— and eventually local—NGOs delivered what they could to where they could, racing against time and pushing against the restrictions placed on them. Despite intense oversight, it was easy to find tarps, bags of rice, high energy biscuits, and mosquito nets on the black market in Yangon.[23]

USAID Administrator Henrietta Fore, Pacific Command (PACOM) Commander Timothy Keating, the head of USAID's Disaster Assistance Response Team, Bill Berger, and Deputy Assistant Secretary of State Scot Marciel flew on the first C-130 flight into Yangon International Airport on May 12, meeting their military interlocutors and US embassy staff on the ground. Admiral Keating was traveling when word of the cyclone hit. He made a refueling stop and diverted his flight to Thailand to strategize and deploy assistance. At his command, Admiral Keating would be able to use amphibious ships, medical assets, marines, and any number of transport vehicles to move supplies. For her part, Henrietta Fore could also move disaster relief supplies and mobilize organizations and funding. The joint efforts of PACOM and USAID were unmatched in terms of resources, reach, and experience.[24 and 25]

Keating and Fore were met at the airport by a three-star general, a mix of military officials, and a smattering of Ministry of Foreign Affairs officials. The US side brought with them photographs of the devastation, including the NASA photo showing incontrovertible evidence of a massive tragedy, to convey the severity of the situation and the need for continued assistance and permission for the US to help deliver aid to affected areas. The Myanmar representatives dismissed the photos, noting that these types of events happened regularly and that if it was that bad, then it was God's will to inflict. They were quite blasé about it.[26] In the *NLOM*, the junta stated cyclone victims did not need supplies of "chocolate bars" and could instead survive by eating frogs and fish.[27]

Keating succeeded in securing additional C-130 flights, but after more than a dozen attempts to convince the military to allow naval ships in to provide medical equipment, doctors, water purification systems, shelter, food, and H-46 cargo helicopters to deliver aid, the ships left on June 4 with all its supplies on board.[28 and 29]

The Vote Goes On

With all the chaos surrounding the cyclone, the referendum was nearly forgotten by everyone except the SPDC. It seemed unfathomable the junta would go ahead with the vote, but they did. The referendum was a key step in the decades-long effort to bring "democracy" to Myanmar through its seven-step "Roadmap to a Disciplined Flourishing Democracy," a process that would not be deterred by a cataclysmic event. Four days after the cyclone, state-run media announced the vote would proceed on May 10 but would be delayed in townships in the delta and parts of Yangon Division until May 24.[30 and 31]

The referendum was the first vote in eighteen years, with the last nationwide general election held in 1990. The 1990 election was highly stage-managed to ensure the approved political party of the former iteration of the junta, the State Law and Order Restoration Council (SLORC), won; however, the people overwhelmingly voted for prodemocracy icon Aung San Suu Kyi's National League for Democracy (NLD) party. Shocked by the outcome and the vitriol aimed at the military, the junta refused to recognize the results, jailed protestors and election winners, and said it would start a process to bring "democracy" to the country, its Seven Step Roadmap. The roadmap called for holding a national convention to conceptualize a new political system, establish a process of implementation, draft a new constitution, hold a constitutional referendum, hold a national election for parliament, convene the new government, and build a "modern and democratic" nation. The roadmap would take two decades to impose, rendering Nargis a minor irritant to the country's political endgame.

The 2008 Constitution of the Republic of the Union of Myanmar, which the country was expected to approve or reject on May 10, formally enshrined the military in politics, providing it an outsized role in government with 25 percent of all parliamentary seats in national-, state- and division-level parliaments; the lead of three of the most powerful ministries (Defense, Border Affairs, and Home Affairs); and several seats in the National Defense and Security Council,[32] an entity seen as the possible successor to the SPDC.

The constitution included several contentious articles that alarmed prodemocracy activists and the NLD, setting the stage for future political conflict between the civilian government and the military that would lead to tragic circumstances less than two decades later.

Article 436 stated that the constitution could only be amended with more than 75 percent of the Parliament, meaning all nonmilitary members of Parliament plus at least one military vote—an unlikely scenario. Additionally, Article 59(f) prohibited anyone with a foreign parent, spouse, or child from becoming president.[33] This seemed specifically designed to prevent democratic icon, Aung San Suu Kyi, from ever attaining the presidency; she was married to a British national and her children are foreign nationals, having had their Myanmar citizenship stripped in the 1990s.[34 and 35]

Finally, Myanmar's most powerful institution—the military, or, known by its Burmese name, the Tatmadaw—endowed itself with the power to legally take charge of governing through declared states of emergency for up to two years if necessary. Given the breadth of the control of government it carved out for itself and no definition of what rose to the level of an emergency, taking control would not be difficult if they wanted to. And it turns out, it wasn't. In February 2021, Commander-in-Chief Min Aung Hlaing used the processes outlined in the constitution to wrest control from the civilian government.

Though the outcome was preordained, there was potential for violence. The Tatmadaw had cracked down on political demonstrations, resulting in thousands of deaths and arrests over the years, most notably in 2007, 1996, 1990, and 1988. The country's myriad ethnic groups, including armed organizations, despised the 2008 constitution. The vote made clear that a political dialogue promised to them by members of the military regime to resolve long-standing issues would not be addressed and that any steps toward a lasting peace with ethnic armed organizations (EAOs) would be dictated by the military. Prodemocracy activists, many of whom spent time in jail for protesting military rule, pilloried the stage-managed affair.

Election monitors from Vietnam and China arrived to witness voting in Nay Pyi Taw. Given that the entirety of the SPDC, the ministries, and government officials lived there, it would be questionable if any voting went awry. Other embassies dispatched officers to observe the vote elsewhere.

A few days after the first round of voting, the junta declared 92.4 percent voted "yes" with a turnout of 99 percent. The cyclone-affected areas would vote on May 24, though the outcome was never in doubt.[36] The official announcement came out on May 29, and the referendum was approved by 92.18 percent of the votes.[37 and 38] The fourth step of the roadmap was complete. A once-in-a-five-hundred-year storm was not going to stop the military from passing the referendum on a document that would encapsulate what they had sought to achieve since 1988: putting the sheen of democracy on what was ultimately a military-controlled government. The military was Myanmar, Myanmar was the military. The vote made it so.

Building Trust between Myanmar and the World

Meanwhile, the international community was desperate to reach cyclone victims. Aid and disaster relief efforts often take time and tend to run into coordination and corruption issues, but this was an effort that was taking a long time, primarily due to the junta's initial intransigence and mistrust. For some perspective, within a week of the 2004 Indian Ocean earthquake and tsunami, foreign governments pledged tens of millions of dollars in aid and shipped sixty tonnes of supplies to impacted areas. Thirty national militaries provided troops, helicopters—which flew 430 sorties a day from Aceh in Indonesia—planes, and ships, and the US put 18,000 armed forces into action.[39 and 40] Myanmar granted the UN thirty-four visas for non-Asian aid workers in the week following the cyclone.

The UN was pressing the junta to let in aid workers more speedily; visas were approved but very slowly. On May 12, UN Secretary-General Ban Ki-moon expressed frustration in a press briefing; the UN had staff on the ground that could not effectively target two-thirds of the affected population. The Myanmar junta was in no rush to really help the UN.[41]

Myanmar has had, and continues to have, a mixed history with the UN. Despite an auspicious start with U Thant, a Myanmar diplomat and educator, as the UN's third secretary-general, Myanmar fell out of favor during the SLORC era. Myanmar's retreat to despotic rule helped it lose global friends, but the UN continued the hard work of diplomacy, resulting in a Myanmar that was subject to a seemingly endless stream of UN envoys, rapporteurs, and resolutions. But dealing with member states with opposing views and an intransigent junta does not an easy situation make, and efforts to push the junta toward democracy largely failed.

The first high-level UN engagement in Myanmar was an unsuccessful one-time visit by Professor Sadako Ogata, a Japanese scholar and diplomat. Following the 1990 elections, she was sent as an independent expert on behalf of the UN Commission on Human Rights, the predecessor of the current Human Rights Council, to make direct contact with the Myanmar government about their refusal to recognize the NLD's win. Secretary-General Boutros Boutros-Ghali sent Rafeeuddin Ahmed to the country in 1994, who delivered a letter to the SLORC from the secretary-general.[42] The first UN special rapporteur,[43] Yozo Yokota, was appointed in 1992 and resigned in 1996, stating that he did not have the resources to fulfill his mandate.[44 and 45] In 1996, Yokota was succeeded by Rajsoomer Lallah of Mauritius, but the Myanmar authorities took offense to him for some reason and never granted him entry during his four-year tenure.[46] The next special envoy, Alvaro de Soto, resigned from his four-year post in 1999 after being unable to facilitate a dialogue between the regime and other political organizations. Razali Ismail, a special envoy for the secretary-general, resigned in 2006 after being refused entry for two years.[47] He was succeeded by Ibrahim Gambari, who had been allowed in the country and had met with senior junta leaders, Aung San Suu Kyi, and a wide range of stakeholders but had ended his tenure humiliated by the junta, given the cold shoulder by the Lady, and stymied by UN members states.[48] The next special rapporteur, Paulo Sérgio Pinheiro, curtailed his trip to Myanmar after finding a listening device under the table while interviewing a political prisoner. Secretary-General Ban Ki-moon selected Vijay Nambiar in 2012 as special envoy, who had the good fortune of working with a regime during its political opening and pursuit of reforms.[49] Appointed by Secretary-General António Guterres in April 2018, Christine Schraner Burgener was the next special envoy and was right back where Ogata started. Several months after the coup, in October 2021, Guterres appointed Noeleen Heyzer of Singapore as the new Special Envoy to Myanmar.[50 and 51]

The UN made resolutions too. Following the nonrecognition of the 1990 election, the UN continually pressed the government to take steps toward democracy, unconditionally free Aung San Suu Kyi from house arrest, and improve its deplorable human rights situation. The UN resolutions started off covering a half page, but in later years, they clocked in at multiple pages.[52]

There was one UN tool that hadn't ever been used but was being considered during Nargis. Bernard Kouchner, the French foreign minister, sought to invoke the UN's "responsibility to protect," or R2P, claiming the SPDC was causing deliberate mass suffering and death, therefore qualifying as crimes against humanity.[53] R2P came to life following the tragedies in Rwanda and the Balkans in the 1990s in the hopes of adequately addressing future atrocities. It was formally adopted in 2005 and declared that should any state fail to meet the responsibility of protecting its people, the international community should act collectively. At the time of Cyclone Nargis, there were breathless legal debates on R2P's parameters and interpretations to see if it rose to this level or would set a precedent. It would be another three years before the UN Security Council invoked R2P, and it did so in Libya, Cote D'Ivoire, South Sudan, and Yemen in 2011, in Syria in 2012, and in the Central African Republic in 2013.[54]

The UN wasn't making too much headway, but one organization was. The Association for Southeast Asian Nations (ASEAN), a regional organization comprised of ten Southeast Asian nations that facilitates cooperation on economic, political, military, and social issues, was losing its patience with Myanmar. ASEAN typically remained quiet on Myanmar's human rights abuses over the years, maintaining a stance of "noninterference." Cyclone Nargis presented an opportunity for ASEAN to be constructive on Myanmar. On May 5, ASEAN Secretary-General Surin Pitsuwan,[55] a widely respected and forward-leaning diplomat, called on all member states to provide urgent relief assistance through an ASEAN mechanism designed to tackle these types of issues, the ASEAN Emergency Rapid Assessment Team (ERAT). Myanmar acquiesced and agreed to work with ERAT to assemble and deploy a team made up of government officials, disaster management experts, and regional NGOs. In the first-ever such mission for ASEAN, ERAT was deployed to Myanmar from May 9 to May 18. The ASEAN secretariat then moved to mobilize full relief and recovery efforts, consisting of ASEAN, the Myanmar government, and the UN (and eventually, local NGOs),[56] which would facilitate day-to-day operations, resource coordination, and daily reporting on recovery efforts and ongoing needs. Eventually, they supervised the creation of another acronymized effort, the Post-Nargis Joint Assessment (PONJA), which included members from international financial institutions and NGOs.[57] More than three hundred people in a ten-day period scoured the cyclone-affected areas to assess the damage, losses, and needs going forward. The final PONJA report presented on July 21 outlined the total damage—USD $4 billion, with total economic losses equivalent to 2.7 percent of Myanmar's GDP. The amount needed for recovery was USD $1 billion to help with recovery and rehabilitation efforts.[58]

In the end, Cyclone Nargis was one of the deadliest natural disasters in the region. Officially, more than 138,000 people were killed or missing. The storm caused billions of dollars in damage. Most villages were abandoned because the villagers either died or moved away. The survivors would tell stories of hearing screams in the night, having the feeling that someone was grabbing their arm, or catching a glimpse of a friend or family member who had disappeared. In a land where ghosts and spirits are an everyday fixture, surely the delta must have been one of the most haunted places. The ecology of the delta completely changed as the topsoil had been stripped by the storm surge. New crops, trees, and mangroves were planted, and villagers found other forms of work. Aid delivery and recovery efforts continued for a few months following the cyclone but ended once there was evidence that the junta was making a profit on aid dollars.[59] The rest of the country fell back to depressing old patterns; the junta refocused on completing the remaining steps of the roadmap, and Aung San Suu Kyi's house arrest was extended for another year.

There were some bright spots, though they were few. Nargis began to chip away at the US's punitive policy fortress on Myanmar. Aid and assistance to Myanmar was significantly curbed after the 1988 crackdown, and almost all US aid programs were directed to the Myanmar-Thailand border, which had been and would increasingly become filled with refugees fleeing civil wars and antidemocratic violence. There were small programs run through the US embassy's American Center, including English-language classes, a library, and a relatively safe place to debate and discuss political issues; these programs were instrumental in keeping the prodemocracy movement alive but they also gave Myanmar citizens the skills to organize and lead, especially during Nargis.[60]

It would also change US and major donor views on local NGO capabilities.[61] and [62] Civil society organizations (CSOs) and NGOs prior to Nargis had limited exposure to working with donors and were often unable to obtain grant money to fund their small programs. Despite this, they spurred into action to get their networks mobilized. These local NGOs became a lifeline, able to get relief and assistance to villages where many donors and foreign governments could not go— or that they didn't know about—and get real-time and unvarnished information back to Yangon.[63] Their work during Nargis and beyond was not without risk; twenty-one humanitarian workers were arrested and jailed for leading the civil society response to Nargis, including the famous Myanmar comedian, Zarganar, who was part of an ad hoc group of 420 relief workers. He was sentenced to thirty-five years in jail, one charge being that he was in possession of video footage of the cyclone's impact in the delta.

Cyclone Nargis was a pivotal event, one that I believe made a significant impression on a member of the SPDC, Thein Sein. He would eventually go on to open the country, providing space for those NGOs that got their start during Nargis and freeing those from prison who helped victims. It was also pivotal for me; a one-month assignment turned into an enduring mission.

2

NATIONAL RECONCILIATION

DRUGS, WAR, AND PEACE

When President Barack Obama came into office in 2009, my colleagues and I were curious if he'd prioritize Southeast Asia. There is always anxiety in a transition; it means a raft of new bosses, preferences, and ways officials consume information. For analysts, we worry where our accounts will fall in the pecking order of importance to new policymakers. My team hoped for opportunities to contribute to the president's daily brief (PDB), a daily summary of high-level, all-source information and analysis on national security issues produced for the president and key cabinet members and advisers.

For many analysts, the chance to write for the PDB is a career highlight. You have the chance to inform and have your words read by the president, cabinet secretaries, and senior officials. I was hopeful that Myanmar would be of interest, especially given its unusual ability to continually capture the attention of very senior government officials from both political parties in both the legislative and executive branches.

Myanmar wasted no time in capturing the president-elect's attention. In November 2008, the Myanmar courts sentenced fourteen activists to sixty-five years in prison for their actions in helping Cyclone Nargis victims and their participation in the 2007 Saffron Revolution and other anti-junta activities.[1] The length of the sentences were unprecedented, and to add to it, the convicted activists were sent to far-flung prisons, hundreds of miles from Yangon. The junta had realized that keeping activists imprisoned in the same location enabled communication and planning, so separating them undermined any efforts to plan a prodemocracy movement once they were released. This was not a good introduction to the incoming administration.

Unending Civil Wars and the US Fuel That Helped Finance Them

The political prisoner issue was not the only long-standing challenge on the US policy to-do list when it came to Myanmar. Human rights abuses in ethnic minority areas, which were found in the country's periphery, occupied space in talking points, legislation, and executive actions. These abuses stemmed from decades of civil war between and among Myanmar's military, anti-government groups, ideological-based armies, and ethnic armed organizations (EAOs). This, above all else, was Myanmar's defining and enduring challenge: national reconciliation and peace with EAOs and unarmed ethnic minorities.

In 2009, tensions were running high in Myanmar's northeastern Shan State. The junta was pushing for EAOs that had signed cease-fire agreements—the country's seventeen armed ethnic armies who forged cease-fire agreements with the military in the 1980s and 1990s in exchange for lucrative concessions—to lay down their arms and join a Border Guard Force (BGF), assimilating them into the Tatmadaw.[2] If they didn't, the cease-fires would be rendered "null and void" and EAOs would be fair game for war. The EAOs with cease-fires in place countered that a political dialogue was to occur first and then a discussion about disarmament, not the other way around.

Myanmar had been engulfed in civil war since its independence, fighting anti-government, student, ideological, and ethnic-based armies. Myanmar's landscape of ethnic conflict includes a veritable acronym alphabet soup of EAOs. This book only gives a brief account of the conflict, peace process, and why it matters, so I encourage those interested in learning more to read Martin Smith's *Burma: Insurgency and the Politics of Ethnic Conflict*, James C. Scott's *The Art of Not Being Governed: An Anarchist History of Upland Southeast Asia*, Bertil Lintner's *Burma in Revolt: Opium and Insurgency Since 1948*, anything by the incomparable Edith Mirante, as well as works by Christina Fink, Andrew Selth, David Mathieson, Mary Callahan, Ashley South, and the nineteenth-century memoirs of Ann Judson and George Scott (aka Shwe Yoe). The Transnational Institute and Myanmar Peace Monitor are also good resources.

Myanmar officially—and controversially—recognized 135 ethnic groups in its 1982 Citizenship Law, with the largest ethnic groups being the Bamar, Shan, Karen, Kachin, Mon, Rakhine, and Chin. Myanmar's diversity is comprised of a dizzying array of linguistic and cultural differences, a complexity that befuddled British demographers and governing colonialists in a country it annexed after three wars in the nineteenth century. This frustration, the lack of effort to understand and account for these differences, and the issues it caused for those in the British Raj were documented in Rudyard Kipling's poem "A Nightmare of Names" published in 1886:

It was a wearied journalist who sought his little bed,
With twenty Burma telegrams all waiting to be read.
Then the Nightmare and her nine-fold rose up his dreams to haunt,
And from those Burma telegrams they wove this dismal chaunt:—

'Bethink thee, man of ink and shears,' so howled the fiendish crew,
'That each dacoit has one long name, and every hamlet two.
Moreover, all our outposts bear peculiar names and strange:
There are one hundred outposts and, once every month, they change.

If Poungdoungzoon and Pyalhatzee today contain the foe,
Be sure they pass tomorrow to Gwebin or Shway-my-o.
But Baung-maung-hman remember, is a trusted Thoongye Woon,
The deadly foe of Maung-dhang-hlat, Myoke of Moung-kze-hloon.

Poungthung and Waustung-chung are not at present overthrown,
For they are near the Poon beyond the Hlinedathalone;
While Nannay-kone in Ningyan is near Mecakaushay,
But Shway-zet-dau is on the Ma, and quite the other way.

Here are some simple titles which 'twere best to get in writing
In view of further telegrams detailing further fighting:—
Male, Myola, Toungbyoung, Talakso, Yebouk, Myo,
Nattick, Hpan-loot-kin, Madeah, Padeng, Narogan, Mo.

Pakhang, Samaitkyon, Banze, Mine-tseil, Mine-the-Kulay,
Mantsankin, Toungbain, Bompan, Aeng, Naung, Banza, Kan-sauÂmya .
Kteepauts, Salung, Enlay, Yindan, Nwa-Koo, Mahan-gyee-kin,
Kek-kai, Nat-lone, Salay, Toung-lone, Yihon, and lastly Tsin.'

It was a wearied journalist—he left his little bed,
And faced the Burma telegrams, all waiting to be read;
But ere he took his map-book up, he prayed a little prayer—
'Oh stop them fighting Lord knows who, in jungles Deuce knows
where!'[3]

Tensions were not limited to the ethnic groups and their colonial overseers but also amongst the majority ethnic Bamar and minority groups. World War II laid bare these tensions, especially as many of the ethnic minorities sided with the Allied forces, including with US armed forces and detachments from the CIA's predecessor, the Office of Strategic Services' Detachment 101, which fought alongside the ethnic Kachin and opened the path for Stillwell's forces, Wingate's Raiders, and Merrill's Marauders to launch a counterattack against the Japanese. A bronze statue of a Kachin Ranger and a Detachment 101 ranger resides on the grounds of the US embassy in Yangon, commemorating the cooperation that helped turn the tide of war in Burma toward the Allies.

Burma's most famous and revered independence leader, Aung San, an ethnic Bamar, sided with the Japanese because they had promised to help unshackle Asian countries from colonial masters. After receiving secret training from the Japanese, Aung San and his so-called Thirty Comrades (luminaries who included members that became the country's first prime minister, a general who would overthrow that prime minister, and a leader of the country's largest insurgent group) led Japanese troops into Burma, mowing down Allied soldiers and the ethnic groups fighting alongside them.

At the end of the war, when Aung San and his comrades switched sides and fought with the Allies, he recognized the challenges in forming a Union of Burma, one that could bring together the dozens of ethnicities that would live in its newly defined borders. He held what he called a Panglong conference to determine how Burma would be formed. Panglong was also a chance for Aung San to make amends and allay fears about inequity and self-determination. Some of the country's largest ethnic minorities, including the Shan, Kachin, and Chin, were willing to cooperate with the ethnic Bamar government. Others either passed or weren't included. Many of the demands tabled by ethnic representatives found their way into the 1947 constitution, including the right of secession for the Shan.[4] Aung San was assassinated on the eve of Burma's independence, and the Panglong spirit would die with him.

As Burma gained independence from the British in 1948 and it was clear any agreements from Panglong or from the independence agreement signed with the British wouldn't protect or provide autonomy to the country's ethnic minorities, many groups chose to rebel, including the Karen National Union (KNU) in 1949, eventually becoming the world's longest-running insurgency. Some groups rebelled for ideological reasons, such as the Communist Party of Burma (CPB), which was led by a former member of the Thirty Comrades, and others rebelled for control over natural resources—including rubies, jade, minerals, gemstones, gold, silver, timber, and narcotics—or transportation routes, all located in ethnic territory.[5] The country was awash in weapons following World War II and later, the Vietnam War; by the 1980s and 1990s, there were roughly forty armed rebellions across the country.[6]

The War on Drugs

Wars have to be financed, and narcotics quickly became an easy revenue stream, partly thanks to the US. The drug trade started in earnest when the Mao-led Chinese communists took over western China and pushed the Koumingtang (KMT) into Burma in 1949. The KMT, covertly supported by the US, used

Burma as its base to fight Mao's troops and recruited ethnic Wa, Shan, Lisu, and Lahu to join their cause. The KMT turned to growing poppies to finance their war, facilitating Burma's entry into the opium trade and earning it the second-place spot behind Afghanistan in terms of poppy production. As the drug trade flourished, Shan State would eventually produce 80 percent of the opium from the Golden Triangle, the drug manufacturing region that covered the adjoining corners of Laos, Thailand, and Myanmar.[7 and 8]

The US support of the KMT would have long-term effects on US-Myanmar relations for decades to come. Once the Burmese discovered US government involvement, they complained to US embassies all over Asia.[9] This would begin to feed their smoldering paranoia about foreign interference within their borders and fears of invasion by powerful countries, especially during Nargis.

The opium trade also created the world's most notorious narcotics traffickers whose products made it into US neighborhoods. Legendary drug kingpins and queenpins cut their guerrilla and narcotics trade teeth thanks to the KMT. Khun Sa; Lo Hsing Han (called the "Godfather of Heroin" by President Richard Nixon);[10] [and 11] and Olive Yang, the glass ceiling breaker on the narcotics trade who broke many social barriers, ran the Golden Triangle with their own armies for decades, earning US bounties on their heads and global notoriety. Decades after building up the Golden Triangle to its notorious reputation as drug central, Yang and Lo Hsing Han were recruited by the military to help negotiate cease-fires with the country's well-armed EAOs. Yang's main success was striking a deal with her distant relative, Peng Jiasheng, and his Kokang army, the Myanmar National Democratic Alliance Army (MNDAA), a cease-fire that held for nearly twenty years until 2009.[12]

The US didn't seem as concerned with the Southeast Asian drug trade or its early role in it until drug-addicted Vietnam veterans returned home and Burmese heroin starting showing up in the US. In the late 1970s, Shan insurgent groups offered to end the narcotics trade. They would sell four hundred tons of opium to the US government for USD $20 million dollars. This would have removed a year's crop from the market and disrupted the narcotics trade at a price considerably less than the US was spending on drug suppression programs. Though there was support in Congress, President Jimmy Carter turned down the offer because he was skeptical about the deal's enforcement based on previous experiences. In 1972, the KMT convinced the US to contribute USD $1 million for the destruction of a twenty-six-ton stockpile. A twenty-seventh ton mysteriously showed up in return for more funds.[13]

The US government chose to engage directly with junta leader Ne Win on major counternarcotics programs, including spraying pesticides on poppy plants, training the military and police forces on counternarcotics operations, and crop substitution programs. The Drug Enforcement Administration (DEA) donated equipment and aircraft to the police and Myanmar's Military Intelligence (MI). The Myanmar regime's efforts earned the praise of the US executive branch and Congress, though the DEA would find that with the exception of the crop dusters, their equipment was hardly ever used.[14 and 15]

The US considered its aerial spraying program to be one of the most successful narcotics control initiatives (though aerial spraying poisoned water and food supplies, spurring the ethnic Shan to write to First Lady Nancy Reagan to stop the program),[16] but the Reagan administration dismissed the cease-fires forged by the MI with the help of Khin Nyunt, Lo Hsing Han, and Olive Yang as a way to end the drug trade, saying that "there is no basis to assume that the realization of the drug traffickers' purported 'political' objectives would cause them to abandon their very lucrative criminal activities."[17 and 18]

That sentiment was mostly true. Though the cease-fires did help bring peace to the country for the first times in decades, it threw an array of illicit businesses into overdrive, creating an unmeasurable black market in gemstones, jade, timber, drugs, and wildlife that would enrich some EAOs and military officers and make it harder to bring everyone to the bargaining table for political and peace negotiations. Following the cease-fires, the Myanmar National Democratic Alliance Army (MNDAA), the United Wa State Army (UWSA), and the National Democratic Alliance Army (NDAA) took over the drug trade and were even encouraged by MI leader Khin Nyunt, who reportedly told them he was upset by the George H. W. Bush administration's cutoff of the aerial spraying program following the SLORC's crackdown on the 1988 uprising. He told them to go for it on drugs to compensate for financial strains.

By 1996, Myanmar shifted toward producing pills and became a regional source country for the production and distribution of methamphetamine. By 2015, the Shan hills had become the global epicenter for the production of meth tablets, with most of the product being exported to Australia, New Zealand, and Japan. The UN Office of Drugs and Crime estimated that the Asian market for illicit methamphetamine is USD $61.4 billion a year, with a large proportion manufactured in Shan State superlabs.[19 and 20] After the February 2021 coup, these numbers are poised to exponentially grow. Meth production has skyrocketed and fighting near superlabs has increased. It looks like there is no near-term end for this scourge in Myanmar.[21]

* * *

According to members of the EAOs I interviewed for this book, Khin Nyunt promised them that a political dialogue would be the next and most important step that would *eventually* lead to discussions of disarming or creating a different type of Myanmar army. The consensus on the EAO side was politics first, with laying down arms or a discussion of joining a Border Guard Force (BGF) a distant second. I'm not sure where the discussion of winding down illicit businesses, especially drug trafficking, came in.[22]

The cease-fires and Khin Nyunt's promises disappeared when the government pushed for the BGF in 2009, leading to the first cease-fire agreement breakdown with the MNDAA—still led by Olive Yang's cousin, Peng Jiangsheng—and putting the rest of the EAOs on high alert. The MNDAA refused to join the BGF, and in August, under the auspices of a counternarcotics operation, Myanmar's security apparatus struck. The resulting violence led to Peng Jiansheng and more than 10,000 residents in Kokang territory fleeing to safety in China. Within weeks, the rebellion was quashed and the Tatmadaw had its first victory against a cease-fire group, a success owed to Min Aung Hlaing, the future military commander-in-chief, who commanded the operation.[23 and 24 and 25] Eventually, other cease-fires began to break down or assume a tenuous position.

The renewed violence caught the attention of the US, and the US embassy watched the Tatmadaw attacks on the MNDAA unfold. They reached out to NGOs, aid organizations, and contacts in ethnic organizations to gather details and cable back developments to Washington. John Whalen, the head of the DEA in Yangon and an encyclopedia on Golden Triangle-based EAOs, had spent much of his time in Myanmar working in Shan State on counternarcotics programs, and he understood the complex dynamics at play. He was particularly interested in how the 20,000–40,000-strong United Wa State Army (UWSA), one of the world's largest narco-armies, which was located in the vicinity of the fighting, would view the developments.[26]

The new US assistant secretary of state for East Asia and Pacific Affairs (EAP), Kurt Campbell, who was leading US policy on Myanmar, started to pay attention to the ethnic conflict and the magnitude of the broader issues at play. The MNDAA conflict was worrying, but the worst-case scenarios for further cease-fire breakdowns would center around Myanmar's two largest EAOs: the Kachin Independence Army (KIA), numbering roughly 10,000 troops and sitting atop amber, jade, gold, timber, and various minerals, and the UWSA. Both the KIA and UWSA had no plans to join the BGF, and they saw the MNDAA conflict as a preview of what they would encounter with the Tatmadaw.[27] Less than two years later, the cease-fire with KIA ended, and conflict spread to ethnic Kokang, Shan, and Ta'ang areas. The UWSA went on high alert and made clear it was in no mood to lay down its arms.[28]

The US, recognizing the impact of seemingly never-ending conflict on the country's political and economic development, invested in the peace process, directed aid and engagement to promoting dialogues, and expanded programs to help the country's most vulnerable populations caught in the crosshairs of war.

US Aid and Assistance to Ethnic Areas

Since the end of full-fledged counternarcotics programming in Myanmar (the DEA maintained its office but was restricted to liaison activities), the US focus on ethnic areas shifted to humanitarian assistance and human rights, especially for ethnic communities that had borne the brunt of abuses from the Tatmadaw and EAOs—forced portering, forced recruitment, being forced to serve as human minesweepers, extortion, and rape. Legislation and Executive Orders (EOs) all included language condemning human rights abuses, and aid was often conditioned on the junta's human rights record. Holding back on aid and assistance was supported by the country's prodemocracy leaders and human rights groups for fear it would really benefit the junta. Prior to Cyclone Nargis, Myanmar received USD $2 per capita in foreign assistance; Laos received twenty-five times that amount.[29]

US aid to Myanmar was required to support democratic activities both inside Myanmar and on its borders and humanitarian assistance to internally displaced persons (IDPs) and refugees. The US started providing assistance for refugees in the mid-1990s through State Department programs, and USAID essentially took over in 2000. Most assistance went to fund the UN High Commission on Refugees (UNHCR), the International Committee of the Red Cross (ICRC), the World Food Program, and other NGOs, some of which undertook sensitive programs like delivering cell phones and computers.[30] Assistance directed to the Myanmar-Thailand and Bangladesh-Myanmar borders went to help refugee camps and medical clinics in the area; an estimated 135,000 refugees lived in Myanmar-Thailand border refugee camps that were first established in 1984. The numbers in the Bangladesh camps would swing wildly from the tens of thousands to the hundreds of thousands, depending on Tatmadaw purges and military campaigns in western Rakhine State.[31]

Cyclone Nargis opened the aid spigots, particularly as local NGOs proved their ability to effectively get to those in need. More US assistance, built on the needs-based assistance for IDPs and refugees, also went to strengthen community-based organizations, train journalists, and improve education services on the border. There was no end date to these programs, and no one expected the situation inside the country to improve enough for the refugees to return and allow the US to wind down border programming. Then Thein Sein assumed the presidency and began to talk about peace.[32 and 33]

Peace in Our Time

Ending ethnic conflicts became a top priority for the Thein Sein government that was elected as the sixth step of the roadmap in 2010. He was a former member of the SPDC and stacked his cabinet with former military officials. But he seemed to be charting a new path, especially with ethnic groups. He appointed an envoy to lead peace talks—Aung Min, the minister of railways and a confidant—and formed a committee to lead dialogues and negotiations with EAOs. He established the Myanmar Peace Center (MPC), a sprawling set of buildings in Yangon, where negotiators and representatives from the government spent innumerable hours working on the peace process. He also set up the Myanmar Peace Fund to direct financing to areas where fighting had ended to help with rebuilding efforts. Thein Sein's approach to the peace process was striking, and the language he used and the authority that he gave Aung Min piqued the interest of EAOs. Aung Min even used the word "federalism," a word that had been taboo to the military for decades because it meant that the EAOs were ultimately seeking autonomy or secession. Thein Sein also acknowledged the devastation that had been wrought on ethnic communities, stating, "The people were going through a hell of untold miseries."[34 and 35]

Thein Sein brokered a bilateral cease-fire with the Shan State Army/Restoration Council of Shan State (SSA/RCSS) in December 2011; the Chin National Front, Karenni National Progressive Party, Arakan Liberation Party, and National Socialist Council of Nagaland-Khaplang faction (NSCN-K) in 2012; and the Pa-O National Liberation Organization and the All Burma Student Democratic Front in 2013.[36]

The agreement reached with the KNU in January 2012, however, was a watershed moment, effectively suspending the world's longest-running conflict and giving hope that the peace talks had real substance. The conflict with the Karen had captured the imagination of many a policymaker, academic, and aid worker, as well as, unfortunately, groupies, opportunists, and mercenary fantasists. Several Westerners went to the Thailand-Burma border, looking to free Burma by passing out leaflets or crossing the border to deliver messages, interview dissidents, or take up arms to fight the Tatmadaw. These adventures have been captured in great detail in books, many of dubious quality and "facts," that perpetuate the exoticism and mystique of Myanmar without delving into the root causes that makes peace so elusive.[37] The conflict even made its way into the movies. *Rambo IV*, released in January 2008, depicted weathered Vietnam vet John Rambo being hired by a church pastor to help rescue a group of Christian missionaries kidnapped by the SPDC. By one movie critic's account, Rambo himself slaughtered nearly three hundred soldiers to rescue the missionaries. The film was banned in Myanmar; however, the opposition youth group, Generation Wave, copied and distributed it. The KNU said the movie boosted morale, with soldiers adopting dialogue like, "Live for nothing, or die for something." That made Sylvester Stallone beam with pride.[38 and 39]

The news of the peace accord came in January 2012, just five weeks after Secretary Clinton's historic trip to Myanmar and while Ambassador Derek Mitchell, the Department of State's Special Representative and Policy Coordinator for Burma, was traveling from Myanmar to Chiang Mai, Thailand, to meet with border organizations. He understood the impact of the news and communicated back to Washington why this was so important.[40 and 41] I myself was in complete disbelief when I heard the news.

As the peace process continued, donors, multilateral organizations, and NGOs got involved. The USAID office in Myanmar, reestablished in 2012, started programming that year that was dedicated to supporting the peace process and providing humanitarian aid to IDP and vulnerable communities. Assistance dollars supported participants in the peace process through activities to build their capacity to effectively deliberate and negotiate. Equally important, USAID established the Women's Participation Fund, providing transportation and daycare costs for women involved in the peace process, allowing them to be able to attend events and meetings.[42 and 43]

NGOs, the EU, Norway, and Japan contributed to the peace process too, funding travel for peace process delegates and the MPC and bringing in mediators from other conflicts to provide best practices and trust-building mechanisms. There was also a smattering of independent consultants and experts, who typically rove from one global conflict to the next, and longtime Myanmar hands offering help.[44]

For the first time in many years, aid and assistance dollars were flowing to ethnic groups and humanitarian support inside the country. European countries began to reallocate funding away from the border, sparking concern among US officials and NGOs who had worked on these issues for years that it was too soon and not safe enough to wind down programming. While hopeful for the prospects for peace, no one who had been working on Myanmar before 2012 believed that a sixty-year-plus civil war could be solved with the stroke of a pen. Refugees on the Thailand and Bangladesh borders didn't feel safe to return, despite assurances from Aung Min. They saw the Tatmadaw attacks against the KIA in 2011 and 2012—occurring after Thein Sein ordered the Myanmar military to halt hostilities in 2011—and those in Shan State and couldn't trust the military to keep the government's word.[45 and 46]

Several organizations reliant on donor money refused to shift their operations to inside Myanmar, understanding the continued need for their work on the border. Dr. Cynthia Maung, who started the renowned community-run Mae Tao Clinic in the Thai city of Mae Sot, felt the impact of the shift in focus almost immediately. Founded in the wake of the 1988 uprising to treat prodemocracy activists escaping the crackdown, the clinic provides an array of services, including basic medical care, psychiatric care, prosthetics for land mine victims, and maternity care. With funding cuts, the Mae Tao Clinic has limited services but has managed to avoid shutting down completely. The US picked up some of the slack, but the needs are still too great.[47 and 48]

Thein Sein was determined to have a Nationwide Ceasefire Accord (NCA) signed before the 2015 general election, despite ongoing clashes between EAOs and the Tatmadaw and ethnic alliances forming and falling apart. By 2014, the peace process was hitting one roadblock after another.[49]

To complicate matters, a new group in town, the Arakan Army (AA), threw the peace process into further disarray. Formed in 2009 and led by a young and social-media savvy major general, Twan Mrat Naing, AA was trained by the KIA, and they fought for the Arakan fatherland and to reinstate the ethnic Arakan Buddhist kingdoms of the past. They began to amass victories and territories as they marched from Myanmar's north toward western Rakhine State. The AA was quite popular with young Arakan men who consumed and drew inspiration from the group's social media posts. The Tatmadaw was taken aback by their success, saw them as opportunists, and didn't think they should be included in the peace process. Other EAOs, especially the more powerful ones, thought they should.[50 and 51] The question on inclusion would become a major point of contention between the Tatmadaw and EAOs as national reconciliation dragged on.[52]

Despite these hurdles, on October 15, 2015 (three weeks before their election), eight EAOs signed the NCA, including the KNU.[53] Seven nonsignatories, who had been part of the negotiations, refused to sign the agreement due to the lack of inclusivity. The country's largest and most powerful EAOs—the UWSA, KIA, and Shan State Army-North (SSA-N)—did not participate, undermining the strength of the NCA. Thein Sein left the door open for the nonsignatories, saying they could join at a later date as they saw fit. The US issued a press statement commending all sides for their effort to end the world's longest-running conflict. The statement also urged the government to continue to engage with the nonsignatories.[54] Thein Sein bet his legacy on the peace process and in opening the country to democracy, and to him, he made good on it.[55 and 56]

The NLD Revives the Spirit of Panglong

When Aung San Suu Kyi's party won the general election in 2015, she put the peace process atop their list. For the ethnic groups, there was some optimism that the NLD would be more open to listening to and incorporating protections for them into legislation and making the NCA process more inclusive. There were concerns, however, about its relationship with the military. If Thein Sein couldn't get the military to stop shooting at the KIA, how could the NLD?

Aung San Suu Kyi invoked the legacy of her father, Aung San, and rebranded the peace process by announcing the "21st Century Panglong Conference," earning the early support of the UWSA and MNDAA.[57] The conference kicked off in August 2016 with a keynote speech from UN Secretary-General Ban Ki-moon to an audience filled with 750 delegates representing political parties, civil society, EAOs, ethnic alliances, and the military. In her opening speech, Aung San Suu Kyi stated that the NLD would bring back the "Panglong spirit and the principle of finding solutions through the guarantee of equal rights, mutual respect, and mutual confidence between all ethnic nationalities." Everyone liked the sound of that.[58]

Despite all the magnanimous speeches, the 21st Century Panglong Conference would be the high point in the NLD's effort to bring peace to Myanmar. Thanks to moves by the NLD, including dismantling the infrastructure Thein Sein put in place that EAOs had become accustomed to and erecting golden statues of the Bamar independence hero Aung San in ethnic capitals, ethnic groups began to feel that the "spirit" of Panglong was really Burmanization.[59] The NLD seemed clueless, and they were. The NLD thought that ethnic gripes were directed toward the military and that once the military was out of power, all would be solved. Both the ethnic Bamar and ethnic minorities had suffered under the military, but what the Bamar couldn't understand was how much worse ethnic nationalities had it. Former political prisoners did through their own experience. For every ten ethnic Bamar in a cell, there were one hundred Kachin. Though the ethnic Bamar returned to their cells bloodied, bruised, and oftentimes missing teeth after torture sessions, their ethnic nationality counterparts would return unrecognizable. The Bamar prisoners began to hear about the human rights abuses in ethnic minority areas and began to understand the depth of the military's depravity in these areas. These Bamar prisoners understood the long road ahead to repair the damage from ethnic conflict; the NLD did not.[60] This realization in the wake of the February 2021 coup has spread beyond prison walls. Now that the streets of Yangon and Mandalay were subject to air force flyovers and neighborhoods were being torched, urban Bamar got a taste of what their ethnic neighbors experienced, perhaps a silver lining in an otherwise abominable period that could result in a real process of reconciliation when the junta hopefully passes from the scene.

The country seemed awash in conflict by 2017 and no closer to peace.[61 and 62] The US started funding the Joint Peace Fund (JPF), an organization established by international donors from Australia, Canada, Denmark, the EU, Finland, Germany, Italy, Norway, Switzerland, and the UK to make the peace process inclusive.[63] The programs looked good on paper, but US development and conflict experts wondered if its funding was being used effectively or was only being used to support stakeholders holding meetings for the sake of holding meetings. It was not just about the representation of people but should also include discussions around women's participation, environmental issues, federalism, fiscal federalism, human rights, and basic capacity-building issues around meeting preparation and the building of negotiation skills.

In the end, these questions didn't have to be considered once the military seized power in February 2021. The peace process is now their peace process, but the military would hardly consider these questions to be important aspects of achieving a lasting peace. The coup destroyed whatever trust had been built, and conflicts are beginning to fester and rage. Protesters against the coup have fled to the jungles to train for a People's Defense Force and are looking for allies among EAOs.

US and global efforts to support the peace process and combat drugs at this stage seem all for naught. As the country descends further into the military's grip, Myanmar's most enduring issue will have to endure for quite a while longer.[64]

3

GEOSTRATEGY

WITH FRIENDS LIKE THESE

In April 2007, North Korean Deputy Foreign Minister Kim Yong-II and Myanmar Deputy Foreign Minister Kyaw Thu formally reestablished diplomatic relations at Yangon's Nikko Hotel. This newfound friendship would benefit both isolated regimes; one had cash and needed ballistic and possibly nuclear weapons, one had ballistic and nuclear weapons and needed cash.[1]

* * *

Myanmar's global isolation had limited it to troubling relations with North Korea and the government of the People's Republic of China (PRC). Though the US had no issue with the country's diplomatic relationships, military trade to North Korea and Myanmar's lopsided and exploitive partnership with the PRC were problematic. This often made sanctions ineffective and undermined the US's ability to undertake the type of development and investment steps the Myanmar government and civil society wanted. These ties also undermined, particularly with the PRC, getting closer to resolving Myanmar's most enduring challenges of national reconciliation and peace.

Friends Become Enemies, Enemies Become Friends

Renewed Myanmar-DPRK ties were suspicious for a number of reasons, but one was how Myanmar was able to move on from how the relationship ended in the first place. Myanmar immediately cut diplomatic ties with North Korea in 1983 after North Korean agents bombed a South Korean delegation visiting Rangoon's Martyrs' Mausoleum (commemorating those killed in 1947, including independence hero Aung San). The bombing killed twenty-one people, most of them senior South Korean cabinet officials, and injured forty-six. The assassination plot was meant to target South Korean President Chun Doo-hwan, who was late because he was stuck in traffic. Chun was visiting Ne Win and his government to improve ties with Myanmar.[2] North Korea denied they ordered the attack and disavowed one of the surviving bombers, Kang Min-chul, who lost an arm trying to blow himself up with a hand grenade to escape arrest. There was an outpouring of shock and sympathy by global leaders who were disturbed by the DPRK's heinous act.[3]

The 2007 Nikko Hotel ceremony sparked concern of a more nefarious relationship. There was unfortunate precedent. In what would be confirmed publicly years later, the North Koreans helped Syria build a facility capable of producing plutonium for the fissile cores of nuclear warheads. In 2006, the Israelis bombed the covert nuclear reactor at Al Kibar,[4] later admitting their role in the reactor's destruction and releasing redacted classified materials from 2007 that read, "Syria has set up, within its territory, a nuclear reactor for the production of plutonium, through North Korea. . . . To our assessment [REDACTED] secretive and orderly [REDACTED] for achieving a nuclear weapon."[5] Myanmar military defectors told the *Sydney Morning Herald* that Myanmar shared similar nuclear ambitions to Syria, hoping to go live with their own production facility by 2014.[6 and 7]

In 2009, exile media outlets published leaked photos of Shwe Mann, an SPDC member, traveling to North Korea in November 2008, signing an MOU for military trade deals and technical assistance. Up to that point, both sides had argued their relationship was purely diplomatic, but these photos and details upended that notion. It seemed clear that the Myanmar military was violating UN Security Council Resolutions (UNSCRs).[8 and 9 and 10]

In addition to photos and rumors, North Korean ships frequently sailed to Myanmar. These were not pleasure cruises and had no other mission than delivering or picking up goods. In November 2006, the 2,900-ton North Korean cargo vessel, MV *Bong Hoafan*, sought shelter from a storm and anchored at a Myanmar port. In May 2009, the MV *Mu San* dropped anchor off the Andaman Islands without permission and was detained by the Indian Coast Guard after a chase lasting several hours. Indian officials tried to determine if Myanmar had been on its route. In June 2009, the US tracked a North Korean ship, the *Kang Nam I*, heading to Myanmar. The ship eventually turned around and headed back from whence it came.[11 and 12] In June 2011, the Belize-flagged MV *Light* motored toward Myanmar ports. The US Navy sent a destroyer, the USS *McCampbell*, to catch up with the vessel, hailing the North Korean vessel four times. The US could legally board the ship per UNSCR 1874, which allows vessels to be inspected if "reasonable grounds" exist to suspect that weapons are being exported. After diplomatic pressure and naval harassment, the ship turned around.[13] Diplomats got creative whenever there were rumors of a ship coming to port from North Korea. Midnight bicycle rides with unexpected flat tires at the port were not uncommon. Midnight strolls for fresh air were also not unusual. One Japanese official disguised himself as a farmer and worked in the fields, binoculars hidden under his traditional Burmese sarong, to catch a glimpse of what the ships were unloading and who was there to receive the packages.

There was also a lot of money trading hands. Officials from Namchongang Trading (NCG) were reportedly setting up shop in Myanmar; NCG was a North Korean trading company sanctioned by the UN Security Council that had provided financial assistance to Syria's reactor project. The North Korean bank, Korea Kwangson Banking Corporation (KKBC), handled transactions numbering in the millions of dollars between the Korea Mining Development Trading Corporation (KOMID), North Korea's primary weapons dealer, and Myanmar. KKBC worked on behalf of Tanchon Commercial Bank, the main financial entity responsible for sales of conventional arms and ballistic missiles, and KOMID. There were reports of suspicious purchases and procurements—like magnetometers and machine tools—and the construction of strange buildings and tunnels. But there was no smoking nuclear or ballistic gun.[14 and 15 and 16]

In June 2010, the government rigorously denied nuclear weapons ambitions, with the minister of foreign affairs stating in a press release to the *New Light of Myanmar*, "it is reiterated that the allegations of Myanmar trying to develop nuclear weapons are unfounded and no efforts have been made to do so. Myanmar only wants peace and has no ambition to become a nuclear power state." Myanmar consistently messaged its peaceful nuclear aims. In September 2000, Myanmar asked the International Atomic Energy Agency (IAEA) for assistance in acquiring a research reactor. The IAEA agreed and would help as long as Myanmar achieved certain milestones, such as bringing its reactor safety and regulatory infrastructure up to a minimally acceptable standard. However, without telling the IAEA or improving its standards, Myanmar started negotiations with Russia over the supply of a ten-megawatt thermal research reactor. Thousands of military students were traveling to Russia to study topics related to nuclear physics. In February 2001, the SPDC and Russia's Atomic Energy Ministry announced plans to build the reactor in central Myanmar, but the project never took off. In July 2001, Myanmar established a Department of Atomic Energy, and at a press conference in January 2002, Military Intelligence's vice-chief, Major General Kyaw Win, reaffirmed Myanmar's peaceful intentions, emphasizing their desire to consider electricity generation from nuclear power.[17 and 18 and 19 and 20 and 21]

Myanmar had uranium deposits and was purchasing dual-use equipment that could have been used for scientific or medical purposes *or* missile and nuclear purposes. Myanmar had a motive to pursue the nuclear option, particularly given their paranoia of a US invasion and what they had witnessed in Iraq and Libya. However, a nuclear program was highly unrealistic because they lacked indigenous knowledge and supplies to build their own program, climate controls, and stable power generation. But more worrying for non-Myanmar-focused policymakers was that Nay Pyi Taw was a major source of hard cash for the North Koreans, violating several UNSCRs and US sanctions.

All of these pieces taken together greatly concerned US policymakers and analysts, and the Myanmar government and military were pressed on this issue at every available occasion. When confronted by Secretary Clinton on her visit in 2011, Shwe Mann became the first official to publicly acknowledge military ties. He held a press conference and denied a nuclear weapons program but acknowledged the content of the leaked photos. While in North Korea, he observed air force defense systems, weapons factories, military aircraft, and naval and other weapons in Pyongyang. He stated, "We observed how they trained their military, and how they upgraded their technology. Afterward, with the aim of improving the quality of our armed forces, we signed an MoU advancing cooperation between the two nations if needed." According to the MOU, North Korea would build or supervise the construction of special military facilities, including tunnels and caves in which missiles, aircraft, and even naval ships could be hidden.[22]

The Thein Sein administration did take significant steps to address concerns. In 2012, Thein Sein agreed to allow more scrutiny by UN nuclear inspectors, earning praise from nonproliferation organizations for a "remarkable decision." Myanmar also signed on to additional IAEA protocols.[23] The NLD government continued to pursue severing its military ties with North Korea, and in 2017, it took action in compliance with several UNSCRs on nonproliferation and North Korea. It kicked out Kim Chol Nam, the second secretary at the embassy of the DPRK in Yangon, who also reportedly worked for KOMID.[24]

This was welcome progress, but the relationship is still in place. Cutting ties to North Korea continued to find its way into talking points and press briefings from Trump administration officials, and in the fire-and-fury days in the summer of 2017, Trump was looking to squeeze North Korea from all sides, including by targeting any sources of hard currency. One of those countries was Myanmar. These issues will likely be in President Biden's points as well, especially as the new junta-government led by Min Aung Hlaing will not see any benefits to ending military ties with the DRPK, especially if it aids in modernizing the military.

The Best of Frenemies

Myanmar would also find itself square in the strategic competition between the US and the PRC. This book scratches the surface of the PRC and Myanmar's complex and long-standing relationship, but there are plenty of scholars and resources to consult, including, among others, assessments by Yun Sun, Murray Hiebert, Bertil Lintner, and Thant Myint-U.

The 1949 Kuomingtang invasion of Kachin State; Chinese communist support for Burma's largest insurgent menace, the Communist Party of Burma; military training and sales to EAOs in Shan State; and the building of large, exploitive infrastructure projects in which the bulk of natural resources and energy supplies went to the PRC all contributed to disgruntled generations of Myanmar military members, political figures, and citizens in the shadows of these megaprojects.[25] However, the increasingly reclusive SLORC, its successor, the SPDC, and now, the new State Administration Council (SAC) had relied on the PRC's protection from UN sanctions, military equipment, and economic investment.[26] By the early 2000s, China touched almost everything in Myanmar, especially its most sensitive development issues.

China shares a 1,400-mile border with Myanmar where the ethnic Kachin, Wa, Shan, Kokang, and other ethnic minorities reside. Chinese citizens, including retired People's Liberation Army (PLA) soldiers, have reportedly trained, sold weapons, and fought alongside EAOs, undermining and complicating an already tricky peace and national reconciliation process. Many of the ethnic groups along the border share familial, cultural, and business ties, so the connections are often beyond the central PRC government's purview. Beijing unlikely approved this support, particularly as its official position on the peace process is noninterference in an internal affair.[27] But Beijing is hardly neutral and has certainly inserted itself, especially when it smells perceived American interference.[28]

Throughout Derek Mitchell's tenure as US ambassador to Myanmar, the PRC was convinced that the US was courting the Kachin against it, and it warned Derek to suspend his travels there and not to lecture the PRC on how to deal with ethnic groups. Derek was accused by the PRC of convincing Thein Sein to suspend the Myitsone Dam in 2011. But Derek had seen the impact of the PRC's investment in the region and retorted that they were the problem in Myanmar; he also noted that the US had ties to the Kachin dating back to World War II. The PRC also made clear they didn't want the US involved in the peace process and that the main reason for their involvement was the shared border, refugee flows that crossed into China during active conflict, bombs that sometimes landed on their side of the border, and the fact that EAOs wanted them involved. They had a real stake in the process; the US did not.[29]

Beijing did not want the US involved in Myanmar, especially in Kachin State where its most lucrative projects were located. PRC entities are active in extracting natural resources there, primarily jade and timber. Myanmar holds the world's largest supply of imperial jade—the highest-quality jade—and Chinese traders and buyers were desperate to get their hands on it.

In 2015, the London-based NGO Global Witness grabbed international attention with its "Jade: Myanmar's 'Big State Secret'" report. Global Witness studied export data and spoke to a cross section of stakeholders to get a sense of the market size, its key players, and the impact of jade mining in Myanmar. Global Witness estimated the value of official jade production in 2014 was over USD $12 billion, though they believed it was much closer to USD $31 billion. At the 2014 annual gem emporium, the average price of jade was more than USD $13,000 per kilogram. To put that in perspective, a gemologist showed me a necklace with forty-three imperial jade beads; just one bead, about the size of a marble, was worth USD $1 million dollars.[30]

Many of the key players were EAOs given concessions in the early cease-fire days, and the two military holding companies—Myanmar Economic Corporation (MEC) and Union of Myanmar Economic Holdings, Ltd. (UMEHL)—and military-connected businesspersons owned jade mines as well. It was often unclear who the true beneficial mine owners were, especially as ownership changed hands over the years without the proper paper trail to track ownership. Gem traders relayed to me that jade mine owners would show up at the annual gem emporium with civilian names, but folks recognized them as active or retired military officers with high-level connections in the country and in the PRC.

Jade exacerbated conflict in Kachin State and generated intense resentment among the civilian population. Companies extracted the riches from their land and never put anything back into the community. As some put it, "the tree is in our garden, but we are not allowed to eat the fruit." Additionally, those working in the mines encountered dangerous labor conditions, where landslides claimed the lives of hundreds of workers and scavengers each year.[31] However, jade was the biggest revenue stream for EAOs and military-related companies, giving both of them reasons to increase their presence and fight for strategic locations to maintain security control. The demand in China wasn't going away, so neither would the problems. US sanctions wouldn't make a dent either as there was no market for jade in the US.

The extractive trades weren't the only deals PRC companies and ethnic groups were engaged in. Mong La, the Shan State border city already notorious for drug trafficking, became home to the 220-square-kilometer Yongbang Special Economic Zone (SEZ), an independent political entity within Mong La's borders vested with independent executive, legislative, and judicial power, a digital economy supported by a newly created Yongbang cryptocurrency, and an "e-citizenship" system open to any country.[32]

The Mong La area is controlled by Lin Mingxian's National Democratic Alliance Army (NDAA) and home to garish hotels, casinos, brothels, nightclubs, and markets selling all manner of things like tiger paws, pangolin scales, elephant skin, live monkeys, and other endangered species. Signs are in Chinese, the currency and phone networks are Chinese, and the clocks are set to Beijing time.[33]

In January 2019, Singapore's Channel News Asia reported that a Chinese tech company, Shanghai Shellpay Internet Technology (SSIT), planned to construct the Yongbang Blockchain Special Economic Zone (SEZ) after it was granted a piece of land by the "Peaceful Liberation Alliance of 7 States" in April 2018. In a press release, the Peaceful Liberation Alliance of 7 States described itself as "a self-governed group, a group consisting of the countless displaced refugees within the Union of Burma, a group with no formal identity; we are war refugees. The Yongbang Special Economic Zone Administration (hereinafter referred to as "the Administration") has taken the role of self-determination and a responsibility to govern ourselves with our people's freedom and prosperity in mind." No one had heard of them before. The *Channel News Asia* report went viral on Facebook and raised the Myanmar government's hackles. Myanmar did not like to be digitally annexed. SSIT's CEO admitted the Myanmar government hadn't been informed but didn't seem too concerned.[34] The Shan State minister for planning and economy, U Soe Nyunt Lwin, told *The Irrawaddy*, "The Shan State government has no knowledge of this project. We, the state government, did not make any agreement with them." In late February 2019, the Myanmar central government reached out to the Mong La authorities, who responded that they had no idea what was going on; they told *The Irrawaddy*, "It's impossible. We don't know what they're talking about . . . it would be such a huge project."[35] The Myanmar government also reached out to the PRC embassy, which also seemed in the dark; the embassy said it would investigate.[36]

Sketchy projects weren't limited to Shan State; Karen State was a target for "development" projects too. The US Institute for Peace (USIP), an independent institute founded by Congress, released a three-part report on efforts to build casino cities that would mask digital transnational networks and a host of illicit activities.

According to the USIP, in 2017, the Yatai International Holdings Group (IHG) planned to launch a "Smart City" on a 120-square-kilometer plot of land along the Myanmar-Thailand border area in a village once known as Shwe Kokko. Yatai IHG is a Hong Kong-registered company headquartered in Bangkok and headed by She Zhijiang, a Chinese entrepreneur with Cambodian citizenship and multiple aliases. The Myanmar Investment Commission (MIC) approved what was pitched to them as an "urban development" project, in line with the government's efforts to develop impoverished communities. It later included plans for high-end housing estates for as many as half a million people, casinos and recreation centers, an international airport, and a "blockchain special economic zone"—not the type of infrastructure typically suited for impoverished communities. Yatai IHG's local partner was to be Colonel Saw Chit Thu, the leader of the Karen Border Guard Force (BGF), a 6,000-strong, Tatmadaw-aligned militia. In exchange for the Karen BGF's loyalty, Yatai IHG was allowed to take control of some aspects of its territory's economic development, and this is apparently what it chose to pursue.[37] The new city would provide its own security, public utilities, health services, and management of land ownership through its own mobile currency exchange and payment app with transactions recorded by its own blockchain ledgers. Yatai IHG and its Singapore-based partner, Building Cities Beyond Blockchain, created Fincy to make the digital infrastructure of Shwe Kokko run and to allow for cross-border payments, currency exchange, and the purchase of cryptocurrency. The purported goal was also to make a "significant contribution to China's Belt and Road Initiative."[38]

Similar to the Yongbang Special Economic Zone, the Yatai IHG project would digitally annex a section of Myanmar that would be beyond the reach of Myanmar law enforcement and regulation. The Myanmar government saw this as an affront to their sovereignty and an undermining of the peace process. They were also concerned about illicit money being laundered through casinos, particularly at a time when the government was trying to clean up its banking system and clear out all the illicit money streams. The state counsellor's office launched an investigation in June 2020 and put it at the top of their talking points with senior officials in the PRC; the PRC embassy in Yangon denied any official Belt and Road Initiative (BRI) connection to the project.[39]

But it was a part of BRI. For the PRC, all roads went through Myanmar.

The PRC kicked off its BRI in 2013 (formerly known as "One Belt, One Road"), a massive global infrastructure and investment initiative that spans up to seventy countries through digital, land, and sea connections. Beijing was setting itself up as a strategic competitor to multiple global efforts, including the US's new Indo-Pacific Strategy (formerly known as "Asia Pivot/Rebalance"), India's Look East Policy, and Japan's East-West Economic Corridor.

Myanmar was an early supporter of BRI, and Aung San Suu Kyi was heavily courted by the PRC, receiving the equivalent of a head of state visit. In January 2020, she signed more than a dozen MOUs to help bring the BRI to Myanmar. The country was a crown jewel for the PRC; the planned infrastructure and transportation links constructed in Myanmar would significantly increase the PRC's regional and global power projection, giving it greater access and control to four-fifths of the container traffic and three-fifths of the world's oil supplies passing through the Indian Ocean.[40]

BRI's China-Myanmar Economic Corridor (CMEC) would be fueled by dozens of signed and publicly championed MOUs that contained vague language on cooperative trade and investment, as well as capacity-building measures and more lofty infrastructure plans. The CMEC featured some enormous and ambitious projects that would certainly benefit China's regional aspirations and throw small advantages Myanmar's way. The CMEC is an upside-down "Y" shape, connecting China's western Yunnan Province with Myanmar's second-largest city of Mandalay in central Myanmar, and stretching southeast down to Yangon and southwest to Rakhine State. The CMEC would include a high-speed railroad from Myanmar's northern border with southern China down to Mandalay and eventually to Myanmar's southern coast, a "New Yangon City" located west of Yangon, a Border Economic Cooperation Zone between the Shan State city of Muse and the southern Chinese city of Ruili, and the Kyaukphyu port project in Rakhine State on the Bay of Bengal.[41 and 42]

The US eyed PRC engagement warily, concerned about the exploitation, environmental damage, and labor issues that often accompanied these types of projects. There was no better example to drive this point home than Sri Lanka's Hambantota port project. The Hambantota port, initially a bilateral deal that was then folded into the BRI portfolio, became the poster child of the exploitive nature of PRC infrastructure projects. In 2002, Sri Lanka's president, Mahinda Rajapaksa, asked the PRC for loans and assistance for an ambitious port project in southern Sri Lanka. Feasibility studies proved that the project was not commercially viable at all, and no one would lend money, so Rajapaksa "negotiated" with one of the PRC's largest state-owned enterprises, China Harbor Engineering Company, which gladly gave him money with huge strings attached. Rajapaksa moved the port's opening timeline up by ten years, coinciding with his sixty-fifth birthday in 2010, and helped himself to the loan money to fill his political campaign coffers. Debt swelled, construction lagged, and in 2012, only thirty-four ships berthed at Hambantota, compared to 3,667 ships at the Colombo port. Sri Lanka couldn't make payments on the loan, so the PRC seized it and 15,000 acres of land around it for ninety-nine years, as per the terms of the contract. In 2017, former Prime Minister Ranil Wickremesinghe changed some of the terms, agreeing to lease the port for ninety-nine years to a venture led by China Merchants Port Holdings Company in return for USD $1.1 billion.[43]

Myanmar got spooked and realized the Kyaukphyu port in Rakhine State might be a Hambantota redux. The Myanmar government turned to the US for technical assistance on renegotiating terms of the original deal, and they got the costs of the port construction down from USD $7.5 billion to USD $1.3 billion and from ten berths to two.[44] The PRC was not pleased, either by the renegotiation or the US's involvement.

Adding to the tension already brewing between the US and the PRC on trade during the Trump administration, the Myanmar issue sparked an op-ed battle in late 2020. George Sibley, the chargé d'affaires at the US embassy in Yangon, called out the PRC for undermining Myanmar's "sovereignty" through debt traps. Sibley pointed out that most of the PRC business ventures in Myanmar were unregulated, plagued by corrupt practices, destructive to the local environment, and of little economic benefit to impacted communities.[45]

The PRC took issue with Sibley's op-ed and wrote a blistering one of their own. The author accused Sibley of "shoddy work" and "unreasonable logic," noting that Myanmar and the PRC have been close neighbors with a long, shared history of cooperation and support. The relationship stood the test of time so the American bandwagoners to the Myanmar team were simply a blip on the radar. The op-ed concluded that the "attempts of some Americans to stigmatize China-Myanmar relations are doomed to fail, just like an ant trying to shake a giant tree."[46]

The PRC, which generally played a peripheral role in the US's Myanmar policy, became a singular focus for the Trump administration. Myanmar policy had been primarily driven by human rights and democratization concerns internal to the country, not outside influences. If the PRC had been the main reason for engaging Myanmar, I believe sanctions would have been lifted long before and we would have had a more robust military-to-military relationship to counter influence and military sales from the PRC, Russia, and North Korea.

Back home, the US was searching for ways to counter PRC expansion and make the Indo-Pacific policy more robust. In 2018, Congress drafted and passed a bipartisan bill with complete buy-in to rethink development, public-private partnerships, and the support of US business engagement overseas: the Better Utilization of Investment Leading to Development (BUILD) Act.[47] The BUILD Act created the US International Development Finance Corporation (DFC), essentially injecting policy and budgetary steroids into the former Overseas Private Investment Corporation by increasing the budget to make commercially viable and strategic overseas investments. The DFC and other US organizations—like the Export-Import Bank of the United States, the Millennium Challenge Corporation, and USAID—were given a mandate to work with allies like Japan, the UK, Canada, Australia, and other partners to pool knowledge, technical assistance, and money to tackle development challenges in emerging markets. Though it couldn't match the seemingly endless amount of BRI funds, and though it was not necessarily created to focus only on countering the PRC, these agencies could invest where the PRC would not, like in small- and medium-sized enterprises, and they could bring high standards to private-sector-led projects.

Congress also doubled down on their commitment to the region and complemented the executive branch's Indo-Pacific Strategy by passing yet another bipartisan law, the Asia Reassurance Initiative Act (ARIA) in December 2018. ARIA would require the Trump administration "to develop a long-term strategic vision and a comprehensive, multifaceted, and principled United States policy for the Indo-Pacific region."[48] ARIA had several objectives, including expanding military relationships with regional partners, conducting regular multilateral and bilateral engagements, strengthening democratic systems, and pushing for free and fair trade, and Congress threw in USD $1.5 billion to help fund many initiatives to support those objectives.[49] While the law outlined how Congress viewed the US's role in Asia and how it intended to counter the PRC, the law was passed in the wake of several Trump outbursts about the cost of alliances and getting swindled on trade deals (in one high-level meeting with ASEAN ministers, the US trade representative's opening remarks included a running list of trade deficits the US had with each Southeast Asian country). Despite high-level travel by several cabinet secretaries and the release of major regional strategies, Congress likely felt slightly compelled to remind Trump that if he was serious about countering the China threat, Southeast Asia was ground zero.

* * *

Myanmar has always found itself operating from a place of insecurity, particularly as it sits between two giants and is the center of several global development schemes. What was once complicated is now even more so, as sliding back into its authoritarian ways once again forces the Myanmar regime to work with limited partners on their terms, not Myanmar's. Even though the country has fewer partners to work with and is further cut off from the US, it is not willingly running into the arms of the PRC as many fear. Its relationship with the country is fraught and uneven and will likely become tenser as Beijing and Yunnan balance their relationship with the Tatmadaw and EAOs and as its megaprojects swallow more land and resources. Myanmar will likely continue to turn to the DPRK as well, further pushing it back to its pariah status so that it can achieve the military modernization it wants and North Korea can get the hard cash it needs.

4

DEMOCRATIZATION

EXORCISING THE GHOSTS OF ELECTIONS PAST

A key indicator of a democratic country is its ability to hold a credible election and a peaceful transfer of power. Myanmar's record was paltry, and the military's electoral experiment in 1990, which resulted in a major loss for its party and a nonrecognition of the outcome, formed the basis of the US and the global community's punishment pile-on. Myanmar intended to try again in 2010, hoping to have learned lessons and looking to formally enshrine the military into the country's political system under the guise of a democratic election.

No one had high hopes for the 2010 election, especially given the country's long history of autocratic rule, bloody coups, and subversion of personal and political freedoms. Myanmar's descent into despotic governance began with General Ne Win's decision to seize power; he was a member of Aung San's Thirty Comrades that led the effort toward independence from British colonial rule only to later oust another fellow independence leader and Aung San associate, U Nu, first in 1958 and then for good in 1962. Ne Win felt U Nu was weak and indecisive, leaving the country vulnerable to dozens of insurgencies. He was convinced, and he soon indoctrinated his views into the fabric of the Tatmadaw, that the military was the only institution that could keep Burma from crumbling and protect its people from the civil wars engulfing the country.

Despite Burma's having a wealth of natural resources and one of the best health and education systems in the world, Ne Win drove the country into the ground. In the subsequent decades, Ne Win nationalized businesses, installed a socialist government with little capability and experience to run a complex economy, reallocated a significant percentage of the government budget to military coffers, and made enormous economic blunders.[1] In December 1987, Burma was granted Least Developed Country (LDC) status, which allowed them to get aid and assistance.[2] Burma would now be among the world's ten poorest nations.

The final straw for the long-suffering Burmese occurred in September 1987, when Ne Win enforced a demonetization that rendered 80 percent of the currency worthless. The government replaced the fifteen-, thirty-five, and seventy-five-kyat notes (the local currency) with denominations of forty-five and ninety, which, coincidentally, were multiples of Ne Win's lucky number nine (numerology was very important to him).[3] Ne Win's intention was to bankrupt black marketeers, but his move destroyed the licit economy. In the ensuing days, university students in the country's largest cities assaulted bus drivers and cab drivers who refused to take their newly worthless money. Government officials were assailed, and one minister's house was torched by an angry mob. Student-led protests grew as shortages of essential goods, and spiraling prices for rice, cooking oil, and medicine, severely impacted daily life. The demonstrations eventually swelled to tens of thousands of people marching in the streets of the country's biggest cities. By July 1988, Burma was in chaos. The military had turned their guns on the people, and soon thousands were dead or wounded.[4]

After twenty-six years in power, Ne Win announced he would step down on July 23, 1988, and he proposed a national referendum to vote on the question of a return to a multiparty system of government. The protests quickly turned from airing economic grievances and shifted toward supporting democratization. This shift was significant and would drive the country's activism and global responses for decades to come.[5]

Ne Win's announcement did little to quell the protests, and on August 8, mass demonstrations occurred across the country in what is now known as 8-8-88 or the 88 Uprising; eight is an auspicious number, making the date and timing that much more significant among the Burmese. Hundreds of thousands of peaceful demonstrators filled the streets, calling for democracy. In response, the government shot and killed an estimated 3,000 protesters. This was the spark that truly ignited Burma's prodemocracy movement.[6 and 7]

Burma's anti-government revolutionaries, political heavyweights, and the family members of well-known and respected leaders—including U Nu—came out of the woodwork to take advantage of the opening. This time also marked the emergence of the global face of Burma's democratic struggle: Aung San Suu Kyi.[8]

Aung San Suu Kyi was the daughter of Burma's most well-known and beloved independence leader, Aung San. Aung San was assassinated in 1947 on the eve of the country's independence and would be placed in the pantheon of Burmese heroes. In the later years of Ne Win's rule, images of Aung San were deemed a threat, as they were seen as a reminder of what could have been; his image disappeared from currency notes, posters, history books, and stories. At the height of the unrest in 1988, Aung San's images reappeared, suggesting that the country was in its second fight for independence.

After years of living abroad with her family, the return of Aung San Suu Kyi in April 1988 to care for her ill mother at the exact time that Burma's old despotic guard was collapsing onto itself seemed like destiny.[9] Aung San Suu Kyi had told her British husband, Michael Aris, that if her country ever needed her, she would go.[10] Seeing the protests and the reemergence of her father's image, Aung San Suu Kyi knew it was time to fight for her country. On August 26, she spoke to 500,000 people in front of the Shwedagon Pagoda, the country's most important religious site.[11] She was incredibly eloquent, wore flowers in her hair, and conveyed the spirit of Aung San, quickly winning the hearts of people both in Burma and overseas.

Aung San Suu Kyi was intelligent and well-educated, having attended the top schools in Burma, India, Japan, and in the UK at St. Hugh's College, Oxford, where she studied philosophy and economics. To the international crowd, she evoked her fellow women leading their own people power movements, including the Philippines' Cory Aquino and Pakistan's Benazir Bhutto.

She formed the National League for Democracy (NLD) party, along with a former military Commander in Chief and minister of defense, Tin Oo, to contest the election that Ne Win had promised.[12]

Fed up with the protests and chaos, on September 18, 1988, General Saw Maung, a Ne Win loyalist, forcibly took power and created the State Law and Order Restoration Council (SLORC). In the first three days of Saw Maung's regime, 1,000 schoolchildren, monks, and university students were slaughtered. Reporters covering the crackdown tearfully pleaded for something to be done. The 33rd Light Infantry Division (LID) shot into a crowd of hundreds of students marching in front of the US embassy. LIDs are Myanmar's shock troops designed for counterinsurgency operations; the 33rd LID would be sanctioned in 2018 by the US and EU for violence targeting the ethnic Rohingya. The death toll in the wake of the coup is estimated at 10,000. Protestors fled to the Thai border, looking to take up arms, garner foreign support, and take back Burma from the generals.[13]

The international community's reaction was swift, transforming Burma into a symbol of the West's fight for human rights. Three days following the crackdown, the US Senate passed Senate Resolution 464, condemning the killings and mass arrests, supporting a return to democracy in Burma, and calling on the Reagan administration to raise the issue of human rights and reconciliation with Burmese officials. The House of Representatives passed House Resolution 529, which was nearly identical in language. The Reagan administration responded on September 23 by suspending all US aid, including counternarcotics programs and arms sales.

When President George H. W. Bush assumed office, he sent a clear message to the SLORC that his administration would continue to press for a free and fair election. On April 13, 1989, President Bush issued Presidential Proclamation 5955, amending the Generalized System of Preferences (GSP) program and suspending preferential treatment.[14] The Bush administration was also fielding calls from human rights activists to try the military in front of an international tribunal for war crimes.[15]

Perhaps in an effort to rebrand, the SLORC renamed the country, cities, and rivers. Many of the British-associated names were changed, and in 1989, Burma became Myanmar. Most countries and international organizations recognized the name change, but the NLD, ethnic-based political parties, the US, and the UK continued to call it Burma because they viewed the SLORC and its new labels as illegitimate. After the name change, the junta arrested 6,000 political activists, including thousands of NLD members, and placed Aung San Suu Kyi under house arrest. The SLORC saw them as their biggest threat; the party members were traversing the country, meeting with people and spreading the ideas of democracy and freedom.[16]

Once key political figures were locked away, the SLORC announced an election for May 1990. Saw Maung said the military would stand by the result and hand over power to the elected government, which they assumed would be their own newly formed National Unity Party (NUP). The SLORC heavily engineered the election through tight restrictions on non-NUP campaigns and continuous political attacks on the NLD. Despite these efforts, the NLD beat ninety-three political parties, including the NUP.[17]

The SLORC was shocked. After months of silence, it ultimately failed to recognize the election results based on the argument that the original election structure did not stipulate a date for Parliament to convene. They issued Order 1/90, proclaiming that the duty of the elected representatives was to draft a new constitution and that the military, which held power under martial law, was not bound by any constitution. The SLORC announced the creation of a "Seven Step Roadmap to a Discipline-Flourishing Democracy," their political do-over. The US cut off economic aid and military assistance to Myanmar and downgraded diplomatic relations from the level of ambassador to chargé d'affaires. Subsequent legislation, executive orders, speeches, press briefings, and sanctions against the regime explicitly and consistently demanded a recognition of the 1990 election results, allowing the winners to convene Parliament.[18]

After 1990, the military grew more powerful, wealthier, and more entrenched in every aspect of Myanmar life, becoming inextricably linked to Myanmar's political and economic fabric. After the nonrecognition of the 1990 elections, it seemed impossible to imagine a time when the military would release its stranglehold on the country.[19 and 20 and 21]

The 2010 election, according to the State Peace and Development Council (SPDC)—the rebranded version of the SLORC—and to some activists in

Myanmar, was just that chance. The junta wanted to convince the world that this was a legitimate process and that Myanmar was indeed on the path to democracy. In March 2010, they issued the electoral laws, which officially annulled the results of the 1990 election and barred anyone currently serving a prison term from membership in a political party; political parties would have to oust those individuals or forfeit their status. This would mean that the NLD could not maintain its political party status unless they ousted Aung San Suu Kyi and the dozens of other members who won their seat in 1990 and were still in jail or under house arrest. Also, parties could not boycott the election and remain registered. So if the NLD called for a boycott, they'd be dissolved.

The electoral laws also posed problems for EAOs and their political representatives. Section 12 of the election law stipulated that if a party "directly or indirectly contacting or abetting an insurgent group launching armed rebellion against the Union, or associations and persons determined by the Union to have committed terrorist acts, or association declared to be an unlawful association" then that political party could not participate in the election. Some armed groups had cease-fires with the SPDC, but it was unclear that if armed groups failed to join the Border Guard Force, even with a cease-fire agreement technically in place, that those groups would be considered as actively rebelling. It was also not clear what "directly or indirectly" meant. Under these unclear terms, many of the ethnic Kachin parties were prevented from voting.[22]

After much international debate, the NLD declined to oust its members, boycotted the election, and was de-registered. The US was preparing to write the whole thing off; however, some prodemocracy activists and members of the NLD and ethnic political parties decided to participate, viewing this as their only chance in nearly fifty years to be a part of the governing system and be able to change the system from the inside. They wanted support from the US. The National Democratic Force (NDF)—formed by several now-former NLD members and led by Khin Maung Shwe, a former member of the NLD's Central Executive Committee—and several ethnic-based parties chose to participate.

The US was grappling with what to do—call the whole process a sham? Offer cautious optimism? How do you support the prodemocracy activists running for office, many of whom benefited from US educational and political training and could use those skills if they were elected? There was intense debate in the US government. Scot Marciel, the Deputy Assistant Secretary (DAS) in the Bureau of East Asian and Pacific Affairs (EAP), spoke to Bill Burns, the Deputy Secretary of State about a US boycott; everyone in the US government was deeply skeptical about the election but was wondering how to tactically play it. Those working on policy couldn't find anyone who said this would lead to an opening, and there were no signs of reforms; however, those in Myanmar were arguing that reforms may not be immediate but could be in the medium- to long-term if they were in office. The NDF and ethnic parties argued that there was the slimmest of hope that the election might lead to unintended consequences, with change happening beyond SPDC leader Than Shwe's control. More optimistic US policymakers offered that the psychology of "elected" military officials might change once they shed their military uniforms and donned civilian ones; since they were no longer in the military, their only source of authority was through new civilian institutions.[23 and 24] Might they make these power centers to continue to support their interests?

In May 2010, EAP Assistant Secretary Kurt Campbell visited the country to push US human rights objectives but more specifically to gather information to inform about how the US should handle the election, push for engagement with the NLD and other parties unfairly targeted by the laws, and get assurances that the process would be fair to those contesting. He went in with the notion that the US could be willing to give the election process a chance, especially if the regime consulted with the NLD and ethnic parties to at least lend credibility to the process. In two days, he met with junta ministers, the Union Election Commission (UEC), and the head of the Union Solidarity and Development Association (USDA), a SPDC-supporting organization with a massive membership made up of military officials and "volunteers." Kurt also met with ethnic groups, the NLD, political leaders, and Aung San Suu Kyi, who was still under house arrest. Despite meeting with the widest array of stakeholders, Kurt did not come away with any clear answers and certainly no assurances from the junta about making the process even slightly more democratic. The SPDC hadn't and wouldn't engage with anyone; to them, the time to do that had been with the first step in the roadmap at the national convention, which had been held more than a decade previously.[25 and 26]

Following the Roadmap

While the US contemplated its policy approach, the SPDC forged ahead. The USDA, replete with millions of members, a nationwide organizational infrastructure, and substantial financial resources, transformed itself into the Union Solidarity and Development Party (USDP) to contest the election. Military officials in the SPDC—with the exception of Senior General Than Shwe and Vice Senior General Maung Aye—retired from the military and joined the USDP as candidates; Thein Sein, the prime minister and now a retired lieutenant general, would lead the party. In late April, all active-duty cabinet members resigned their commissions, and on April 29, the USDP registered their party with the UEC, joining twenty-nine other parties contesting.[27]

Thein Sein's appointment came as a surprise because there were many, including myself, who thought that the charismatic SPDC member Shwe Mann would lead. But Shwe Mann was also known for being ambitious and not always following orders, which concerned Than Shwe.[28] Thein Sein was perceived as a pliable, quiet, less corrupt, dutiful soldier who would follow Than Shwe's orders. As the prime minister, he was the official that traveled overseas to ASEAN meetings and other diplomatic ventures, and he gained some positive recognition during the Nargis recovery efforts. He was perhaps the kinder, gentler SPDC official and a more palatable public face. No one expected him to rock any boats.[29]

In the end, the US did not support the election, but with an eye toward supporting those prodemocracy activists who were participating, they didn't completely throw it under the bus either. Despite a highly orchestrated event where everyone knew the outcome, Washington watched the election closely. The good news was that the election day was relatively peaceful. At the regional level, the Shan Nationalities Democracy Party, Rakhine Nationalities Party, and All Mon Region Democracy Party beat the USDP and won 28 percent, 51 percent, and 30 percent of their local seats in Shan, Rakhine, and Mon States, respectively. The NDF won twelve seats in both the upper and lower houses of Parliament. Forty-three women won. The unsurprising/bad news was that the USDP "won" 77 percent of all contested seats, meaning that with their presence in Parliament and the constitutionally mandated clause allocating 25 percent of all parliamentary seats at national and local levels to the military, they had a supermajority and the ability to block any constitutional amendment attempts to make the constitution more democratic.[30]

President Obama said the election was "neither free nor fair" and didn't come close to meeting international standards. Secretary of State Hillary Clinton said she was "deeply disappointed" at a "severely flawed" process and that Myanmar "missed an opportunity." The international community called the election a sham and felt that the Parliament would be nothing more than a rubber stamp for Senior General Than Shwe's whims.[31 and 32]

In March 2011, the new government sat, and the country's top leaders and ministers were selected by the elected and military-appointed members of Parliament. Thein Sein became president, and the two vice president slots went to Tin Aung Myint Oo, a former SPDC member and antidemocracy hardliner, and an ethnic Shan politician, Sai Mauk Kham. Shwe Mann became the Speaker of the lower house. The last member of the SPDC, Tin Aye, became the head of the UEC. Senior General Than Shwe and Vice Senior General Maung maintained their military titles but retired quietly to their homes in Nay Pyi Taw, now having accomplished their Seven Step Roadmap to a Discipline-Flourishing Democracy.

Though the political landscape looked dark, there was one bright spot. One week after the election, Aung San Suu Kyi was released from house arrest. Swarms of people gathered outside of her home on University Avenue; she met them at the gate, waving and giving her thanks for their support.

Foreign governments heralded her release. President Obama said, "She is a hero of mine and a source of inspiration for all who work to advance basic human rights in Burma and around the world." Secretary Clinton noted that she "has endured enormous personal sacrifice in her peaceful struggle to bring democracy and human rights to Burma. . . . Through it all, Aung San Suu Kyi's commitment to the Burmese people has not wavered."[33] Her husband's family in the UK were elated. She hadn't seen her sons in a decade. Aung San Suu Kyi's brother-in-law, Adrian Phillips, said, "We are obviously very pleased if it means we can contact her again after so many years of silence. . . . She has a granddaughter, Jasmine, who she has never seen." Even the former president of South Africa who helped dismantle the country's apartheid system, F. W. de Klerk, said, "For years we have been asking . . . for her release. We welcome it, and we hope it will last, and there won't be a regression of any nature." Other fellow Nobel laureates were ecstatic.[34]

Soon after, she began to realize how much she had missed and how isolated she had become. The section of road in front of her house was blocked with barbed wire, barricades, boulders, and armed police. Through the years, her friends, colleagues, and supporters were able to sneak magazines, books, and news to her, but it was limited. Cell phones were also quite new to her (and to the country), and she had no idea that the modern telecom age had arrived; someone even had to explain that people were taking photos of her with their phone. Aung San Suu Kyi was upset; she had missed out on so much and felt her connection to the world was tenuous. She also felt very disconnected with Myanmar's youth. Aung San Suu Kyi reached out to the US embassy and requested to meet with the young people who visited the American Center. She sat with them and listened about their world, their anxieties, and their hopes for the future. She felt a renewed sense of purpose.[35]

Flickers of Progress

Things were changing in Myanmar. The country's new president, Thein Sein, took up his office in March 2011 and began speaking publicly about political reform that was unlike the droning yarns junta officials had spun in the past. In the first six months of his term, Thein Sein reached out to political dissidents and NGOs, inviting them to help develop the country; established a National Human Rights Commission; started discussing national reconciliation and outreach to EAOs; allowed unions to organize; and eased media restrictions.[36 and 37]

Most shockingly, he reached out to Aung San Suu Kyi and met with her in August 2011 in an effort to build a relationship.[38] The SPDC often refused to meet her and spent decades spreading ugly rumors and lies about her, calling her a "whore" and a foreign stooge. When she did meet with them, it was often unproductive and meaningless theater. During Ambassador Derek Mitchell's first visit to the country in late August 2011, after his confirmation as Special Representative and Policy Coordinator for Burma, he met with Aung San Suu Kyi and asked her about the changes he was seeing. He felt that she could give him a much clearer view and dismiss any unrealistic optimism. She, too, was cautiously optimistic. Her relationship with Thein Sein was developing positively, and they were even talking about the NLD reregistering to run in a by-election to fill forty-four seats vacated by the appointment of senior government leaders as ministers. Her note on the election and NLD reregistration were of keen interest to US policymakers back home; it would be significant to them if the Thein Sein government paved the way for the return of the NLD—a big risk for him but a step toward meeting the international community on its demands.[39 and 40]

In April 2012, a newly reregistered NLD and its chairwoman, Aung San Suu Kyi, prepared for their first step in exorcising the 1990 electoral specter. The NLD was contesting a by-election to fill seats vacated by ministerial appointments. Despite less than fifty seats up for grabs, it was an important test for the Thein Sein government to allow for a credible election and to potentially hand NLD victors their seats.

The campaign was not all smooth; the NLD cited major irregularities, including candidate intimidation, election poster vandalism, vote buying, and voter rolls filled with dead people. Skeptics of the reforms thought the Thein Sein administration was just "old wine in new bottles"; the junta's successor was tricking everyone and lulling domestic constituencies into a false sense of hope while it was only poised to crush prodemocracy forces once again. Derek urged the government to hold a credible election and noted that the US would support the results if the people deemed them acceptable and credible. He also noted that voting day was only one step in the democratic process; Myanmar still had to hand power to the winners and allow them to govern.[41 and 42]

Despite the concerns, voting took place on April 1 and went relatively well. Aung San Suu Kyi, as well as forty-two of her colleagues, won their parliamentary seats, bringing them one step closer to fulfilling a twenty-two-year-old dream.[43]

Accolades came rolling in. The US's UN ambassador, Susan Rice, applauded the "critical step on the path to consolidating and strengthening Myanmar's democratic reforms." Senator Jim Webb praised Aung San Suu Kyi and Thein Sein for their work in bringing about reform. He was in the country after the election and spoke with parliamentarians and other prominent figures and called the developments a "profound moment" in Myanmar's history. Senator John McCain, who also closely followed the issue, stated, "This is a historic moment for Burma, as 'The Lady' finally takes her rightful place as an elected leader of her fellow citizens." Both Webb and McCain also recommended that the US's stringent sanctions policy be revisited and that an easing should be considered.[44 and 45] It was unimaginable to be talking about lifting sanctions that had been in place for years, but it was also unimaginable to have Aung San Suu Kyi and her party in office. Maybe things were really changing.

Preparing for a Democratic Test

The biggest test of all for the country would be the upcoming 2015 general election. By this time, I had left government and was running the consulting firm I founded, Inle Advisory Group. Though politics wasn't my primary focus, I planned to be in Myanmar for the 2015 election. I wanted to witness it for myself.

There was significant pressure on the UEC, headed by former SPDC member Tin Aye, to hold a credible process. The UEC had received support from international NGOs and foreign governments; however, the stakes and expectations were so high. Tin Aye was constantly berated by the international community, activists, and his own government. The UEC set the election date for November 8, 2015 and invited the Carter Center and the EU to monitor it, the first time in at least sixty-five years that the country would permit Western poll observers.[46] Other organizations were later added, including the International Republican Institute, the National Democratic Institute, the International Foundation for Electoral Systems, and various individuals from global governments, universities, and multilateral organizations.

However, there were steps the UEC took that drew criticism from the international community. The UEC disqualified almost all of the Muslim candidates running, as well as some prodemocracy activists, and disenfranchised ethnic Muslim Rohingya from voting despite them being able to vote in the 2010 election.[47] The US delivered a sharp rebuke, saying, "the move to disqualify some 100 candidates, through an opaque and discriminatory process, risks undermining the confidence of the Burmese [Myanmar] people and the international community in these elections."[48] Likely due to global pressure, the UEC reinstated a handful of candidates, all of them Muslim. Worried about further shenanigans, the Yangon-based embassies of Australia, Canada, Denmark, France, Norway, Japan, Sweden, the UK, and the US issued a joint statement saying, "we are supporting efforts to promote a credible, transparent and inclusive election, underpinned by healthy competition that ensures freedom of expression and respect for human rights." The joint press release went on to say that the signatories "are concerned about the prospect of religion being used as a tool of division and conflict during the campaign season."[49]

Other vestiges of the past spooked the policymaking community and the NLD. In August 2015, Thein Sein, the military, and those loyal to them removed a significant rival and competitor—the lower house Speaker and former SPDC member, Shwe Mann, and his ally, Deputy General Secretary Maung Maung

Thein—from their respective positions within the party. Security forces surrounded the USDP headquarters during the ouster, preventing some of those present from leaving, and police forces were at Shwe Mann's residence following his removal. It drudged up bad memories of SLORC and SPDC members taking out their "colleagues" through trumped up corruption charges, mail bombs, or helicopter crashes. Ye Htut, Myanmar's candid presidential spokesperson and minister of information, said President Thein Sein sacked Shwe Mann because the Speaker supported controversial bills in Parliament and had ties to rival party leaders (he and Aung San Suu Kyi had been working quite closely together in Parliament).[50] Aung San Suu Kyi canceled a planned trip to Shan State and met with Shwe Mann on August 17. She echoed widespread concerns on the USDP's ouster tactics, noting, "With regard to the happenings in the middle of the night, this is not what you expect in a working democracy."[51 and 52] The day following the ouster, Shwe Mann posted a picture and a short note on his Facebook page, thanking citizens for their concerns. He later noted that he would "continue to serve in his full capacity until the very end" and would abide by the USDP's decision.[53]

Shwe Mann's ouster reverberated throughout the US government. At a Washington, DC-based think tank event, Danny Russel, the new EAP assistant secretary of state, stated, "The internal leadership dispute within the USDP had a chilling effect on the political climate. . . . The government and the ruling party have to act in a way that reinforces, not undermines, public confidence in the government's commitment to democratic processes." Danny went on to say that the ruling party had the right to make its own internal personnel decisions, but "whatever the rationale . . . the government and the party really needs to bend over backwards to demonstrate that the bad old days are in fact over and they will not avail themselves of the tools of oppression that marred Burma for so many decades."[54]

The NLD was not without their problems either, particularly on matters of inclusivity and democracy in practice. Members of the 88 Generation Students, who had risked their lives during the 88 Uprising and subsequent political protests in the country, were willing to campaign as NLD members, rather than maintaining a separate identity, to bring together the major forces in the prodemocracy movement under one banner for the first time. Ethnic minorities also hoped to be a part of the NLD; Aung San Suu Kyi evoked the spirit of Panglong, her father's efforts to recognize ethnic rights and inclusivity.

That's not what happened.

The NLD's candidate list failed to include anyone outside of the party, ignored nominations from local NLD chapters for qualified candidates, and did not include any Muslim candidates who applied. Ko Ni, a respected and well-known Muslim lawyer and NLD member, said the NLD leadership intentionally excluded over a dozen Muslims from its candidate list to placate Buddhist nationalist hardliners who threatened the party.[55]

The NLD's political machinations were met with protests. A prominent political activist said the NLD's exclusion of most of the 88 Generation applicants would fragment the pro-reform camp, saying, "This is an insult and their decision will make the opposition force shatter. It's such a shame for them to make this kind of decision without even thinking for the country."[56] Prominent prodemocracy activist and founding 88 Generation Student member Ko Ko Gyi was excluded from the candidate list after joining the NLD.[57] It was essentially too late for him to register his own party so he concluded, "I've decided not to run in the next election as an independent candidate because I don't want the votes for the democratic forces to split."[58] Despite his anger, he knew how fractiousness could spell the end of the prodemocracy movement.

* * *

The US needed to see a credible election; any policy step, punitive or positive, would hinge on its conduct and acceptance by the Myanmar public. Ben Rhodes, Obama's deputy national security advisor and a key aide on the Myanmar issue, as well as other US policymakers, stated that they could accept that the election would have flaws, but they wouldn't stand for violence, over-the-top electioneering, or anything close to what happened in 1990.[59] Rhodes, fully invested in Myanmar policy following a 2012 trip by Obama, traveled to the country in 2015 to relay the views of the White House, assess the political climate, and press on the Rohingya issue. He packed his short trip with meetings with US and international election observers, the UEC's Tin Aye, President Thein Sein, Commander in Chief Min Aung Hlaing, the minister of home affairs (a ministry in charge of security and policing, a critical component for protecting the polls and electorate during the election), and Aung San Suu Kyi. Rhodes reiterated the call for transparency and a credible election process and raised concerns regarding the intrusion of religion into politics and the ongoing plight of the Rohingya. Rhodes stressed the importance of international observers in assessing whether the vote would be properly conducted and disputes fairly adjudicated, noting, "In any country, you are able to compile a body of reporting from different sources and evaluate whether there is an appearance that decisions disadvantage one political or ethnic faction over another, so that will be apparent. Our hope is that this election is truly inclusive and that if there are problems, they are problems of capacity, not will."[60]

In an October 21 congressional hearing, EAP Assistant Secretary Danny Russel was questioned on how the Obama administration could shape US policy after the election. He stated the US government "will make our assessment based on what we hear and see. It is critically important that all parties accept the results of the polling. . . . Our ability to assist the new Burmese [Myanmar] government, let alone to look at relaxation of sanctions . . . will depend on our assessment of the integrity of the overall process. . . . The conduct and results of these elections will fundamentally shape our engagement with the Burmese [Myanmar] government in 2016 and beyond."[61]

* * *

In November, I traveled to Myanmar to be in the country on what was going to be a historic day. I had to be there and witness it myself, to see if the changes were real, and probably because of FOMO.

There was a lot of excitement and fear. I decided to stay with my friend and her husband. I wanted to be with friends to celebrate what would hopefully be a celebratory event. But if shit hit the fan, I also wanted to have access to a car and resourceful friends if we needed to get out of town quickly.

Myanmar's election booths opened at 6:00 a.m. on November 8. Voters had already been in line for hours, ready for what they felt was their first real vote since 1990.

I'd be spending the day tagging along with Josh Hills from the International Republican Institute (IRI) in Yangon. He was an official election monitor and had an extra spot in his car. Some 12,000 domestic and 1,000 international accredited observers and thousands of political party agents were observing the vote across the country with mostly unrestricted access, including to polling stations inside military compounds.

We managed to visit several polling stations, though I couldn't go in as I was not a credentialed observer. I could see voter rolls, voting instructions (including in cartoon form for those who had difficulty reading the ballot instructions), UEC volunteers to assist voters, and pots of indelible ink to be applied to the forefinger to prevent double voting.

Josh had his Myanmar IRI colleague with us as well, and we drove him to his polling station. He lined up with his neighbors and chatted with them to gauge how the day was going. Most of the polling stations were at schools and the volunteers were former or current schoolteachers, so everyone fell back to old habits of listening to their teacher for fear of being yelled at. It was more effective than staffing the stations with police or military. Indeed, a few people in line got too rambunctious, prompting the teacher/polling station head to yell at them to be quiet and show some respect for the process. Everyone immediately went quiet, even me.

We also visited Aung San Suu Kyi's district polling station, which was complete chaos. The place was teeming with journalists, voters, and people who just wanted to catch a glimpse of the Lady casting her vote. There was a scuffle to get her picture, causing some folks to be pushed and trampled. It was one of the few reports of "violence" that day in Yangon.

We went to check in on an NLD campaign office that was brimming with activity. It was an electoral nerve center, with members on phones scribbling down information, including any complaints they could register with the UEC or early voting results. There were whiteboards and paper sheets taped to the walls with voting districts and candidate information, maps strewn across the floors, and a few people cooking to sustain everyone for what was likely going to be a long day.

We drove by the USDP headquarters in Yangon to see how they were monitoring the polls and tallying the votes. The gates were locked. The driveway was empty except for a few plastic bags and some crows. We rang a bell, but no one answered. The place was a ghost town. At first, we joked that it looked like they had already given up, but then those sentiments gave way to paranoia. What if they knew something we didn't? What if they skipped town because the military was going to roll in after the polls closed and arrest everyone? We slowly drove away, completely unnerved.

Putting the Ghosts of 1990 to Rest

Most of the results came in that evening, though votes from further locales would drip in over the next few weeks. One polling station was located up a mountain in the far reaches of Kachin State. The person bringing the ballots back to the nearest town with an accessible road had to walk the ballots down through a densely forested mountain, a trip which took several days.

When the UEC announced the official results on November 20, 2015, it confirmed the NLD had won a landslide victory, winning nearly 80 percent of the elected seats in the People's Assembly, more than 80 percent of the elected seats in the National Assembly, and more than 75 percent of the elected seats in the state and regional parliaments. President Thein Sein's USDP was demolished, securing forty seats at the national level and seventy-six seats in the state and regional parliaments. With the exceptions of the Arakan National Party (ANP), which focused its efforts in Rakhine State, and the Shan Nationalities League for Democracy (SNLD), which campaigned primarily in Shan State, few of the ethnic-based political parties won seats, a surprise to many, including myself, who thought that they would have won their own districts. It turns out that voters wanted a show of force in government against the military and that instead of creating a fractious government, the way to secure at least a small guarantee for continued democratization and the recognition of ethnic rights and freedoms would be to vote for the NLD. There would be one prodemocracy voting bloc.[62]

Election observers from the EU and the US-based Carter Center deemed the election credible. The EU said 95 percent of its more than one hundred election monitors rated the balloting as either "good" or "very good" and that voter list inaccuracies were uncommon and not systemic. The Carter Center highlighted some election day issues, including transparency problems with advanced voting in military barracks and other government-controlled areas.

Almost everyone expected the NLD to win the majority of votes except the USDP, who were mostly left in a state of shock. Zaw Htay, the deputy director general of the office of the president said, "All of our calculations were wrong. It was like a tsunami. . . . This is payback for the last 50 years."[63] Top USDP officials were quick to concede their electoral loss, allaying fears of a repeat of the 1990 election. Lower House Speaker Shwe Mann announced his loss first, followed by the chairperson of the USDP, Htay Oo, and President Thein Sein. They also congratulated the NLD on their win; even Commander in Chief Min Aung Hlaing offered his congratulations.[64]

World leaders, including UN Secretary-General Ban Ki-moon, British Prime Minister David Cameron, Canadian Prime Minister Justin Trudeau, French President François Hollande, Indian Prime Minister Narendra Modi, and the Dalai Lama all commended Aung San Suu Kyi on her win.

US President Barack Obama called both President Thein Sein and Aung San Suu Kyi to congratulate them on the election. In his conversation with Thein Sein, Obama praised him for his reform efforts and praised the government, political parties, civil society, the UEC, and the people for holding and participating in a credible election. In his call with Aung San Suu Kyi, the official White House readout stated, "The President commended her for her tireless efforts and sacrifice over so many years to promote a more inclusive, peaceful, and democratic Burma. The two leaders discussed the importance for all parties to respect the official results once announced and to work together in the spirit of unity to form an inclusive, representative government that reflects the will of the people."[65] Josh Earnest, the White House press secretary, said the election process was encouraging and "represents an important step in Burma's democratic process. . . . What is clear is that for the first time ever, millions of people in Burma voted in a meaningful, competitive election."[66] US Secretary of State John Kerry issued a press release, praising the conduct of the election and commending "all of the people and institutions in the country who worked together to hold a peaceful and historic poll." The US highlighted concerns too, including reports of electoral fraud, disenfranchisement, and the seats allocated to unelected military members of Parliament.[67]

Hillary Clinton, the former secretary of state and a presidential candidate, who had a significant personal and professional interest in Myanmar, also praised the election and the Myanmar people for having "shown once again that they are determined to keep moving forward toward a better future."[68]

Probably the person most relieved about the whole election was Tin Aye. He had weathered attacks from all sides and the death of his wife in the midst of everything. He had done his job and had done it well.

Senator Mitch McConnell, a long-time Myanmar watcher and Aung San Suu Kyi's biggest congressional advocate, was quite pleased about the results but was wary of the constitutional issues that would prevent an Aung San Suu Kyi presidency and whether the military would peacefully hand over power in March 2016. For him, until he saw clear indications that the political transition was complete, there were not going to be any major policy changes.[69]

McConnell didn't have to worry too much. Following the election, Aung San Suu Kyi and members of the NLD met with outgoing USDP and top military leaders, including Thein Sein, Shwe Mann, and Min Aung Hlaing. By all accounts, the meeting went well, and afterwards, both the USDP and military chiefs publicly reiterated their recognition of the election results and support for a smooth transfer of power, with Min Aung Hlaing stating, just one month prior to the USDP handing over power to the NLD, that he did not want to "let Myanmar become an Arab Spring failure," suggesting that the military would observe the will of the people and their votes and ensure a peaceful transition.[70] Those words would come back to haunt him nearly five years later.

Thein Sein ordered all ministries to "open the books" and provide complete information to the NLD about their operations. The outgoing and incoming governments established committees to oversee the transition and met regularly up until the official handover in March 2016. News spread that even Senior General Than Shwe met with Aung San Suu Kyi. Than Shwe called Aung San Suu Kyi Myanmar's "future leader" and pledged support for her.[71]

For the US and for the NLD, one item remained: Aung San Suu Kyi could not be president per Article 59(f) of the constitution, which stated anyone who had a spouse or children with foreign citizenship could not be president. Her children held British citizenship. The NLD, at the direction of the party's advisor and lawyer Ko Ni, pulled together a bill to create a position called state counsellor, a role guaranteeing her the right to contact government ministries, departments, organizations, associations, and individuals. She would be accountable to the Parliament and would technically be the second-in-command in the civilian government (though she made comments about being "above the president") and effectively be in charge. Legal experts said the state counsellor bill was "airtight" and that the military could do little to stop or veto it. Aung San Suu Kyi's new role immediately caused tension with the military, which was seemingly blindsided by the legislative action. Other MPs criticized the bill, stating that the NLD should be using its early days in power to enact policies that benefitted the public, including the release of political prisoners, rather than focusing on consolidating power in the person of the party's leader. Fair point, but this bill revealed what had actually long been the NLD's main goal: bring Aung San Suu Kyi into power.[72]

5

ENGAGEMENT

PROVE THE SKEPTICS WRONG

Ambassador Larry Dinger, the chargé d'affaires at the US embassy in Yangon in 2009, held a US presidential inauguration event at the American Center. The American Center was and is an important resource in Myanmar; it provides internet connectivity, a library, research and writing resources, English-language courses, events, and a safe place to meet and discuss politics. Many young people enthusiastically attended that night. As President Obama spoke, he uttered one line that stood out: "To those who cling to power through corruption and deceit and the silencing of dissent, know that you are on the wrong side of history, but that we will extend a hand if you are willing to unclench your fist."[1] Dinger heard an audible gasp in the room, with the participants saying, "He's talking about us." Ben Rhodes, Obama's deputy national security advisor, noted that Myanmar was one of the countries in mind when writing that line.[2 and 3]

A Relationship at Its Nadir

Since 1988, bilateral relations were so abysmal that any engagement from the deputy assistant secretary-level (DAS) and above was considered controversial. Any engagement was seen as a reward, and its allowance was predicated on the junta making efforts on human rights, which they were absolutely not doing. This resulted in few lines of communication, making efforts to come to any bilateral understanding impossible. If some US official wanted to take a chance and try to find a Myanmar conduit, this effort would likely negatively impact their career trajectory because human rights groups and like-minded policymakers would pile on the criticism for giving the junta something for nothing. After a while, the risks were not worth the effort to even bring up engagement as an idea. Additionally, the junta often refused to give visas, so any high- or mid-level official who did want to go often couldn't.

US companies also gave up on reaching out to policymakers about easing restrictions, particularly American sanctions programs, to enter the Myanmar market. Successive administrations and Congress were so allergic to the idea of allowing US investment, or even pursuing the smallest of economic openings, that exploring the idea became a waste of time for them too.

Obama came into office with an idea that if a government, no matter where it was located on the pariah scale, wanted to make a genuine effort to open, the US would work with them. Myanmar was one country where Obama was curious to see if it would unclench its fist.

In February 2009, Secretary Hillary Clinton ordered a Burma policy review, noting that neither the Western approach of purely punitive measures nor ASEAN's "constructive engagement"—a diplomatic strategy characterized by dialogue, consultation, consensus-building, and strict adherence to the policy of noninterference and noncommentary in the affairs of fellow members[4]—succeeded in changing Myanmar. There were several chronic issues to address, such as human rights abuses, but there was also a growing concern that Myanmar's isolation had pushed it to develop exploitive and questionable military and business ties to a number of countries of concern, including Russia, Belarus, North Korea, and the People's Republic of China (PRC). The review was to determine if the US was pursuing the most effective policy. The effort would include consultations with counterparts and colleagues in ASEAN, the broader international community with interests in Myanmar, NGOs, academics, business leaders, and Myanmar civil society and opposition political parties, including (and especially) the NLD.[5]

Clinton wanted to think creatively and test ideas. She met with Senator Mitch McConnell, who led policy on Myanmar in the Senate and was the principal defender of Aung San Suu Kyi and the sanctions regime against the military. She explained to him what the Obama administration wanted to do. McConnell wanted assurances that prodemocracy icon Aung San Suu Kyi would be consulted, and on the way out of the meeting, he pointed to a handwritten note from her on his wall and said, "As long as she's alright with it and she agrees, I'm ok with it." McConnell was pessimistic but asked the State Department to keep him informed. Clinton also spoke to Senator Jim Webb and Congressman Joe Crowley, key figures on Myanmar policy in the Senate and House of Representatives.[6]

The State Department also had to bring the White House on board. This fit within the administration's outreach/unclench policy, but they wanted to be informed on the plan as it was risky. Ultimately, they supported it. Clinton made some calls to various Asian leaders and brought up the policy review on travels to Singapore, Thailand, and Malaysia. Southeast Asian leaders were supportive and noted that there was an opportunity: the junta's prime minister, Thein Sein, realized how far behind his country was in comparison to the region and he knew something needed to be done.[7]

Dr. Kurt Campbell was leading the main effort for the State Department on the policy review. He was confirmed as the Bureau of East Asian and Pacific Affairs (EAP) assistant secretary in mid-2009 and was one of the few Washington foreign policymakers who traded in big think and visionary concepts and who had a personality to match. Kurt had worked a bit on Myanmar issues at the Pentagon in the 1990s but mostly on projects designed to interdict or block operations in which the Tatmadaw was involved, such as the illicit drug trade and ethnic conflicts. After he was nominated for the EAP job, he spoke with his good friend and colleague, Dr. Mike Green, a senior staffer at the National Security Council (NSC) on Asia issues under the Bush administration. Green followed the issue closely and conveyed its importance to Kurt. Kurt became intrigued by the prospect of diplomatic engagement; he saw the faintest signs of a Burmese Spring with indications that the insular military regime was ready to dip their toe in the waters of political reform. After he joined the government, he saw how much we didn't know and how significant the limitations of our understanding were about the junta and about what was animating politics. That had to change. With Obama's call to take risks in foreign policy, Kurt saw an opportunity.[8]

His initial plan was to meet with Myanmar's UN representative in New York, Ambassador Than Swe, to set parameters for a step-by-step approach for the release of political dissidents and a modest opening around Aung San Suu Kyi and the NLD. The DAS for Southeast Asia, Scot Marciel, had met with Than Swe in the past and found him to be a decent interlocutor and the best chance of opening a communication line. Kurt choreographed his first meeting with Than Swe carefully, meeting him in an ornate room at the Waldorf Hotel in New York that would inspire diplomatic conversations. However, they had a fairly unproductive four-hour meeting in which Than Swe digressed on the history of Myanmar. Kurt tried to lay out the plan for engagement but wasn't getting anywhere. He ended the meeting with an ask to visit the country but with no hope for an affirmative answer. It would be three months before Kurt got that answer.

One event nearly derailed the entire policy review and initial engagement with Than Swe. In May, an American citizen named John Yettaw swam across Inya Lake in the middle of the night to Aung San Suu Kyi's doorstep, telling her he was there to save her from an assassination attempt.[9] He was in extremely bad shape, and Aung San Suu Kyi, who was under house arrest and banned from having guests, especially foreigners, let him in to rest and recover. When her housekeeper begged Aung San Suu Kyi to tell him to leave, she told her, "After seeing so many people get arrested without any reason, I no longer want to witness one more get detained because of me. I will take care of everything. Just let him in."[10]

The timing could not have been worse: Aung San Suu Kyi's house detention was set to expire, and the junta had run out of legal excuses to keep her imprisoned. Yettaw presented a perfect solution. Aung San Suu Kyi and her two caretakers were sentenced to three years in prison with hard labor for allowing a US citizen to stay at her home without first getting permission from the government. But Senior General Than Shwe magnanimously reduced the punishment to eighteen months of house arrest. Yettaw was sentenced to seven years in prison with hard labor.[11 and 12]

In a stroke of perhaps good timing, Senator Jim Webb was coming to visit Myanmar.

An Opening at Last?

Senator Webb was no stranger to tackling difficult issues or to Myanmar. Webb worked on Southeast Asian issues for decades, including as a marine rifle platoon and company commander in Vietnam, with the Vietnamese diaspora in the US, as a journalist, and in his role as a senator. When the trade embargo with Vietnam was lifted in 1994, he saw firsthand the benefit of "face to face transactions" and growing ties on a personal, professional, and government level, leading to what he assessed as the most important factor in creating a more open society. He wanted to apply those lessons to Myanmar.[13 and 14]

His meeting with a US businessman in 2001 further shaped his thinking on sanctions and investment. The businessman said that the ban on new US investment allowed for PRC investments to flood the market, undermining the remaining vestiges of the US business community and US policy objectives. Webb traveled around the country, met with members of the military government, and saw PRC economic and diplomatic influence in Myanmar's markets and along the country's northeastern border. Over the years, he disagreed with the US's policy of isolation and increasingly punitive sanctions and said the policy was amounting to a "predictable cycle of outraged condemnation and 'feel good' legislation" that "accomplishes almost nothing," especially when there are trading partner alternatives like the PRC. Webb was also a big proponent of engagement, noting that the US has a national interest in confronting authoritarian regimes to change their ways and that by isolating them, the US is "ignoring the circumstances we supposedly condemn."[15]

Senator Webb was elected to the Senate in 2008, and when he arrived, he fought to get on the Senate Foreign Relations Committee (SFRC) to work on Asia. Once he was on the committee, he wanted to go to Myanmar and started meeting with "validators" so that a trip could be productive and worthwhile. Validators are subject-matter experts who can assess all the angles of developments in country and offer thoughts on outcomes. They can be academics, businesspersons, philanthropists, NGOs or development organization officials, or former government officials.[16]

When he announced his trip in 2009, everyone was trying to figure out its true purpose—was this a sign that Obama was looking to pursue more engagement with the junta? Was Webb on a fact-finding mission for Obama? Were sanctions going to be lifted? The fear of a less punitive policy sparked several of Webb's congressional colleagues to write a letter to Secretary Clinton, saying Myanmar "continues to perpetuate crimes against humanity and war crimes so severe that Burma has been called 'Southeast Asia's Darfur.'"[17] The State Department wouldn't block his trip, but they were concerned any statements from Webb might not align with executive branch thinking, particularly as his trip was coming in the midst of the Burma policy review. There was also confusion on the Myanmar side as to who he represented; Myanmar didn't grasp the nuance of separate but equal branches of government and that Webb was representing his own congressional interests.[18 and 19]

In mid-August 2009, Senator Jim Webb arrived in Myanmar, the first American political leader to visit in ten years. Webb met with the SPDC in its entirety and was the first-ever high-level official to meet Senior General Than Shwe. He also met with ethnic groups, political parties planning to contest the 2010 election, the NLD, and Aung San Suu Kyi, which was a meeting he had requested with every senior SPDC official he met and one that UN Secretary-General Ban Ki-moon had been denied only weeks before.[20 and 21]

Webb chose his words carefully in his meetings, focusing on similar themes with each interlocutor, including long-standing US demands on human rights, Aung San Suu Kyi's release from house arrest, and democratization. He also asked for the release of John Yettaw. Webb brought his lessons in Vietnam, his experience as a soldier, and a shared history of British colonization to develop some baseline of commonality. The SPDC revisited the desire for better relations with the US repeatedly, asking for ways to communicate directly with Washington, restore diplomatic ties, and of course, lift sanctions. Thein Sein commented that the government thought Webb's trip was important and would help build the relationship. Webb responded that there were still differences to work through, but under the right conditions, the relationship could find a way forward. Than Shwe granted two of Webb's wishes: allowing a visit with Aung San Suu Kyi and releasing John Yettaw.[22 and 23 and 24]

The trip elicited mixed reviews among the pro-engagement and activist crowds but was largely seen as a positive step, especially given his meeting with Aung San Suu Kyi and the release of John Yettaw. Khin Maung Swe, who would later break away from the NLD to run in the 2010 election with the NDF, encouraged more engagement, saying, "Don't wait. Don't waste time." The NLD was also quite curious about Webb's Aung San Suu Kyi meeting; they weren't allowed to meet with her very often and were looking for guidance as to what to say publicly about his trip. She conveyed to Webb that she supported more engagement with the SPDC and encouraged visitors to Myanmar to get a "balanced impression." This was a one-eighty from her previous position; she had called for a tourist boycott many years prior, noting that any money spent on tourism would only line regime pockets and undermine the prodemocracy movement. Aung San Suu Kyi also warned the Uncles, the elderly NLD leadership that maintained the party while she was under house arrest, to refrain from criticizing the trip.[25]

Upon his return to Washington, Webb authored an op-ed for the *New York Times*, saying that though sanctions came from a thoughtful place, they were counterproductive. Webb reflected on his 2001 trip, looking at how US sanctions had caused businesses to flee, ushering in giant PRC state-owned conglomerates to dominate the landscape. He saw an opening for the US, seeing opportunities for greater engagement, cooperation on humanitarian projects and locating World War II soldier remains, and the removal of sanctions, noting that the US engaged with the PRC and Vietnam despite their human rights records.[26 and 27]

His op-ed failed to convince policymakers to follow up with significant engagement.

A Push for Accountability

The Burma policy review continued after Webb's trip and remained contentious on what to do with the military to hold them accountable for human rights abuses and how this could fit with potential increased engagement. David Pressman was running the War Crimes and Atrocities shop at the NSC and sought a mechanism for accountability so that when the country did open up and reintegrate into the world, Myanmar could begin to process its trauma and develop more fruitfully. There was precedent in other countries, like South Africa, and Pressman thought it would be a worthwhile endeavor for Myanmar. He didn't expect it to be easy within the interagency, which is comprised of representatives from all US agencies and departments—including State, Treasury, and Defense, depending on the issue— because in his experience, regional-focused teams viewed human rights issues as unserious obstacles that were in the way of grand strategies. Pressman wanted to push for a Commission of Inquiry (COI), an independent investigative body with a mandate to collect evidence of and data on suspected war crimes related to specified incidents. A COI sounded much more damning than it was, and it made those that supported more engagement nervous that a COI would send mixed messages and stop engagement in its tracks. For the pro-COI crowd, it was merely a fact-finding mission that would carve out space for a human-rights-respecting, democratic Myanmar to emerge. It wasn't right to give the military a free pass to get away with war crimes; at some point, the people would demand justice.

In his engagement with the US interagency, Pressman kept hearing the same argument: a COI could shut the door completely on engagement and never open it again. He understood that but countered that no one wanted to shut the door, but the doorframe on which it was hanging needed to be understood. The reality was, there were a lot of people who had been enslaved, killed, raped, and exploited. There were ways to deal with this that didn't result in automatically referring Myanmar to the International Criminal Court (ICC). A COI would allow the UN Office of the High Commission on Human Rights (UNHCR) to investigate and report what was happening. It was meant to be a modest fact-finding mission.[28]

In the end, the COI got killed. Pro-engagement folks were too concerned that the COI would undercut burgeoning engagement and the gain of incremental openings on democratic and human rights goals. At the time, I harbored the same concerns about the COI for similar reasons. I perceived it as one step below a war crimes tribunal and that it could shut down the emerging communication lines with a hermetic regime. In speaking with David Pressman for this book, his framing of the COI changed my perception. Looking back, I don't know if casting the COI in a different light or using different language would have mitigated the response from the pro-engagement crowd. However, given what happened in the aftermath of the Rohingya crisis in 2017 and the coup in 2021, this really was a modest step.

Same, Same, but Different

Secretary Clinton announced the policy review conclusions at the end of September 2009 on the margins of the UN General Assembly (UNGA). The changes in policy seemed imperceptible, but to longtime Myanmar watchers, it was a major shift to officially call for engagement. The US would aim to build better ties with the SPDC through a dialogue focusing on democracy and human rights, cooperation on nonproliferation issues, and areas of mutual benefit such as counternarcotics and the recovery of World War II-era remains of soldiers missing in action. Engagement also extended to regional and like-minded partners; the US would pursue a more robust and consistent effort with global partners such as ASEAN, Japan, and Europe. The US would also increase its assistance funding, building on the expansion of humanitarian assistance programs launched during Cyclone Nargis. The US also planned to appoint a special envoy as required by the Congress's 2008 JADE Act.[29 and 30]

Despite the carrots, there were still sticks. The US was maintaining its existing sanctions program and would only discuss an easing if the military took demonstrable actions concerning the release of political prisoners, the peace process, human rights abuses, and political and economic reforms. The US would also add names to the US Department of the Treasury's Specially Designated and Blocked Nationals (SDN) List if necessary; the SDN List is enforced by the Treasury's Office of Foreign Assets Control (OFAC) and includes individuals and companies owned, controlled by, or acting for or on behalf of targeted countries. Their assets are blocked, and US persons are generally prohibited from dealing with them.

The policy review reaffirmed the core issues on which the US demanded progress and noted that if meaningful progress was made, the bilateral relationship could improve in a step-by-step process. The State Department acknowledged this could be a long process but that the stakes were high enough to warrant a try, noting, "We need to change our methods, not our goals." Clinton herself noted, "Engagement versus sanctions is a false choice in our opinion."[31]

Though it didn't look like much, it was risky at the time. It was practically verboten to even discuss policy changes unless you were discussing ways to squeeze the junta more. High-level engagement was seen as a reward, and to many activists, the junta had done nothing to warrant such a gift.

Selling the Policy

The State Department went on a road show to discuss the new policy with Congress, European and regional partners, and stakeholders in Myanmar.[32 and 33] In early November 2009, Kurt, DAS Scot Marciel, and the State Department's Burma desk officer, Laura Schiebe, traveled to Myanmar to put its new engagement part in action. Kurt was the first senior diplomat to visit the country since Madeleine Albright, then-US ambassador to the UN, in 1995. Marciel had been to the country before in his role as director for mainland Southeast Asia, but his meetings were limited to Ministry of Foreign Affairs counterparts, the NLD Uncles, political activists, and former political prisoners.[34 and 35]

Kurt was excited to go to Yangon and Nay Pyi Taw. The team flew directly to Yangon from Bangkok, using a US military air flight. It was an older prop airplane, and as they were boarding, the pilot yelled to them over the whirs of propellers, "DR. CAMPBELL! THERE'S A FEW THINGS YOU SHOULD KNOW ABOUT! ONE, YOU SEE THAT THERE! THE CABLE? DON'T TOUCH THAT! ALSO, THERE ARE PARACHUTES IN THE BACK FOR EACH OF YOU! YOU PROBABLY WON'T NEED THEM BUT KNOW THEY'RE THERE!"

They survived to engage in one of the most interesting diplomatic engagements Kurt has ever had: Aung San Suu Kyi. Looking out the window, waiting for her arrival, Kurt saw a small Toyota pull up, and when she came out of the car, he thought, "Hey! That's Aung San Suu Kyi!" It was as if she had walked out of a photograph and into real life.

Aung San Suu Kyi spoke effectively about her ongoing fight for democracy and noted that the junta was concerned about PRC influence and falling behind its ASEAN neighbors. She was gracious and friendly and asked about his family. The three hours passed like nothing. He and his team carefully drafted cables, making sure they conveyed the nuances of the conversation. When he got back to the US to brief Clinton on the trip, she had all the cables on her desk marked up with red pen and she peppered him with questions.[36]

Kurt and Marciel met with Thein Sein but not Senior General Than Shwe. Kurt pushed hard on key US concerns, especially the release of Aung San Suu Kyi, but got nowhere.[37] In a press briefing following the trip, Marciel stated, "We did not anticipate that one trip to Burma by us would solve all the problems that so many able people over many years have not been able to solve." Privately, in a note back to Clinton's key advisor, Jake Sullivan, Marciel noted that the "Burmese had an opportunity if they were willing to move, but that window wouldn't stay open forever."[38] To Larry Dinger, the chargé d'affaires at the time, Nay Pyi Taw missed an opportunity to build on the first positive steps made during the Webb visit. The US wasn't going to have meetings just to have meetings; progress needed to happen to justify continued engagement.[39]

As time went on, Kurt felt like he was not getting anywhere. He turned to his new DAS for Southeast Asia, Joe Yun, a veteran of difficult diplomatic issues who was armed with a good sense of humor, and asked him to take the lead to see if he could make any headway.[40 and 41] Marciel encouraged Joe to build on the relationship that was growing with Than Swe. Despite Kurt's unremarkable first engagement, he thought there was potential to find a way to bridge the gap between the US and Myanmar. There were indications that Than Swe could be someone to talk to. These indications would later prove right.[42]

Herding Policy Cats

In August of 2011, the Obama administration had its nominee for the Office of the Special Representative and Policy Coordinator (SRPC) for Burma confirmed. Earlier that year, it had decided to fulfill an obligation outlined in the 2008 JADE Act—a piece of legislation passed in the wake of egregious human rights abuses following the crackdown on the 2007 Saffron Uprising—in appointing someone to this role. In August 2007, the SPDC caused a steep jump in fuel prices, raising the costs of everyday items and further straining the household budgets of people who were already struggling. The public grew angry and eventually, prodemocracy and student activists, including many organizers from previous mass protests held in 1988, 1990, and 1996, began filling the streets, calling on the junta to address the issue. Eventually, the country's most revered institution, the Buddhist monkhood, took their place at the forefront of the demonstrations. In line with naming protests movements after colors, this was named the "Saffron Revolution," the color associated with monks' robes (Myanmar monks' robes are maroon, however). Protests spread across Myanmar, and the monks used their most powerful tool, evoking *thabeik hmauk*, or the overturning of the alms bowl. This meant that soldiers and their families could no longer make merit and were spiritually condemned, a serious issue for devout Buddhists. After allowing demonstrations to go on for few weeks, the junta decided it was time to violently crack down, killing more than a dozen and injuring and arresting hundreds. Congress decided it was once again time to act with the JADE Act and, among other policies laid out in the legislation, find an individual to start bringing ideas and policies together to move the needle significantly on Myanmar.[43 and 44]

The SRPC would have the rank of ambassador, meaning the nominee would be appointed by the president and would also have to endure a hearing and confirmation by the Senate. He would also be responsible for rallying and consulting with the international community, including the PRC, India, Japan, ASEAN, and the EU, to coordinate policies, support efforts to release all political prisoners, promote a dialogue between the junta and the prodemocracy crowd, address other human rights concerns, and regularly consult with Congress.[45]

The most important part of the title, aside from its rank, was "policy coordinator." This meant that in addition to working with international partners, the SRPC had the authority to wrangle all parts of the US government to implement the office's vision and mission. That was not only the most important job but also the most difficult.

The Obama administration announced Derek Mitchell as the first SRPC. Obama could not have picked a better person for the role; Derek was a longtime Asia hand and had been involved in Myanmar for decades. He held roles in Senator Ted Kennedy's office, at think tanks, and at the Department of Defense. Like so many drawn to the Myanmar issue, Derek's involvement seemed fated. In 1992, he visited his friend Greg Craig, a lawyer who had also worked on Senator Kennedy's staff, for career advice. Craig urged him to go to an event on human rights where the focus was on a woman in Burma whose name Derek could not pronounce. Derek went, picked up a copy of Aung San Suu Kyi's book, *Freedom from Fear*, and began to read. At first, he thought this was diverting him from his focus on the PRC, but there was something about this book that sparked a deep interest. Three years later, while working at the National Democratic Institute (NDI), he traveled with NDI President Ken Wollack to Myanmar to meet with Aung San Suu Kyi (this time, Derek knew how to say her name). She asked them to keep a light shining on Burma's quest for democracy. It was hard not to be captivated by the cause; here was a woman who was holding up the whole country and asking for Americans to use their freedom to fight for the freedom of those in Burma. The NDI selected her as a recipient of their democracy award that year. Though she couldn't come to the US to accept it, Derek put together a short film around her acceptance speech and cause, introducing the issue to a wider audience around the world. Derek was now completely tied to the country.[46]

Several years later, he drafted a piece with Dr. Michael Green for *Foreign Affairs* called "Asia's Forgotten Crisis." It was published two months after the 2007 Saffron Uprising, when Congress and the Bush administration were holding hearings and interagency meetings on what to do about Myanmar. The piece assessed that US policy was stuck with no clear direction on what to do next. The West kept imposing more sanctions and diplomatic isolation while Myanmar's Asian neighbors pursued "constructive engagement." Neither was working. The paper discussed the importance of working with ASEAN, particularly because some countries, like Indonesia and the Philippines, could serve as examples of a successful democratic political transition, and engaging with Japan—a US ally with a strategic soft spot for Myanmar—as well as the PRC and India. Derek and Green argued that it would take US leadership to bring disparate policies and opinions together to channel them to help the prodemocracy movement in Myanmar and improve human rights. In a prescient view, they suggested an envoy be appointed by the president to do just that. Both Derek and Green had outlined a job description they'd each be nominated for. Green would be nominated by the Bush administration in its waning days, but time ran out before confirmation.[47] The position went unfilled for years until one day, while out walking his dog Bernie, Derek got a call from Kurt offering him the job. It took some convincing, but he stepped up to the plate.[48 and 49]

Go Big or Go Home

Two weeks before Derek arrived at the State Department, Kurt called Southeast Asia hands into his office, including the Burma desk officer, Kate Nanavatty, the Director and Deputy Director of Mainland Southeast Asia, Patrick Murphy and Eric Barboriak, and now Principal Deputy and Assistant Secretary Joe Yun. Kurt kicked off the meeting saying, "What do you think about Secretary Clinton visiting Burma?"

For Kurt, the US had exhausted nearly all options on Myanmar and saw this trip as a way to push open the door, if even a crack, to get Myanmar to start moving on a path toward democracy and an improvement of its appalling human rights record. The Obama administration had taken the view that if an opportunity, however small, to effect change presented itself, the US should take it. There was a new opportunity with the SRPC's office implementing its mandate and using a possible Clinton visit as leverage.[50]

There was a bit of a stunned silence. Any small policy step that wasn't punitive generated an uproar from Myanmar human rights groups, powerful people in Congress, and the State Department itself. This would be the first secretary of state trip since the 1950s. This small team could be crucified, but they all agreed it was an intriguing proposition.[51]

Old Wine, New Bottles?

In August, Derek officially started as the SRPC, also known by those unable to string those letters together as the special rep. The country was a black box, and it was unclear who the possible changemakers could be. He wanted to find out who they were and assemble a cadre of people he could work with.

Derek had a vision for what the office would do. Since he and Green wrote the piece, the conversation on Myanmar had hardly changed, even after the Burma policy review in 2009. The same debate was raging—more sanctions, more engagement—from the human rights and the pro-business sides. The US needed to get out of old patterns.

But things seemed to be changing in Myanmar. The country's new president, Thein Sein, was publicly talking about political reform. In his inaugural speech in March 2011, he called for workers' rights and an end to corruption, welcomed international expertise, and called for peace with the EAOs, a noticeable departure from his predecessors.[52] Thein Sein reached out to political dissidents and NGOs, inviting them to help develop the country; established a National Human Rights Commission; started discussing national reconciliation and outreach to ethnic armed groups; allowed unions to organize; and eased media restrictions. He was building a professional relationship with Aung San Suu Kyi. Thein Sein did not strike anyone as a take-charge kind of guy who would risk his livelihood to push for reform. What was driving him?[53 and 54 and 55]

It was possible that Cyclone Nargis and the killing of monks in the 2007 Saffron Uprising triggered a change within the SPDC apparatchik. Thein Sein was a devout Buddhist, and he was from the delta; witnessing monks being gunned down on the streets must have hit hard. Born in the delta, the callous response by the SPDC after his home was erased in a storm may have hit hard too. He also witnessed the speed at which neighboring countries were developing and how far behind Myanmar was falling. As the former prime minister, Thein Sein often traveled around the region and saw firsthand that Singapore was a first-world country, that Thailand had a booming tourism industry, and that the Laos government officials came to ASEAN meetings with iPads (and a higher per capita GDP).[56 and 57]

Since the 2010 election, Thein Sein worked with several advisors to provide analysis of key issues and political advice. He relied on a group called Myanmar

Egress, an organization of businessmen, journalists, and academics who sought ties to the military to find potential reformers. Local and international communities had mixed views of Egress, seeing them as too close to the military and more interested in improving their business prospects than in real reform. In addition to their reports, Myanmar Egress gave Thein Sein DVDs of *The West Wing*, hoping to inspire good leadership. Who says television and movies don't influence kids these days?[58 and 59 and 60]

When Thein Sein took office in March 2011, he formed his own presidential office of ministers, which included Soe Thane, former commander of the navy, and Aung Min, a former intelligence officer. Soe Thane would focus on economic and major diplomatic matters while Aung Min would tackle the peace process with Myanmar's myriad of EAOs and—in a surprise to many Myanmar watchers—student groups and activists.

The combination of Thein Sein's management style, which included listening to experts, delegating authority, and seeking out stark reporting on the state of Myanmar's economy, helped build the steps of what the political transition would look like.[61]

Derek had to get to Myanmar and see what was going on. This was to show the US was serious about assessing the sincerity of reforms and implementing an engagement strategy. In September 2011, Derek, along with Kate Nanavatty, took a US military air flight from Bangkok to Nay Pyi Taw, a deliberate move to go to the capital first to meet with government officials. This was symbolic but also a trust-building mechanism; Derek was there to hear their side of the story first. Derek was going to press the government "to prove the skeptics wrong," a mantra the US would use repeatedly.[62]

Nay Pyi Taw was an odd place. EAP Assistant Secretary Danny Russel described it as the "Emerald City with crazy fucking buildings." The roads were eerily empty, and all of the government buildings looked alike. The first set of meetings was at the Upper House of Parliament, an imposing set of gigantic buildings surrounded by a moat and connected to the empty sixteen-lane highway by a cable-stayed bridge. The delegation met with the Upper House Speaker Khin Aung Myint in a cavernous room adorned with floor-to-ceiling paintings of traditional Myanmar scenes. He was joined by several of his parliamentary cohorts, including some from opposition parties, and many were dressed in ethnic garb. The Naga representative was particularly memorable, with a large, feathered headdress that included bones and teeth from animals.[63]

Khin Aung Myint welcomed the team, providing a brief history of reforms and offering cautionary words of encouragement about building the US relationship. Derek responded, saying he was pleased to be in Burma. He was quickly interrupted by Khin Aung Myint, who reminded him that he was in Myanmar. Derek knew the name issue was going to be a stumbling block and had run right into it at the outset. Derek quickly recovered and the meeting went as smoothly as it could.[64 and 65]

Derek shuttled around the seemingly vacated capital, meeting with other ministers and parliamentarians, including the Lower House Speaker Shwe Mann. Shwe Mann also was joined by colleagues from across parties with uniforms reflecting ethnic heritage. He spoke of reforms and about his readiness for change, and he insisted the reforms were genuine. Shwe Mann was an ambitious politician and sounded convincing, but he was also a highly intelligent military strategist who had earned his military title, "Thura," meaning "Bravery," by outwitting and ultimately breaking the strength of the KNU insurgency. He said all of the right things, but it was difficult to believe him.[66 and 67 and 68 and 69]

The US delegation was asked by their hosts if there was anything they wanted to see or do in Myanmar. They asked to go to the military parade grounds, a place off-limits to civilian foreigners except for the US defense attaché, who attended the annual Independence Day military parade held at the grounds. The thought was that if the government officials allowed them to go and walk around, it might offer them a chance to engage military officers in a less formal setting and gauge their thoughts on recent developments. To their great surprise, the Myanmar officials said yes and escorted them to the grounds.

Towering over the main parade grounds are thirty-foot-high statues of Myanmar's most revered warrior kings: Anawrahta, Bayinnaung, and Alaungpaya. The team was allowed to take photos of the statues and ask questions. It was surreal, not just because they were in the most bizarre city surrounded by towering Burmese kings of yore, but that they were here, talking openly with the military about everyday things.

Over the course of the Nay Pyi Taw trip, Derek heard a lot of interesting things, and for the most part, they seemed sincere. Of course, there were flashes of the past, including dry history lessons, calls for the full removal of "undeserved" sanctions, and a large portrait of Than Shwe in the Ministry of Information building. But something felt different. Derek wrapped up in Nay Pyi Taw and headed to Yangon to get a reality check from ethnic groups, civil society, political activists, businesspersons, former political prisoners, and, of course, Aung San Suu Kyi.

It is no secret that US policy took its cues from Aung San Suu Kyi, the face and voice of Myanmar's democratic struggle. Countless activists' campaigns, legislation, executive orders, and speeches were informed by and dedicated to her struggle. She had lost everything; the junta took away her children's Burmese citizenship (they had held dual British/Burmese citizenship), forcing her to choose to fight for her country or be with her family. This was made exponentially more difficult when her British husband was dying of cancer and her children were young teenagers; she chose to remain in Myanmar to fight for her country, an agreement she had made with her husband years before. He passed away, having gone years without seeing her.

Aung San Suu Kyi had more face time with the generals and knew how wily and conniving they could be. She was an important part of the gut check to see if the changes were real.

Derek shared his thoughts from his government meetings, noting that while he was cautiously optimistic, he knew the generals had made and broken promises in the past. Aung San Suu Kyi shared the same cautious optimism but noted that her burgeoning relationship with Thein Sein was intriguing and that they were even talking about the NLD reregistering to run in a by-election in April 2012 to fill seats vacated by appointed ministers. She mentioned having dinner with him and his wife, whose company she enjoyed, and that his tone differed remarkably from the old SPDC. Derek also discussed US policy, and she expressed concerns about moving too quickly to reward the government; the early signs were positive and seemed genuine. But the hopes of the Myanmar people had often been dashed in cruel and bloody ways.[70]

He also asked about the Burma/Myanmar name issue. She said she still preferred the use of "Burma," noting the illegitimacy of the name "Myanmar." She also noted how no one knew how to pronounce Myanmar, mocking the versions she had heard over the years. I've heard all of them too—Mininmar, Miranmar, Meye-an-mar, Malaysia, Muammar. If there is an "ar" at the end of a word in the Myanmar language, it's to denote a double "a." So "Myanmar" should look to the English-speaking eye as "Myanmaa." So the easiest way to pronounce Myanmar is like trying to sound like a Boston-accented cat—Myan-maa.

Derek held a press conference in the Yangon airport before flying off to Thailand. This was also a signal from the US on the new engagement strategy. Visiting foreign government officials, mostly Western, chose to hold a press conference in Bangkok and bash the government. Even when the generals had thought the meetings had gone well, they were sometimes taken aback by these press conferences, and they questioned the sincerity of being so open once they left the country for the safe haven of Bangkok. Derek spent the conference discussing early assessments of Thein Sein's policies and noted that the US still needed to see the unconditional release of thousands of political prisoners, a credible path to peace and national reconciliation with the country's EAOs and political activists, improvements on human rights, a halt to military trade with North Korea, and forward momentum on political and economic reform. Thein Sein and the USDP had to prove the skeptics wrong.[71]

The Ground Shifts

After Derek's trip to Myanmar, the Myanmar policy team traveled to New York to meet with Myanmar's foreign minister, Wunna Maung Lwin, as well as the Myanmar permanent representative to the UN, Than Swe, and his other diplomatic colleagues who were there for the UN General Assembly (UNGA), an annual event for country leaders to address the world. The foreign minister was also invited to come to Washington, a policy carrot from the US. Myanmar officials were under a twenty-five-mile rule restriction; when Myanmar officials traveled to the US for UN meetings, they were barred from traveling twenty-five miles outside of New York. The State Department would allow a trip to DC to show the US acknowledged reforms.[72]

Derek, Kurt, Joe, and Kate met the Myanmar delegation in New York in what became a very tense meeting; the team was starting to get to brass tacks of policy action. Kurt was very eager to get bilateral ties more normalized and felt if the Burmese were to release some political prisoners, then the US could go forward with some significant steps. Derek felt the US was finally in a position to push for action on long-standing concerns like the release of all political prisoners, as well as push for more openings on the peace process and Myanmar's military ties with North Korea. Kurt and Derek couldn't argue in front of the Myanmar delegation so they moved to a separate room to hash it out. Hopefully, it looked to the delegation like a good cop/bad cop discussion, and it prompted them to think of what they could deliver. After mostly agreeing on the way forward, Kurt and Derek told the foreign minister that the US needed to see real progress and that no country claiming it was a democracy would imprison political activists. Wunna Maung Lwin countered by asking for the names of prisoners, all 2,000-plus of them.[73]

Several organizations and foreign governments had prisoner lists, and the State Department's Democracy, Human Rights, and Labor (DRL) Bureau was undertaking the herculean task of verifying names and prison locations to ensure they had the most accurate list. DRL Assistant Secretary Mike Posner had dealt with enough authoritarians to know that being armed with irrefutable evidence was a trump card and could get the most difficult conversations moving. His Burma desk officer, Stacey May, led the painstaking process of comparing several political prisoners lists from the EU, the Association of Politics Prisoners-Burma (AAPP-B), the US, the UN, and Myanmar's prison system. She visited prisons and met with former political prisoners and NGOs to cross-check and get the most accurate information. It needed to be airtight, and Stacey did it with the help of many dedicated organizations and governments.[74]

The US side didn't have the DRL list with them, and Kurt asked the team to rattle off some names. The team stated that the US would deliver the DRL list, but in the meantime, they discussed the umbrella under which so many had been arrested, including participating in protests in 1988 and 2007, running in the 1990 election, helping victims of Cyclone Nargis, and engaging in labor and human rights activism. The team identified well-known prisoners such as the 88 Generation student activists Min Ko Naing, Ko Ko Gyi, Jimmy, and Nilar Thein; labor activist Su Su Nway; comedian and activist Zarganar; and Shan Nationalities League for Democracy leader Hkun Htun Oo. They emphasized there were thousands more who did not benefit from such recognition. Wunna Maung Lwin said he'd look into it.[75]

Less than a month later, on October 11, Thein Sein released more than 6,000 prisoners in a general amnesty. Junta officials typically did these amnesties around major Buddhist holidays. The DRL, Burma desk, and the special rep's office frantically went through the list of names and identified one hundred political prisoners from DRL's political prisoner list. The most prominent remained behind bars, making it feel like a hollow victory of sorts, but it was a step in the right direction. At least two of the names mentioned during the meeting in New York, Zarganar and Su Su Nway, were released.[76 and 77 and 78]

The US's new approach, and Thein Sein's embrace of reform, was tested once again just days after the meetings at UNGA. In September, a group under the banner "Save the Irrawaddy" began demonstrating against the PRC-backed Myitsone Dam being built in Kachin State at a major confluence of rivers, including the lifeblood of the country, the Ayeyarwady.[79] The proposed dam would generate 6,000 megawatts of power; however, it would also displace tens of thousands of people, cause untold environmental destruction, and threaten the use of the Ayeyarwady for those that lived alongside it. It was a lopsided deal. Myanmar certainly wasn't going to get 6,000 megawatts of electricity; most of that would go to the PRC. The number of protesters grew to crowds not seen in years and spread throughout the country. In Washington, we were getting nervous. Protests never ended without bloodshed in Myanmar. We thought there was no way the government would back down.[80]

A miracle happened. On September 30, 2011, President Thein Sein sent a letter to Parliament stating, "Our government, being elected by the people, has to take great consideration of public opinion. Accordingly, we have an obligation to respond to the public concern with seriousness. Therefore, we will suspend the Myitsone project during the term of our government." I screamed for joy. The crowds calling for the end of Myitsone started cheering *for* Thein Sein. The people had fought for something and had finally won. It was such an incredible moment and that made this skeptic really believe.[81 and 82]

By the time Derek's first trip to Myanmar was complete and change in Myanmar seemed to be going at a rapid pace, Kurt started reaching out to the White House and Secretary Clinton's senior advisors to see if they could proceed with her trip.

President Obama's Deputy National Security Advisor for Communications, Ben Rhodes, and the State Department's Director for Policy Planning, Jake Sullivan, were key to getting the White House and the Secretary's support.[83 and 84 and 85]

While working with the US side, they also needed to get approval from Myanmar. Derek and Patrick Murphy went to Myanmar to discuss the trip. Joined by the chargé d'affaires, Michael Thurston, they had to convey the scale of this undertaking, the secrecy around it, and US expectations. In late October 2011, they snuck into Nay Pyi Taw to quietly meet with Wunna Maung Lwin. He was surprised; in our interview for this book, he said he was impressed by the idea and thought it a very bold step for US foreign policy. Wunna Maung Lwin also saw it as an opportunity to show Secretary Clinton that Myanmar was serious about reforms and to earn her trust. But he was also worried about the repercussions if this went horribly wrong. The responsibility would be on him to make the trip successful from his side. He was cagey and said he had to talk with Thein Sein. Derek, Patrick, and Michael understood his concerns but told him they needed an answer by the end of the day. Thein Sein must have seen the opportunity because when they met with Wunna Maung Lwin later in the evening, he was all smiles. He ordered a bottle of wine and toasted to a new chapter in the relationship.[86 and 87]

Derek took advantage of the trip to meet with Shwe Mann to follow up on key issues, including Myanmar's ties to North Korea. In 2009, dozens of leaked photos of former SPDC member Shwe Mann showed him meeting with North Korean officials, touring military sites, and signing agreements and contracts. Shwe Mann shocked Derek and confirmed the meetings, saying he sought a military relationship to modernize the Tatmadaw and that there were few places for the military to get the weaponry it needed to do so. He was willing to work with the US to unwind this relationship. This trip was going better than expected.[88 and 89]

More important was securing the support of Aung San Suu Kyi. She had been positive about her interactions with Thein Sein, but Derek wasn't sure if this was a step too far for her. Derek had previewed this idea with her on his first trip to Myanmar, and she was lukewarm. On this visit, she was hesitant and asked a lot of questions. Aung San Suu Kyi always had to view things from a leverage perspective; to give away too much would lessen her ability to bring democracy to Myanmar, to free members of her party languishing in prison, and to fulfill the promises forged in the 1988 student uprising. She was quite tepid but told him she would have a good think.

On the way to the airport, he got word that Aung San Suu Kyi was on board and sounded downright excited about the prospect.[90]

It was time to make the secretary's trip happen.

The Trip That Launched One Thousand Trips

Hillary Clinton was no stranger to Myanmar. Even before she was First Lady, the country and the travails of Aung San Suu Kyi were on her radar. Her roommate during her second year at law school was Burmese, and she had learned about the country's history, culture, dance, and food. As First Lady, she sent Madeleine Albright to Yangon to see if the regime would loosen its grip on power. Albright brought a poster to the 1995 UN Women's Conference in Beijing that was signed by Clinton and others, urging the release of Aung San Suu Kyi. In 1996, in Chiang Mai, Thailand, Clinton called for a real dialogue between Aung San Suu Kyi and the regime, and President Bill Clinton awarded the Lady the Presidential Medal of Freedom. When Clinton first heard about the trip, she thought it seemed like such an outlandish leap. She had heard enough crazy stories from Kurt and from her own experiences to wonder if this place was too weird. But it seemed like a Hail Mary pass to push for change in the country.[91 and 92 and 93]

President Obama was expected to announce her trip a few weeks later in Indonesia at the November 2011 East Asia Summit, a gathering of ASEAN countries, the US, Australia, China, India, Japan, New Zealand, Russia, and South Korea. There was still no guarantee the trip would take place. Obama wanted to doubly make sure the trip had Aung San Suu Kyi's blessing. Aboard Air Force One, Obama called her, and the two Nobel Prize winners discussed the parameters of the trip, Aung San Suu Kyi's views, and then the important stuff, like dogs. The trip was on.[94 and 95]

The following day, President Obama announced that he was sending Secretary Clinton to Burma. He noted that "after years of darkness, we've seen flickers of progress" and that her trip would be an important step in showing America's commitment to Myanmar, the region, and to human rights. Secretary Clinton would be the first American secretary of state to travel there in more than half a century, the last being John Foster Dulles in 1955.[96]

The team had less than two weeks to put on the finishing touches. A visit by a senior US official requires a lot, but even more so in a country with sanctions implications, little digital connectivity, and slow visa approvals.

Clinton's delegations had to avoid sanctions and bad optics. A travel waiver allowed stays in hotels and the refueling of cars at gas stations owned by sanctioned individuals, but the optics would have been horrible; Secretary Kerry ran into this issue during a stay at a hotel owned by a sanctioned individual during a 2014 ASEAN meeting in Nay Pyi Taw.[97] The State Department managed to find a hotel that was owned by a nonsanctioned individual but had to send Secretary Clinton's plane to Bangkok overnight to be refueled by a nonsanctioned company.

They also had to get the staff, security detail, and journalists traveling with the secretary hip to the idea that their Blackberries, cell phones, and wi-fi weren't going to work in Myanmar. Myanmar's mobile connectivity was worse than North Korea's, and the satellite phones or the few handset cell phones that the State Department could acquire would be limited in number and usage.

The schedule for Yangon included a stop at the Shwedagon Pagoda, Myanmar's most famous and revered site. To enter the grounds of the pagoda, one had to remove shoes and socks and any weapons, something Clinton's security wasn't pleased with. The women quickly called all the nail salons for emergency pedicures.

There were more issues with the plane. The pilots weren't sure if the runway was long enough for takeoff and landing or if the passenger stairway was the right size. They figured they could land on the empty sixteen-lane highway in front of Parliament if Nay Pyi Taw's was too short. For the stairs, they would figure it out.

Meetings were another issue. These trips require careful choreography, and every move and word is dissected and analyzed. The planning team reached out to those people the US government calls validators and human rights and prodemocracy activists to get their views. They were cautious of the US giving away too much to a government no one still really trusted; they strongly urged that the secretary not relent on pushing for the unconditional release of all political prisoners, an end to the human rights abuses, and the removal of the military from politics.[98] For the most part, the trip had a lot of support. Almost everyone saw this as a necessary step to both acknowledge what was happening and push, at the highest levels, for more action.

The trip team also met with senators, congresspersons, and their staff. Myanmar was a rare bipartisan issue in Washington and had the attention and cooperation (mostly) of both the executive and legislative branches. This cooperation was critical to the process. Secretary Clinton reached out to Senator Mitch McConnell—who was supportive because Aung San Suu Kyi was and who thought the trip might help boost her position vis-à-vis the military and her ability to eventually ascend to a leading role—and to Senator McCain. The special rep's office was in close contact with Senators Webb and Lugar, the Senate Foreign Relations Committee, the House Foreign Affairs Committee, and what seemed like an endless list of folks who had worked on the issue through the years. The special rep, EAP, and DRL were committed to a whole government effort; this was beyond any one department, person, or bureau.[99 and 100]

* * *

On Monday, November 28, the secretary's delegation headed to Andrews Air Force Base. They came equipped with a mobile library that included David Steinberg's *Burma/Myanmar: What Everyone Needs to Know*, Thant Myint U's *River of Lost*

Footsteps, Pascal Khoo Thwe's *From the Land of Green Ghosts*, Emma Larkin's *No Bad News for the King*, and a copy of George Orwell's *Burmese Days*. They also had movies to play, including *Beyond Rangoon*, and they were trying to track down a copy of *The Lady*, a new film that detailed the life of Aung San Suu Kyi. It was a complete hassle to get *The Lady* on the plane; the director, Luc Besson, tried to FedEx the movie to the hotel in Busan, the first stop on the trip for an aid and assistance conference, but apparently it proved "impossible." Instead, Besson put a courier from Paris on a plane to Busan to hand-deliver a copy so everyone could watch it on the way to Yangon.[101]

Derek, Patrick, and Kate were already in Myanmar, getting the details settled and waiting for the Washington team to arrive. Kurt; Danny Russel; Jake Sullivan; the chairman of the joint chief's advisor and liaison to the secretary, Admiral Harry Harris; Counselor and Chief of Staff to Secretary Clinton, Cheryl Mills; Deputy Assistant Secretary of State for Strategic Communications Philippe Reines; protocol officers; and a host of journalists filled the secretary's plane on a historic trip to Myanmar.

The plane landed in Busan very late at night. Derek, Patrick, Kate, Kurt, and Joe (who was safely tucked away in DC) did a call around 2:00 a.m. with folks in DC, Korea, and Myanmar to see how the details were coming along. At one point, Kurt said, "Guys, I think it would be a nice gesture to get Aung San Suu Kyi a dog gift. Both Secretary Clinton and Aung San Suu Kyi love dogs. I'll do everything in my power to get that gift." The next morning, a poor State Department staffer had to navigate Busan's cobblestone streets to find a shop that was (a) open; (b) selling dog toys; and (c) could understand the request in English. After several back-and-forths, drawings of dogs, and a desperate shout of the word "puppy," the store owners excitedly pointed toward an entire wall filled with dog toys, bowls, food, and everything a dog would ever need. The poor staffer found toys not labeled "Made in China," including a water bowl with some cute paw print designs and a red, white, and blue rope toy. The toys were wrapped by the concierge desk, handed over to the protocol team, and appreciated by Aung San Suu Kyi.[102]

At the conclusion of the aid and assistance conference, the team was on its way to Myanmar, watching *The Lady*, which had been successfully obtained. As Nay Pyi Taw came within sight, Kurt said he couldn't believe they had made it and were actually going to pull this off.[103] As they descended the stairs and got their first taste of Nay Pyi Taw, Secretary Clinton was greeted by a big, red banner with bold, white letters welcoming the deputy economic trade minister from Belarus.[104]

Engagement in Action

Secretary Clinton was excited but nervous. She had received protocol advice prior to the trip (often given to avoid a diplomatic incident) and was advised to avoid wearing white, a color associated with mourning. She had already packed a white jacket for her meeting with Aung San Suu Kyi and wondered if she'd have to make a costume change. When she descended the stairs and saw a sea of people in white, she knew it was fine. Either that, or everyone was acting like this trip was a funeral. She would also wear a white jacket when she accompanied President Obama on his historic trip in November 2012; she really stuck it to those who gave her that "advice."[105]

The delegation piled into the vans, drove along the empty highways to the Thingaha Hotel, and planned for the next few days. Mercifully, as they were pretty isolated and blessed with slow internet (the military opened some bandwidth for journalists and the delegation to use), most of that evening was spent in excited conversation. Secretary Clinton met with the hotel and kitchen staff, shook hands, posed for photos, and enjoyed her meals, specially made with massive amounts of chili peppers at her request.[106]

Her first meeting was with the foreign minister, Wunna Maung Lwin. Wunna Maung Lwin was understandably nervous; he was terrified that Clinton would issue ultimatums or push for something the government wasn't ready to or couldn't deliver.[107] To his likely relief, the meeting went fine. It was cordial, and each side had their chance to express hope in where bilateral ties would go and where the problems remained. He also took care to point out the women at the table; he said he knew Clinton supported women representation and so he rustled some up. Clinton appreciated the effort.[108 and 109]

The next stop was the Presidential Palace. Thein Sein greeted Secretary Clinton and escorted her to a large ceremonial room that housed golden tables, oversized stuffed chairs lined with satin, and what looked like an enormous Broadway stage behind them. Thein Sein discussed the steps his government had taken and, in a change from junta speeches past, openly discussed the difficulties in the country and the junta's responsibility. He spoke about the relationship with North Korea and that he was open to working with the International Atomic Energy Agency (IAEA) on the Additional Protocols, a safeguard agreement that allows for stricter verification processes on nuclear capabilities.[110] Clinton praised these steps but emphasized they should only be seen as a beginning. There were still close to 2,000 political activists languishing in prison, and their release would be a major trust-building step. Mike Posner, the assistant secretary for DRL, brought the most updated list and offered to work through it with the government. Clinton was also clear that a release was not enough and that there needed to be a commitment to not detain people for exercising universal freedoms of expression, assembly, and conscience.[111 and 112]

The lunch that followed was, to Clinton, more important. Meals such as these were typically held for heads of state, but Thein Sein recognized the importance of the trip and rolled out the red carpet. He also invited his wife to join, and the conversation was real and substantive. For Clinton, Thein Sein struck her as someone who was trying to find his own way politically through this new world his government was embracing; he was much more open to suggestions and advice than she expected. The delegation left the lunch, and the conversations in the lobby were deafening. People were excitedly talking to their respective counterparts, and everyone was in a good mood, filled with ideas of the possibilities ahead.[113 and 114]

The delegation headed to Parliament and onto the famed sixteen-lane highway. Nay Pyi Taw first-timers audibly gasped as they navigated the empty roads until the imposing parliamentary buildings came into view. They were escorted to the Upper House of Parliament to meet Speaker Khin Aung Myint. At this stage, Clinton had the nomenclature down and was deft at avoiding saying the word "Burma" or "Myanmar." She used terms like "this beautiful land," "your country," "Nay Pyi Taw," or "the golden land."[115] They sat in another enormous room, this one replete with several members of Parliament from a variety of political parties attired in their traditional ethnic garb. The room was the size of a football field, maybe two. Clinton talked about her time in Congress and the importance of representation. Khin Aung Myint outlined the responsibilities of the Upper House, with an emphasis on checks and balances on the president and his ministries. His remarks were fairly formulaic but pleasant enough; he did not come across as gung ho about reform as his executive branch cohorts, but he took his job seriously.[116]

As the delegation filed out of the room, Khin Aung Myint had gone over to his colleagues. He broke out into a huge smile, pumped his fists in the air, and then shook hands with everyone. Everyone started smiling, and it was a genuine moment of elation. They had held their own, had a decent first conversation with one of their strongest critics, and had come out the other side. It was a sense that they were on the right track.

The schedule was planned to the minute, and meetings had to be ended at the designated time. This was even more important for the next meeting as Secretary Clinton needed to get to Yangon before sunset. Nay Pyi Taw was not built to handle flights after dark, and she needed to get to the Shwedagon Pagoda as the sun was setting. For Shwe Mann, however, this was his chance to meet with the secretary of state from the United States, and he was not going to be confined by time limitations. He had been notified by the US embassy that he was only going to get a ten-minute courtesy visit. He said he needed at least forty-five minutes.[117]

The delegation was led to yet another large ceremonial room and a cast of ethnic parliamentarians. Shwe Mann had an agenda and wanted to get right into it; he figured Clinton had received enough history lessons and was a smart lady, so there was no need to waste time. She ended up meeting with him for more than an hour; when they hit the forty-five minute mark, he said this was too important for Myanmar and this conversation had to happen. Myanmar had no experience with democratization, and he wanted her advice. He also wanted to see if it was possible for sanctions to be fully lifted if the transition continued (he and his son, Aung Thet Mann, were on the SDN List). Finally, he wanted to find ways to build a bilateral relationship with effective communication lines. He wanted his government to be able to contact US officials more readily without faxes or endless layers of bureaucracy on the US side to approve a ten-minute conversation.

Clinton vividly recalled the meeting and noted that Shwe Mann was charismatic and very energetic. He said they were learning all about America through watching *The West Wing* (I guess he borrowed Thein Sein's copy). Clinton thought that was touching in that they were trying to learn, but she was quick to point out that though *The West Wing* was a fantastic show, it was not the most realistic tool to use to build a democracy and run a government.[118 and 119]

The team rushed back to the hotel where Clinton was set to speak to the press. This was her first press conference of the trip, and she had a lot of ground to cover. She started by saying that she was here to see if the time was right for a new chapter in the US's long history with the country and briefly discussed the meetings and areas of continued concern. She also discussed a package of "deliverables," a set of policy measures or carrots that high-level officials are prepared to offer on trips like these. It should be noted that with the small exception of donor assistance following Cyclone Nargis in 2008, Myanmar had not received any carrots since the 1980s. Myanmar received few assistance dollars, had no help from organizations like the World Bank or the Asian Development Bank, and had relatively little economic ties to foreign countries with the exception of the PRC and some regional neighbors. Myanmar was mired in poverty, and although decades of gross economic mismanagement and civil war helped put them there, it would be nearly impossible for the Thein Sein administration to get Myanmar back on the economic track alone without some form of international assistance.

Clinton announced the US would also allow the World Bank and International Monetary Fund to conduct assessment missions to identify specific development needs, especially in rural areas. The UN Development Program would be allowed to expand its very minimal presence in the country to do more health, microfinance, education, and training programs. The US would also allow Myanmar to be an observer of the State Department-led Lower Mekong Initiative (LMI), established in 2009 by the US, Cambodia, Lao PDR, Thailand, and Vietnam to encourage inclusive growth and to address development challenges through capacity-building projects and programs with the close cooperation of LMI governments.[120] The US was also going to resume joint counternarcotics operations and remains-recovery efforts of the hundreds of American pilots and military officers who were lost in the country during World War II.

These may seem like small deliverables, but it was a huge deal. The US was finally chipping away at a punitive architecture that had been built over decades. Clinton closed her remarks by reflecting on the flickers of progress and saying that the US was "prepared to walk the path of reform" if Myanmar chose to move in that direction.[121]

The team left the press conference and hopped into the vans, tearing their way through the empty streets to get on the plane. They bid farewell to the government officials waving on the tarmac and to the big red sign welcoming Belarussians, and they headed to Yangon to visit the famed Shwedagon Pagoda.

"I felt as if we had known each other a lifetime..."

Rudyard Kipling visited Shwedagon Pagoda in 1889, writing, "'There's the old Shway Dagon' (pronounced Dagone), said my companion. 'Confound it!' But it was not a thing to be sworn at. It explained in the first place why we took Rangoon, and in the second why we pushed on to see what more of rich or rare the land held. Up till that sight my uninstructed eyes could not see that the land differed much in appearance from the Sunderbuns, but the golden dome said: 'This is Burma, and it will be quite unlike any land you know about.'"[122]

The Shwedagon Pagoda is reportedly one of the oldest Buddhist stupas in the world, houses hairs of the Buddha himself, and is an awe-inspiring sight.

Once the shoes and socks of the delegation and security officers were reluctantly removed, they were escorted up the elevators to receive a tour of the pagoda. They waded through the crowds of tourists and locals praying. People spoke in hushed tones, perhaps surprised as a turquoise-pant-suited US Secretary of State wandered around and who broke their silence by banging the King Therawaddy Bell with a large stick. They slowly made their way to the symbol of her day of birth, and she poured water over a Buddha that stood by the garuda, the symbol of Sunday.[123]

Following the magical Shwedagon visit, Clinton prepared for her most anticipated meeting: a dinner with Aung San Suu Kyi. After years of supporting the Lady, whom Clinton characterized as the "imprisoned conscience of her nation" who carried "the hopes of the nation on her shoulders," this would be the first in-person encounter. The dinner was to be held at the chargé d'affaires's residence to allow for privacy and a chance for the two icons to speak uninterrupted at length. Clinton donned her best funeral coat and was greeted by Aung San Suu Kyi, who was also wearing a funereal white. Clinton said, "I felt as if we had known each other a lifetime, even though we had just met." Secretary Clinton found her to be very engaging, smart, strong, and dedicated to her life's mission to democratize Myanmar. They talked about how she played her cards, as an icon and the NLD leader, working on building relationships with several of the key retired military leaders like Thein Sein and Shwe Mann. This was more than a strategic play to work with the military. There was a familial angle as well due to her father founding the current military's predecessor organization, the Burma Independence Army, during World War II. She believed she had to take her time in trying to respect them, but she still wanted to move them along on political reforms and demilitarizing the political sphere; for her, this was a necessary step on the way to the vision of Myanmar she held. She didn't go into her political plans for the following year's by-election. Instead, the conversation veered toward how she spent her time under house arrest listening to the BBC, reading, and meeting with the people who were permitted to visit her. She had to be highly disciplined to keep it together and carved out a routine for herself. She also wanted to talk about Clinton's family. The dinner flew by because it was such an easy conversation.[124 and 125]

It was powerful for longtime Myanmar observers to see Clinton and Aung San Suu Kyi bonding as women in politics and as women with few peers.[126]

The last day was spent ground truthing what the delegation had heard in Nay Pyi Taw with people who had borne the worst of what the Tatmadaw threw at them. The first stop was Aung San Suu Kyi's house, where she was joined by NLD party members and Uncles. Aung San Suu Kyi said she knew there were a lot of groups in the US opposed to engagement, but she said it was important for those outside of Myanmar to listen to the voices inside the country.[127] In comments to the press after the meeting, both women were exuberant and embraced each other like sisters. Aung San Suu Kyi said, "If we move forward together I am confident there will be no turning back on the road to democracy. . . . We are not on that road yet, but we hope to get there as soon as possible with the help and understanding of our friends." As the team piled back into the vans, a reporter shouted a question to Danny Russel about how the trip was going. He shouted back, "I'm having the time of my life!" They all were.[128 and 129]

Following the meeting, the delegation traveled to the Beik Thano art gallery, both to look at the newly booming art scene in Yangon and to meet with ethnic representatives. The representatives discussed the conditions on the ground in their respective states—Shan, Rakhine, Kachin, Karen, Kayah, Mon—and urged the secretary to push for a national dialogue. The government had promised when the cease-fires had been initially forged that a political dialogue would happen before a discussion on laying down arms, but the opposite was happening. Even as ethnic groups pushed for peace, the military was shooting at them. There was little trust on either side.[130]

The team headed back to the embassy for the trip's final meeting with the growing civil society community. The representatives talked about their responsibilities, their impact, and the "flickers of progress" they saw emerging. They were especially excited about Secretary Clinton's trip and the possibility for increased American engagement and technical assistance in education, health, and other areas of critical need. They were ready to serve communities and wanted US help.[131]

Overall, nearly everyone welcomed US engagement but acknowledged there was still a long way to go. People were cautiously optimistic as there had been precedent for having hopes dashed in brutal ways.

A Different Time

In her book *Hard Choices*, Clinton noted that the opening of Myanmar was one of the "most exciting developments" during her tenure at the State Department and that "Burma was giving the world new hope that it is indeed possible to transition peacefully from dictatorship to democracy." Journalist and author James Fallows said of her trip and the US government's work, "Much like Nixon's approach to China, I think it will eventually be studied for its skillful combination of hard and soft power, incentives and threats, urgency and patience, plus deliberate— and effective—misdirection." Academic Walter Russell Mead labeled her trip as a "decisive a diplomatic victory as anyone is likely to see." Clinton's trip would be what Derek branded as the trip that launched a thousand trips. Soon after, foreign ministers and leaders from around the globe would travel to Myanmar to see the changes for themselves.

Clinton acknowledged the challenges and difficult work that lay ahead for the fledgling democracy, including the spasms of anti-Muslim sentiment, finding ways to overcome decades of military rule, and controlling the chaos democracy sometimes brings. "The end of Burma's story is yet to be written," she wrote, but for one moment, they'd take the time to live in the moment and celebrate the small victories that were slowly piling up.[132]

The hard work could start tomorrow.

The Need to See the Changes for One's Self

And boy, did it. Everyone wanted a piece of Myanmar.

Perhaps the most important trip was Senator McConnell's in January 2012; he was the gateway to major policy changes. He had been introduced to the Myanmar issue by his staffer Robin Cleveland, who showed him a magazine article about

Aung San Suu Kyi's Nobel Peace Prize in 1991. Over the years, he developed a relationship with Aung San Suu Kyi through correspondence and worked with Senator Dianne Feinstein and others to put together legislation to help get the country out from under a military dictatorship. McConnell had a poster of Aung San Suu Kyi and a framed letter from her in his office, a reminder of the cause he had dedicated himself to support. It would be critical for him to hear from her directly and meet with the former military leaders his legislation had targeted to see if these changes were genuine.[133]

For him, meeting with Aung San Suu Kyi for the first time in person was an emotional moment. There was no need for clandestine communication anymore. At a press conference at the end of his trip, McConnell stated, "I'm convinced he [Thein Sein] is a genuine reformer, and more importantly, so does Aung San Suu Kyi." He went on to say that after meeting with top government officials and NLD members, ethnic groups, and prodemocracy activists:

> The one clear impression one gets from everyone with whom I have spoken here is that reform is for real.... So as somebody who has watched events in this country for some 20 years, I must say this is the first time that I have been genuinely optimistic about the future. I'm convinced as I go back to Washington and review these matters with my colleagues that reform is clearly on the agenda here and likely to stay on the agenda. My view of that is similar to what Secretary Clinton has already said publicly, which is that what we're looking for is reciprocity. As the country moves forward down the path of reform, then we will review the sanctions.... So it's going to be step-by-step.[134]

Congressman Joe Crowley, a key policymaker on Myanmar issues on the House Foreign Affairs Committee (HFAC), was also in the country in January 2012. He was the first member of the US House of Representatives to visit in twelve years. Crowley had a long history on Myanmar issues. He initially became involved because his diverse constituency included Burmese, Bangladeshi, and Indian communities that brought the issues home to him. His staff later included Jeremy Woodrum, the cofounder of US Campaign for Burma, an NGO that advocated for the protection of human rights in Myanmar. Crowley worked closely with his mentor, Tom Lantos (for whom the JADE Act is named for) and became the primary person on Myanmar issues when Lantos passed away. Crowley also admired Aung San Suu Kyi and her sacrifices. He felt she was a genuine leader and was inspired by her cause.[135]

Crowley went to Myanmar, and like many US government travelers, he was going to fly into Nay Pyi Taw via a US military airplane from Bangkok. He was set to meet with former military leaders to push for human rights and action on political reform before meeting with Aung San Suu Kyi in person. Once he was on board, the pilot yelled over the engines, "CONGRESSMAN! I HAVE TO GO THROUGH A FEW THINGS WITH YOU! THERE'S A PARACHUTE BEHIND YOU, YOU PROBABLY WON'T NEED IT! WE'LL BE GOING LOW OVER THE JUNGLE BETWEEN BURMA AND THAILAND! WE SHOULD BE FINE BUT IF WE CRASH, THERE'S A LOT OF WILD ANIMALS DOWN THERE! WE SHOULD BE FINE!" Crowley looked down at his shoes, thinking that there was no way he'd be able to outrun a tiger in them.[136]

After surviving the flight, he delivered some tough messages to the Thein Sein government but felt that there was a genuine desire to change. He also discussed ethnic issues and mentioned the plight of the ethnic minority Rohingya. As his constituency included a large Bangladeshi population, he was aware of the refugee camps filled with Rohingya who had been driven from Myanmar by the military. He didn't get anywhere on that topic with Thein Sein, nor did he with the prodemocracy and NLD crowd.

Crowley then went to Yangon to meet with Aung San Suu Kyi. It was a significant moment for him to finally meet with the person whose cause he had been supporting for years. Crowley, like the others who traveled to Myanmar after Clinton, was convinced something incredible was happening in Myanmar.[137]

With Clinton, McConnell, Crowley, and also Senator McCain and Webb's support, Derek had room to move on policy. But he also had to talk with international partners. Derek thought it was important to go to Europe to collaborate, as the US often did on foreign policy measures of mutual interest. Sanctions, aid, and assistance work most effectively when everyone is on board and aligned. It doesn't help if the US has imposed sanctions to effect change but everyone else has let their businesses invest.

He set off for Paris, Rome, Brussels, and London in February 2012. In Paris, he met with US embassy officers and French foreign ministry officials to discuss developments inside Myanmar and what steps to take next. Derek told them he had heard the French were eager to suspend all sanctions on Myanmar, an action the EU would debate and likely pass in April. The French told him they wanted to keep some leverage but felt it was the Italians and Germans who were really pressing for it.[138]

He flew off to Rome and met with three US missions: the US embassy in Rome, the US mission to the UN agencies, and the US embassy to the Holy See. Derek met with Italian parliamentarians and delivered the same message he had to the French, expressing concern about lifting sanctions too soon. His interlocutors were sympathetic and said that the French and Germans were the ones pushing for the suspension of sanctions.[139]

Perhaps the most exciting meeting of the trip was to the Vatican. The Catholic Church had a long history in Myanmar, and many Burmese political leaders and tycoons had attended Catholic schools. Catholic charities were active in education, food security, refugee and internally displaced persons issues, and peace efforts. Derek was escorted into St. Peter's Basilica to meet with the Vatican's head of foreign affairs to talk about political developments. Toward the end of the meeting, Derek expressed how exciting it was to be among such history, so his host took him on a little tour. He first led him to an adjoining room lined with gray brick speckled with artistic sketches, cracks, and holes. At one time, this was artist Raphael's sketch room where he tinkered with ideas and images for his paintings. It then served as a bathroom for one of the popes. The holes in the walls were from the sacking of Rome in 1527, which was reenacted by the cardinal; he mimicked taking a hammer to the wall and shouted, "Bang! Bang!" He then led Derek to a map room, which housed all of the old Vatican maps of the world as they knew it.[140]

After a history-filled trip to Rome, Derek went to Brussels to meet with all of the EU representatives. This was where decisions on sanctions, aid, and other policy maneuvers would be made. Derek had been regularly holding roundtables with the EU mission in Washington, so it was good to go to the main mission to speak directly about US views. Derek spoke with the German representative and conveyed what he heard from the French and Italians on sanctions. The German diplomat very directly said, "Yes, it's us. And the French and Italians. The only ones with real reservations are the Czechs."[141] With that bit of news, Derek kicked off the roundtable and shared views and insights gained from trips and engagements, including the recent visit by Secretary Clinton and Senator McConnell. Derek tried to convince them to consider a sector-by-sector approach on sanctions-easing to keep leverage for reform in problematic sectors, like sectors with extensive military-business entities or exploitive businesses like jade mining, gas, or timber. However, the EU had already decided that they were going to suspend all sanctions that year with the exception of military sales, noting that they could be reimposed if necessary.

Slightly dejected, Derek took off for London. The US traditionally had been more aligned with British policy on Myanmar. The UK still used the term "Burma" and were avid supporters of Aung San Suu Kyi, partly due to her husband being British; to the UK having a vocal advocacy community; and to the colonial connection. Derek discussed the meetings in Brussels, and the UK felt the same way he did about the sanctions-easing but were going to be on board with the EU regardless. They told him to hold the line and keep some restrictions in place to leverage further change and keep Myanmar on the path of reform. Derek agreed about maintaining leverage but noted it was unfair that the EU would allow all of their businesses to enter Myanmar while the US would be expected to hold the line and tell their businesses to wait. Plus, the bite of sanctions could hardly be felt if Myanmar had other viable investors.

* * *

In April 2012, President Obama and Secretary Clinton announced that Derek was to be the first ambassador to Myanmar in twenty years, and on June 27, he appeared before the Senate Foreign Relations Committee (SFRC) led by Senator Webb for his confirmation hearing. Derek spoke about his work as special rep and how he would work to keep Myanmar on the path of political reform. He also noted that he was under no illusions about the challenges that remained; reform could be reversed and democratization was not inevitable. Derek also discussed national reconciliation and peace, including renewed sectarian violence in western Rakhine State.[142] He was then questioned by members of the committee. Senator Inhofe wanted to make sure the US had full access to gas blocks.[143] Others wanted US businesses to stay out of the fossil fuel industry. Senator Rubio focused on trafficking issues.[144]

Despite contradictory policy wants from the SFRC, Derek was confirmed two days later as the first ambassador to Myanmar—and Than Swe the first Myanmar ambassador to the US—in decades. Within days, he, his wife Min, and their pup, Bernie, headed off to move in and join the first US business delegation to Myanmar in years.

The Icon Comes to Washington

Patrick Murphy, the director for mainland Southeast Asia and deputized special rep, was tasked with temporarily taking Derek's role. Patrick had been working on the Myanmar issue forever—as a desk officer, an embassy officer, and in his current role. He had been working as tirelessly as everyone while also working on Vietnam, Laos, Cambodia, and Thailand. His first task was to host Aung San Suu Kyi in the US for a nine-city, seventeen-day tour. She would attend sixty events and meet 40,000 people on her first trip to America in decades. This trip would prove more daunting than Secretary Clinton's trip.

The State Department had to consider necessities like security, costs, and logistics as the Myanmar embassy was not prepared to and would not provide the assistance for her trip despite her status as an elected member of Parliament; the Myanmar embassy did not view her as an official representative of the Thein Sein government and had no instructions to support her. Patrick was able to borrow a seasoned protocol officer, Shilpa Pesaru, and Medora Brown, who had been providing administrative support to the special rep's office, to provide full-time support for Aung San Suu Kyi's trip. They were also working closely with the

State Department's security officials to assist the two officers who were joining the trip to protect the Lady. Aung San Suu Kyi would be joined by her friends and associates who would help with logistics. The team was also working with florists on the ground in each city to ensure they had a fresh supply of flowers for Aung San Suu Kyi's hair.

The trip team had to help prioritize the hundreds of meetings requests, outline her goals and strategy, and find a way to politely decline invitations. Aung San Suu Kyi wanted to meet with policymakers, business leaders, activists, and philanthropists who had supported her cause. She also had to pick up the many awards she had been awarded in abstentia.[145]

The special rep's office was getting hounded and bullied with requests to meet with Aung San Suu Kyi. Medora seemed to get all the good ones. Annie Leibovitz called to see if she could have ten minutes to do a photo shoot of Aung San Suu Kyi. She even offered Medora a print. Patrick was only offered threats to his career and livelihood.[146]

Aung San Suu Kyi's first day in the US was in Washington, where she met with Secretary Clinton and later joined a State Department-led rule of law roundtable, an issue on which she was laser-focused and which she thought would be one of the cures for Myanmar's many ills. She also discussed the HIV/AIDS crisis with US agencies, met with reporters from Radio Free Asia and Voice of America, picked up an award at a joint Asia Society-US Institute for Peace event with an introductory speech from Clinton, met with World Bank President Kim, and had a dinner with Secretary Clinton.[147 and 148]

The following day, she met with President Obama and later received the Congressional Gold Medal, initially awarded in 2008. Secretary Clinton; former First Lady Laura Bush; Congresspersons Nancy Pelosi, Joe Crowley, Don Manzullo, John Boehner; and Senators Harry Reid, Mitch McConnell, John McCain, and Dianne Feinstein joined Aung San Suu Kyi onstage, and each spoke of what the Lady and her struggle meant to them. Laura Bush, a longtime advocate for Aung San Suu Kyi and who continued to support educational activities in the country through the Bush Institute after President Bush left office, spoke at the event.[149] She said that the new hope growing in the country was a tribute to Aung San Suu Kyi. McCain called her "my personal hero," going on to say, "I want to thank you . . . for teaching me, at my age, a thing or two about courage." Clinton said, "It's almost too delicious to believe, my friend, that you are in the Rotunda of our Capitol, the centerpiece of our democracy as an elected member of parliament." Aung San Suu Kyi, who described herself as a "a stranger from a distant land" was clearly affected by the ceremony and the speeches. She said, "This is one of the most moving days in my life. . . . From the depths of my heart I thank you, the people of America . . .

for keeping us in your hearts and minds during the dark years when freedom and justice seemed beyond our reach."[150 and 151]

One person who was not on the dais was Senator Webb. As everyone patted each other on the back for all the work they and their colleagues had done, no one mentioned Webb, the risks he took, the cover he provided for the administration to do hard things, or the support he offered. Though his name had been mentioned for his critical role in Myanmar policy quite often in the past year, including by Clinton, Kurt, and Derek, Webb felt that his work on Myanmar policy was slowly being lost to history.[152]

Aung San Suu Kyi went to New York twice. She was thrilled to be back for the first time since she lived there when working for the UN in the 1960s, saying, "I lived in Manhattan for more than three years, and I loved this city at a time when people thought it terrible."[153]

Complicating matters was that Thein Sein was also in New York to speak as head of state at the UNGA's General Debate. There was concern that Aung San Suu Kyi could upstage Thein Sein's first global foray since the reforms had started.[154] It should have been a celebratory moment for him as well and was made a little sweeter when on September 19, days before Thein Sein left for New York, Thein Sein and Shwe Mann were removed from the SDN List for their role in political reforms. According to the US Treasury, "Thein Sein and Thura Shwe Mann have taken concrete steps to promote political reforms and human rights, and to move Burma away from repression and dictatorship toward democracy and freedom, warranting today's delisting action."[155]

Thein Sein and Aung San Suu Kyi decided to meet while in New York, but Aung San Suu Kyi was under the impression it would be a one-on-one engagement with a possible short press briefing. When she arrived, there were cameras everywhere and she felt ambushed by a perceived public relations stunt. She was stunned but tried not to let it overshadow the rest of her trip. Aung San Suu Kyi also met with fellow female Nobel laureates, the most elite of clubs, in what turned out to be a very frosty meeting. It was an early sign that many were making the wrong assumption in viewing her as a human rights activist and not a political figure. She had insisted she was the latter, something that became quite clear a few years later and was not welcomed by her Nobel cohort.[156]

Senator McConnell extended an invitation for her to visit the McConnell Center at the University of Kentucky, and, for something a little less taxing, McConnell and his wife, Secretary Elaine Chao, took her to see a horse farm. The trip for McConnell was an emotional one. He said of the visit, "I must confess, I don't easily tear up, but after passing notes all those years, it was a real thrill to bring her to Louisville. . . . That was the moment of euphoria."[157 and 158]

Aung San Suu Kyi's marathon trip continued. She managed to squeeze in Columbia University, Yale, and Harvard, and the cities of San Francisco and Los Angeles, before finally calling it a trip. Congresswoman Nancy Pelosi hosted an event at the University of San Francisco, awarding Aung San Suu Kyi with an honorary degree. She also got a key to the city and later hobnobbed with celebrities in LA.[159 and 160]

One key goal for Aung San Suu Kyi was outreach to diaspora communities throughout the US. It was important for her to thank them for their sacrifice and support. Large communities of Burmese refugees, mostly from Karen and Chin ethnic groups, reside in New York, Washington, DC, Maryland, Kentucky, Indiana, Washington State, and California. She visited Crowley's district and spoke at his alma mater, Queens College. The rather large room was filled with Burmese diaspora, generations of people who had fled both Ne Win and Than Shwe. Their children had been born in the US and had only heard about Aung San Suu Kyi in family stories and recollections. Here she was, speaking to them, acknowledging their struggle, and asking for them to consider returning to help rebuild the country. Carole King, a Queens College alum, came by to sing "You've Got a Friend," adding to the feel-goodness of the event.[161] Aung San Suu Kyi spoke to crowds in Kentucky and in San Francisco. At the latter venue, she embraced the "Mother Suu" image, speaking to the crowd of 5,000, smiling constantly and telling funny stories about her dog. The most difficult part of the trip was Fort Wayne, Indiana. It was a microcosm of the fractiousness that troubled Myanmar. There was fighting on who was organizing the event, where it would be, who would be allowed to come, and who spoke for the community. The infighting and inability to compromise nearly derailed the event. The one thing that was under control there was the florist who provided flowers for Aung San Suu Kyi.[162]

Obama, Oburma

It was finally time for the ultimate visit: President Obama was set to travel to Myanmar as part of a broader trip to Asia in November 2012.

Human rights groups demanded he cancel it. In their minds, the Thein Sein government was only doing surface-level and easily reversible changes. The senior director for multilateral affairs and human rights, Samantha Power, didn't necessarily agree with all of the US's policy changes, particularly on sanctions, but publicly supported Obama and Clinton's steps toward normalizing the relationship. She saw Obama's trip as furthering progress on issues on which the US was getting traction, saying it supported the president's policy of being willing to engage with countries that concretely showed a will to reform, stating, "The reason we engage is not to reward but to lock down progress and to push on areas where progress is urgently needed."[163]

Power traveled to Myanmar in October 2012 to push for progress on human rights before the visit but also to convince Aung San Suu Kyi to support it. Aung San Suu Kyi called Obama's trip a "dreadful idea" and a "mistake" and that it would legitimize a military-flavored regime that stood in the way of democracy. At this stage, Aung San Suu Kyi's relationship with Thein Sein was starting to fray, and she was increasingly frustrated about the prospects of amending the divisive constitution. Power, who recounted the meeting in her book, *The Education of an Idealist*, was excited to meet with her, having admired her courage and sacrifice. But she was consistently interrupted by Aung San Suu Kyi as she attempted to explain the rationale behind the trip. Failing to sway the Lady, Power turned to an easier topic: the ethnic Rohingya. Power, who had witnessed genocide firsthand in the Balkans in the 1990s, urged Aung San Suu Kyi to speak up against the increasing violence and call for the protection of rights for all people in Myanmar. Aung San Suu Kyi said it would not be good for her to take sides and told Power to stop relying on propaganda to inform her opinion; to Aung San San Kyi, the violence was hyped up by Muslim countries. Power was shocked by her tone and lack of open-mindedness and hoped the meeting was an aberration.[164]

DRL's Mike Posner also pushed to get solid commitments on improving human rights, helping to provide justification for Obama's trip. In October 2012, weeks before Obama's scheduled visit, Posner led an interagency human rights dialogue that included Derek, now three months into his role as ambassador; State Department officials from labor rights, economic development, conflict resolution, and rule of law offices; senior officials from the White House and vice president's office; USAID; the Department of Homeland Security; and the Department of Defense, including both civilian officials and uniformed military. The delegation met with President Thein Sein, his office, ministers, the military, and Aung San Suu Kyi in her capacity as a parliamentarian.

Bringing US uniformed military officers was deliberate; though the dialogue was DRL-led, Mike felt that those who needed to hear and understand the message would be more interested in hearing it from people in uniform. The Myanmar side, expecting to be lectured by activists in government guise, suddenly started calling colleagues and running out of the room. Next thing everyone knew, thirty people from the military joined the discussion. With a captive audience, both the DRL and the US military were clear that there would be no legitimization or public recognition of the Tatmadaw until significant and verifiable efforts had been made on human rights. It felt like a significant step had been made in getting uniformed officers to talk about human rights.[165 and 166]

But it was not enough—Power and Posner would have to go to Myanmar again to secure promises on reforms to make Obama's trip palatable. After three grueling days, the Myanmar government signed off on a communique that included commitments on releasing political prisoners, granting access for humanitarian workers to conflict areas, more action on political reforms and on the rule of law, and a strategy for allowing refugees and activists to return to Myanmar safely. Power and Posner got what they came for.[167]

Obama arrived in Yangon less than two weeks after the US election, becoming the first sitting US president to go to Myanmar, a country he implored to unclench its fist in one of his first speeches as president. Obama's limo and motorcade pulled onto the Myanmar streets to head to his first meeting. His key advisor, Ben Rhodes, thought that the largest crowds would be near the airport, but as the motorcade drove on, the masses of people grew to five deep, and thousands of people were on the streets waving flags, wearing T-shirts adorned with Obama's face and with children sitting on their parents' shoulders to catch a glimpse of the US president.[168 and 169]

On the drive in from the airport, Derek and Kurt regaled the president with tales of Burmese history and Yangon. The golden Shwedagon Pagoda appeared on the horizon, and Obama asked what it was. Kurt gave a brief explanation of it, emphatically noting that no trip to Myanmar was complete without visiting the revered stupa. Unbeknownst to Kurt, a Shwedagon stop was ruled out because of security issues. Obama looked at his team and asked, "Why are we not going there?" The Secret Service agents, already exasperated with Kurt (they had chased him around the tarmac as he was jettisoning stolen Air Force One tchotchkes he had stuffed in his pockets—they only wanted to let him know that his car assignment had changed), said they'd make it happen.[170]

Obama, joined by Secretary Clinton, visited Aung San Suu Kyi at her home. Aung San Suu Kyi spoke of matching the high expectations of the country's youth and then delved into the inanities of the Myanmar parliamentary system. Obama pivoted to talking about issues of US concern, including the violence targeting the Rohingya. In a less chilly response than what she gave to Power, she said the human rights of all the country's people should be respected.

In a joint speech to the press, Obama expressed his admiration for Aung San Suu Kyi, seeing her as a charismatic icon and leader and a person who had sacrificed so much to bring democracy to her country. He also praised Clinton for her service and for the powerful message that she and Aung San Suu Kyi send about the importance of women as leaders and for embracing and promoting democratic values and human rights.[171 and 172 and 173]

Obama made a speech at Yangon University, the birthplace of the country's anti-colonial and prodemocracy movements. Obama focused his themes on reconciliation and the power of diversity, speaking on the troubles in western Myanmar, saying:

we look at the recent violence in Rakhine State that has caused so much suffering, and we see the danger of continued tensions there. For too long, the people of this state, including ethnic Rakhine, have faced crushing poverty and persecution. But there is no excuse for violence against innocent people. And the Rohingya hold themselves—hold within themselves the same dignity as you do, and I do. I say this because my own country and my own life have taught me the power of diversity. The United States of America is a nation of Christians and Jews, and Muslims and Buddhists, and Hindus and non-believers. Our story is shaped by every language; it's enriched by every culture. We have people from every corner of the world. We've tasted the bitterness of civil war and segregation, but our history shows us that hatred in the human heart can recede; that the lines between races and tribes fade away. And what's left is a simple truth: e pluribus unum—that's what we say in America. Out of many, we are one nation and we are one people.[174]

I thought it was a timely and important speech. But in Myanmar, it got mixed reviews. His use of "Rohingya" riled ethnic Buddhist Arakan members of parliament. The crowd expected a speech that evoked his inspiring razzle-dazzle and audacity of hope but received a lecture on diversity. One audience member said that compared to other speeches she'd seen Obama give, this one was "just average" and "not very inspired." Tough crowd![175]

Obama met with Thein Sein, telling him that the more he did on reforms, the more the US could do to help with economic development. The Myanmar government agreed to the points in the Power communique from a few weeks prior and reiterated their commitment to provide more access for the International Committee of the Red Cross to prisoners, to create a process to adjudicate remaining political prisoners, to bring in the UN high commissioner for human rights to help deal with human rights issues, to pursue a ceasefire in Kachin State, to address the underlying issues in Rakhine State, including returning displaced people to their home and addressing the issue of citizenship for the Rohingya, to sign onto IAEA additional protocols, and to adhere to UN Security Council Resolution 1874, which further committed them to ending the military relationship with North Korea.[176]

All in all, it was a busy and successful six-hour trip.

A New Administration Joins the Ranks of Burma Hands

When President Trump assumed office in 2017, he inherited a Myanmar on the downswing. The National Security Council's new Asia team helped staunch the loss of momentum that typically occurs in a presidential transition and refocused attention to Myanmar. Led by Matt Pottinger, a China hand, journalist, and US Marine, the team sought to develop a constructive engagement strategy to mitigate the worst outcomes that could spin out from the peace process and violence in Rakhine State while keeping Myanmar interested in maintaining a relationship with the US to work together on the hard stuff. Interagency meetings on Myanmar once again were on the rise as the Rohingya issue garnered more attention and as the administration sought ways to limit PRC influence and North Korean military sales in the region.

The White House was set to host Aung San Suu Kyi around August 2017, a chance to signal that the US wanted to do more with Myanmar, improve economic and investment ties, and talk through Rohingya and human rights issues. Of course, discussing Myanmar's treatment of Muslims was going to be a tricky topic because Buddhist nationalists generally supported Trump's Muslim travel ban and thought the Rohingya crisis was "fake news." In the end, the meeting coincided with the long-awaited release of the Kofi Annan Advisory Commission on Rakhine State report for which Aung San Suu Kyi needed to be present; the following day, the military retaliated for an attack led by a Muslim insurgency that resulted in the eventual purge of 750,000 Rohingya. The White House could not host Aung San Suu Kyi after that.[177]

With the trip scuttled, the Trump administration still found ways to signal the importance of Myanmar and Southeast Asia more broadly, releasing in late 2017 its Free and Open Indo-Pacific Strategy that advocated for free, fair, and reciprocal trade, open investment environments, good governance, and freedom of the seas. The strategy called for high-level engagement at the senior-most levels and ongoing work with (despite presidential threats to) the US's five treaty allies in the region.[178 and 179] Though not a significant priority within the document, Myanmar remained indirectly and directly tied to key national security priorities, such as North Korea, the PRC, and human rights issues. The NSC drafted a specific Myanmar strategy that same year, which pushed back on recommendations for blunt punitive actions, sought to deploy targeted, effective measures, and looked to find ways to work on the harder issues, like military professionalization, drug trafficking, and the Rohingya crisis. The low-hanging fruit of policy had been done; this was the hard stuff and needed to be met with bold, flexible, and well-thought-out actions.[180]

In June 2018, Pottinger went to Myanmar to meet with senior government leaders and civil society to discuss a range of issues, including how Myanmar fit into the broader Indo-Pacific plan, and offer support to help them turn things around. Pottinger said that while the US certainly criticized the military-led violence against, and the government's lack of protection of, the Rohingya, the US continued to demonstrate its support for Myanmar's future by spending USD

$120 million since 2017 on issues critical to Myanmar's economic and political development, including improving health and banking systems, building skills and capacity of local ethnic leaders to contribute to peace efforts, providing technical assistance and training for law enforcement and judicial officials, and training teachers to support the education sector. Pottinger wanted to show that though the US would condemn human rights abuses, that didn't equal abandonment.[181]

On the same trip, Pottinger secured separate private meetings with Aung San Suu Kyi and Deputy Commander-in-Chief (CINC) Soe Win. The new US ambassador to Myanmar, Scot Marciel, had warned Pottinger that if he discussed the Rohingya issue with Aung San Suu Kyi, she might get frosty and end the meeting. Marciel wasn't suggesting Pottinger avoid the topic but rather preparing him. Pottinger delved right into the topic, saying clearly that the US wanted to do more to enhance the bilateral relationship and help her on constitutional reform but could not with the ongoing violence and the government's denial of the situation. He asked her to publicly acknowledge what was going on. Aung San Suu Kyi was nonfrostily noncommittal.[182]

The meeting with the deputy CINC went slightly better, but Pottinger received the old line that the Rohingya were illegal immigrants and terrorists. Like Senators Webb and McCain, he could talk to them soldier-to-soldier, which aided in creating an atmosphere for a more productive dialogue on military professionalism and rule of law that were critical to stopping human rights abuses. He shared his experiences in Iraq and Afghanistan fighting terrorism; he said the US could help on those issues (he was not suggesting the Rohingya were terrorists as the Tatmadaw was) and the rules of battlefield. The military had to be accountable for what they did, and it was important for it to be under civilian control.[183]

Back in Washington, Congress, human rights groups, the international community, and some in the Trump administration remained fixated on the Rohingya issue to the detriment of pressing for progress on other critical issues. It's fair to note it was hard to focus on anything else; the situation was growing more tenuous by the day for the hundreds of thousands of refugees in Bangladesh. Cox's Bazar, the site of the camps, was a prime spot for cyclones and was vulnerable to flooding and mudslides. The camps were overcrowded, significantly raising the risks of communicable diseases, fires, community tensions, and domestic and sexual violence. School-aged Rohingya fell further behind their peers in Rakhine State thanks to a lack of structured education in the camps. Despite being a nonsignatory to the 1951 Refugee Convention, which obligates a nation to take on refugees, Bangladesh continued to house hundreds of thousands of Myanmar refugees in its country. The needs were overwhelming, and this was not an issue Bangladesh wanted to be handling for the long term; it had its own problems.[184]

The Trump administration would continue aid and assistance programs and support investment in the country, but it would be pressured to deal with the seemingly intractable challenge of ethnicity and identity in Myanmar, the very same challenge it faced at home.

Independence leader Aung San with his family, including his wife Khin Kyi, his sons Aung San Oo and Aung San Lin, and his daughter and future prodemocracy icon Aung San Suu Kyi (bottom center). Source: *Freedom From Fear: And Other Writings*, Aung San Suu Kyi, 1991. https://commons.wikimedia.org/wiki/File:Aung_San_and_family.jpg

Junta leader Ne Win, who wrested control of the Burmese government in 1958 and again in 1962. Source: Government of Israel, 1959. https://commons.wikimedia.org/wiki/File:General_Ne_Win_PM_of_Burma_1959.jpg.

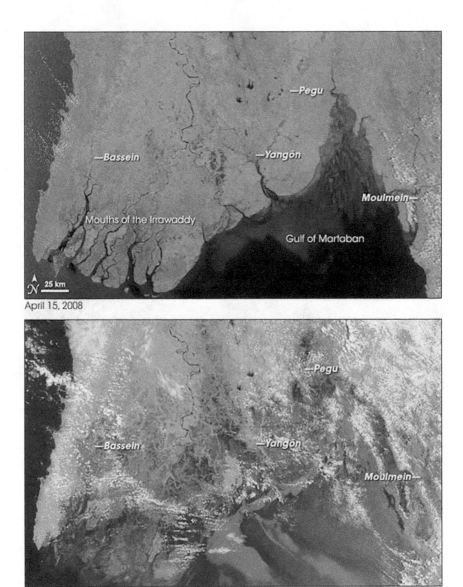

April 15, 2008

May 5, 2008

NASA satellite photos show the extensive damage done by Cyclone Nargis in 2008. Source: NASA/MODIS Rapid Response Team, 2008.
https://upload.wikimedia.org/wikipedia/commons/0/0d/Cyclone_Nargis_
flooding_before-and-after.jpg

Assistant Secretary for East Asian and Pacific Affairs Kurt Campbell and U.S. Embassy Chargé d'affaires Larry Dinger meet with Aung San Suu Kyi in 2010 as part of the new U.S.-Burma policy. Source: U.S. Embassy in Burma, 2010. https://upload.wikimedia.org/wikipedia/commons/a/a7/Larry_Dinger%2C_Kurt_Campbell_and_Daw_Aung_San_Suu_Kyi_on_Inya_Lake.jpg

Secretary Hillary Clinton and Aung San Suu Kyi, both wearing funereal white, meet for a private dinner in 2011 at the Chargé d'affaires residence. Source: U.S. Department of State East Asia and Pacific Media Hub, 2011. https://commons.wikimedia.org/wiki/File:Secretary_Clinton_Meets_Daw_Aung_San_Suu_Kyi_for_Dinner_(6437451337).jpg.

President Barack Obama insisted he add a stop at the iconic Shwedagon Pagoda during his short, but historic, visit in 2012. Source: White House, Pete Souza, 2012. https://commons.wikimedia.org/wiki/ File:Barack_Obama_poses_in_front_of_Shwedagon_Pagoda.jpg.

Dogs were a common theme that could bring all leaders together. Aung San Suu Kyi got a chance to pet Bo on her trip to Washington, DC in 2012. Source: White House Flickr Account, Pete Souza, 2012. https://upload. wikimedia.org/wikipedia/commons/0/0f/Aung_San_Suu_Kyi_with_Barack_ Obama_20120919_%28cropped1%29.jpg.

The famed leg rower of Inle Lake, the inspiration for the name of my consulting firm. Source: Erin Murphy.

President Obama meets with President Thein Sein at the White House in 2013. Source: White House, Lawrence Jackson, 2013.
https://upload.wikimedia.org/wikipedia/commons/8/89/Thein_Sein_and_Barack_Obama_in_the_Oval_Office.jpg

(R-L) Ambassador Derek Mitchell, Deputy Secretary of State Tony Blinken, and Assistant Secretary for Democracy, Human Rights, and Labor Tom Malinowski speak at a press conference in Nay Pyi Taw in 2016. U.S. Department of State East Asia and Pacific Media Hub, 2016

https://upload.wikimedia.org/wikipedia/commons/9/99/105_-_Flickr_-_East_Asia_and_Pacific_Media_Hub.jpg

My work introduced me to all sorts of experiences around Myanmar, many of which pushed my risk tolerance. Source: Erin Murphy.

U.S. Secretary of State John Kerry is briefed by State Department Spokesperson John Kirby, U.S. Ambassador to Myanmar Scot Marciel, Assistant Secretary of State for East Asian and Pacific Affairs Daniel Russel, State Department Deputy Chief of Staff Tom Sullivan, U.S. Embassy Rangoon Deputy Chief of Mission Kristen Bauer, and State Department Speechwriter Andrew Imbrie on May 22, 2016, at the Kempinski Hotel in Naypyitaw, Myanmar, before bilateral meetings with Myanmar Foreign Minister Aung San Suu Kyi and Commander-in-Chief Min Aug Hlaing. The Kerry team got in trouble because the hotel was owned by a sanctioned crony. Source: U.S. Department of State, 2016. https://commons.wikimedia.org/wiki/File:Secretary_Kerry_is_Briefed_(26560488863).jpg.

Aung San Suu Kyi and Vice President Mike Pence in a tense meeting
on the sidelines of the ASEAN Summit 2018. Source: U.S. Embassy in
Burma, 2018. https://upload.wikimedia.org/wikipedia/commons/e/
e6/VP_Mike_Pence_and_Aung_San_Suu_Kyi_at_33rd_ASEAN_
Summit_%281%29.jpg.

U.S. Secretary of State Rex Tillerson and Commander-in-Chief and
2021 coup leader Senior General Min Aung Hlaing discuss the crisis in
northern Rakhine state in November 2017. Source: Myanmar's Defense
Services Commander-in-Chief's Office, 2017.

6

SANCTIONS

PUTTING THE "SPECIAL" IN SPECIALLY
DESIGNATED NATIONALS LIST

Like Cuba and Iran, Myanmar became synonymous with sanctions. If things went south in Myanmar, as they often did, sanctions were the first tool deployed in the foreign policy tool kit.

Over the years, Myanmar would be subjected to foreign assistance restrictions, sanctions, and regulatory restrictions related to the Child Soldiers Prevention Act of 2008, the Victims of Trafficking and Violence Protection Act of 2000 (also known as Trafficking in Persons or TIP), the USA PATRIOT Act, the International Religious Freedom Act, the Trade Reform Act of 1974, the Arms Export Control Act of 1976, the Foreign Corrupt Practices Act, and the Dodd-Frank Act. These restrictions had far-reaching consequences. For example, the TIP sanctions empowered the US executive director, a person nominated by the US president, confirmed by the US Senate, and representing the US on the board of directors of the World Bank Group,[1] to use their "best efforts to deny a board vote" on any assistance for Myanmar. That meant no development finance institution support for years.[2]

Economic and trade sanctions began during President Clinton's second term (Presidents Reagan and Bush suspended aid and assistance programs and downgraded diplomatic ties). Both Congress and Clinton determined that the SLORC had committed large-scale repression of the democratic opposition in Myanmar, and Clinton issued Executive Order (EO) 13047 prohibiting any new investment by US persons or entities.[3] "New investments" came to be defined as entering new contracts, purchasing equity interests, or participating in royalties, earnings, or profits from investment in a nearly all sectors. US business could, however, sell products to Myanmar. So if you found Doritos or Pepsi on Yangon store shelves, it was legal. Some companies already in Myanmar, like Chevron and Caterpillar, were grandfathered in, but their engagement was quite limited.[4]

During the George W. Bush administration, both the executive and legislative branches felt that the continued repression by the junta warranted more sanctions, so President Bush signed Congress's Burma Freedom and Democracy Act of 2003 (BFDA) into law. The BFDA banned products of Myanmar origin in the US (so Americans couldn't bring home tchotchkes or large teak logs) and froze the assets of, and applied visa bans to, senior government officials. The BFDA and the accompanying EO 13310 prohibited the exportation or re-exportation of any US financial services to Myanmar and blocked three state-owned banks— Myanma Foreign Trade Bank, Myanma Investment and Commercial Bank, and Myanma Economic Bank (MEB)—meaning these banks could not conduct any transactions in the broader international banking system, especially if it involved US persons or entities or the US dollar.[5 and 6 and 7]

Congress passed the Tom Lantos Block Burmese Junta's Anti-Democratic Efforts (JADE) Act of 2008, and Bush signed it into law. It was named for Tom Lantos, a Holocaust survivor, congressman in the House of Representatives, and staunch human rights advocate. He passed away from cancer earlier in 2008 and the JADE Act, aimed at punishing a regime for gross human rights violations, seemed an appropriate memorial. The JADE Act expanded the SDN List criteria to include the current and former junta leaders and their families, enforced a visa and travel ban, and specifically targeted the import to the US of any jadeite and rubies (get it? JADE/jade?).[8]

President Obama put a pause on strengthening sanctions until the Burma policy review was complete. At the end of the review in late 2009, the administration chose to pursue engagement and sanctions. However, once the Thein Sein government began enacting political and economic reforms, rumors started flying about easing sanctions. After the April 2012 by-election that brought Aung San Suu Kyi and the NLD into government, a key requirement of the EOs and legislative acts, the rumor mill went into overdrive. The EU suspended its sanctions regime at the end of April 2012, allowing their businesses to fully enter the market without restrictions for the first time in years.[9 and 10]

There was fear among the human rights activist crowd and skeptics in Congress that the US was getting overly excited about Thein Sein's actions, and they wanted leverage in place to keep key reforms going. Many thought the Thein Sein government's reforms were only surface-deep, that there were no significant structural changes in Myanmar, and that the government was "old wine in new bottles."

Others thought the US wasn't doing enough. With the EU out of the sanctions game, US businesses were at a disadvantage. Additionally, the impact of US sanctions was significantly weakened; Myanmar had other options now. How could the US push for change by dangling the prospect for investment when Myanmar could get investment from the Germans, French, British, Japanese, or South Koreans?

There were calls to lift sanctions coming from the US policymaking community as well. Senator Webb, who had been advocating for the lifting of sanctions for years, said that they must be lifted "as quickly as possible." He was in the country after the 2012 by-election and spoke with parliamentarians and other prominent figures, calling the developments a "profound moment" in Myanmar's history.[11] Senator McCain, also an avid Aung San Suu Kyi supporter, said it was time to work with international partners in easing sanctions. He didn't want them lifted wholesale but in an incremental way in consultation with Congress.[12]

The Easing Begins

In late April 2012, Secretary Clinton's team was preparing remarks in response to the NLD's win in the by-election and the culmination of positive developments that had occurred since the beginning of the year, including the release of hundreds of political prisoners and the cease-fire with the KNU. There were several interagency discussions, as well as outreach to validators, interlocutors, stakeholders, activists, and anyone who had a stake in the game. Her remarks would include the first indications of a new US stance on economic relations with Myanmar.[13]

Easing the restrictions on financial services had broad support. As Myanmar was opening up, it needed access to the international financial system to be able to grow, generate wealth and income for its people, and get the necessary financing to rebuild its country. What wasn't clear was whether the 1997 ban on new investment would be eased. For activists, there was a fear of a "gold rush" of businesses to Myanmar. They felt that large corporations would not care about labor and human rights standards, would be exploitive, and would do little to press the government on core issues such as political prisoners and violence against minorities.[14]

What was clear was that the SDN List would stay in place; there were still many "bad actors," including the SPDC members and cronies. But the SDN List criteria for adding individuals and entities needed to be updated to reflect a rapidly developing situation. The criteria for sanctioning any member of the government could technically apply to the NLD. Current US sanctions criteria also didn't reflect the developments and complexities in the peace process and national reconciliation.

Clinton ended the debate on what would be eased and what wouldn't by announcing:

> We are prepared to take steps toward: first, seeking agrément for a fully accredited ambassador in Rangoon in the coming days, followed by a formal announcement of our nominee; second, establishing an in-country USAID mission and supporting a normal country program for the United Nations Development Program; third, enabling private organizations in the United States to pursue a broad range of nonprofit activities from democracy building to health and education; fourth, facilitating travel to the United States for select government officials and parliamentarians; and fifth, beginning the process of a targeted easing of our ban on the export of US financial services and investment as part of a broader effort to help accelerate economic modernization and political reform. Sanctions and prohibitions will stay in place on individuals and institutions that remain on the wrong side of these historic reform efforts.[15]

For the first time since 1997, US businesses would be allowed to invest.

There were a few key figures in Congress who still had to be convinced to support the policy, most notably the House Foreign Affairs Committee's Ileana Ros-Lehtinen. Ros-Lehtinen represented a congressional district that was majority Cuban American. She was the daughter of anti-Fidel Castro activists and thus viewed sanctions through a Cuba lens. The possibility of rolling back Myanmar sanctions could have implications for Cuba. In 2010, Raúl Castro began implementing his own set of economic reforms, a small but notable chipping away of the revolution's communist platform. Castro loosened regulations on farmers to favor market forces and prices (this was reversed in 2015), liberalized small business regulations, pushed for state-owned enterprises to be more autonomous and competitive, authorized the sale and purchase of homes and cars, adopted a comprehensive tax code, and implemented a new foreign direct investment law. Several of these moves mirrored reforms Thein Sein had undertaken, which earned him praise and diplomatic carrots. The White House was considering revising Cuba policy, Castro's being another fist to unclench. Ben Rhodes, Obama's deputy national security advisor, made this and Myanmar a focus during Obama's second term, looking to pry open Cuba, and for those who were working on this issue with him, he used the efforts on Myanmar as a model. Both dealt with human rights issues, vocal activists, an engaged Congress, and a policy stuck in amber.[16] and 17

Convincing skeptics in Congress and within the interagency was extremely difficult, but on May 17, Secretary Clinton announced the outlines of the new sanctions policy in a press conference with Foreign Minister Wunna Maung Lwin, who was visiting Washington, DC. The US had decided to allow US businesses to invest in all sectors and not exclude them from the traditionally problematic extractives sector in Myanmar. Clinton was also careful to note that the US maintained leverage and other means to bring sanctions back should reform and human rights protections go off the rails. US businesses would be encouraged to invest responsibly and be an agent of change through employment and adhering to the gold standard of corporate governance and utilizing the rule of law.[18] One way to hold them to these standards was a new Responsible Investment Reporting Requirement to be filed by new investors that would include questions on their corporate, human rights, and labor policies, their anti-corruption efforts, and their stakeholder engagement. Most businesses felt these were an undue burden and provided an opportunity for human rights groups to pick apart their reports and shame them publicly. It spooked small- and medium-sized companies with limited budgets and resources. The reporting requirements were meant to help the US government understand what was making life difficult for US companies and use it as a way to showcase the good the US companies were doing, but you could never convince investors of that.[19]

Like Getting a New Car without Wheels

Despite the initial easing of sanctions, the SDN List, the so-called blacklist enforced by the Treasury's Office of Foreign Assets Control (OFAC), whose inclusion of individuals and entities prohibited from engaging in US-dollar-denominated transactions and from business dealings with US persons and entities, was fully in effect. Roughly one hundred names and companies of the country's notorious "cronies" were added, making most of the economy completely off-limits to US businesses.[20]

Further complicating the landscape was OFAC's 50 percent rule. The SDN List didn't include every name that was off-limits. By the 50 percent rule, any company that was owned 50 percent or more in the aggregate by entities or individuals that were sanctioned were also blocked, resulting in a cascade effect.[21] Given that cronies owned multiple companies, US companies could not work with a plethora of business interests. Despite fears of a gold rush, the specter of sanctions violations made it hard to convince US businesses to consider the Myanmar market.

So who are the cronies?

Myanmar's crony class is comprised of about two dozen families who grew rich from patronage ties to top military leaders, including Senior General Than Shwe, Vice Senior General Maung Aye, General Shwe Mann, and, before his fall and subsequent arrest, Khin Nyunt, the former prime minister and head of military intelligence. The new junta leader, Min Aung Hlaing, is also cultivating his own crony class, reveling in the advantages the SPDC had once bestowed upon themselves.

These linkages resulted in special import and export licenses, banking licenses, land and mining concessions, stakes in state-owned enterprises, and infrastructure and other commercial tenders, and they allowed tycoons to eventually control large swaths of the economy—hotels, real estate, roads, gas stations, ports, airports, hospitals, banks, mines, forests, agriculture, shopping malls, restaurants, cafes, soccer teams, and airlines. For the US government, the cronies were an ideal target given their proximity to the junta; the idea was if you squeezed those closest hard enough, they would eventually complain to the top to make changes. The US targeted the three richest cronies—Tay Za, Zaw Zaw, and Steven Law—and their businesses, as well as what could be considered "second-tier" cronies who also had vast business interests.

The most well-known crony was the CEO of the Htoo Group of Companies, Tay Za. Tay Za was the most flamboyant crony, known for a collection of sun bears and fleets of luxury cars. He once handled uranium with his bare hands at a press conference.[22 and 23 and 24]

According to Tay Za, Htoo Group of Companies started with a loan from his mother-in-law to set up a sawmill. From a sawmill, he would go on to own a 668,000-acre tract of rainforest along with another 162,000 acres of palm oil concessions in the southeast. Under the Htoo umbrella, his business interests grew from logging (exports for teakwood can run into the hundreds of millions of dollars per year), to roughly twenty-two companies with 40,000 employees in the tourism, hotel, airline, bank, agriculture, food and beverage, construction, and weapon trading sectors. Tay Za forged his military connections right to the top with SPDC leaders like Senior General Than Shwe and General Thura Shwe Mann, numbers one and three in the SPDC hierarchy, respectively. He also made decent connections with Russian defense suppliers and managed to secure spare parts for air force planes and MI-17 helicopters from Russia's Export Military Industrial Group and Rostvertol. He allegedly also secured the purchase of MiG-29 jets.[25 and 26 and 27]

Tay Za was also connected to military trade with North Korea, putting him in a different stratosphere of trouble. Singapore's United Overseas Bank closed nine of his accounts after transfers he made to a company in China were reported to have links to a North Korean bank sanctioned by the UN for being the main "financial entity responsible for sales of conventional arms, ballistic missiles and goods related to the manufacture of such items." Tay Za says he made the payments on behalf of the SPDC and the Thein Sein governments. This was in violation of both UN Security Council Resolutions and US sanctions on North Korea.[28]

Given the overwhelming evidence that Tay Za was providing material support to the junta, he, his wife, Thida Zaw, his oldest son, and his brother Thiha were added to the SDN List. In a 2011 interview for *La Republica*, he affirmed to his interviewer that he was "the wealthiest man in Burma. . . . My holdings show that actually your Western sanctions don't bother me. In fact, they suit me fine, and that goes for everyone on your blacklist, including the generals themselves. But I don't like seeing our economy depending on Chinese trade alone. . . . I say to the Americans—come and see Myanmar [Burma] and have faith in its opening up, don't just swallow the nonsense invented by the CIA."[29]

The sanctions definitely had an impact on his airline, Air Bagan. Two American tourists got caught up in sanctions issues when their Air Bagan flight crashed on Christmas Day in 2012. Even though a general license from the Department of the Treasury allowed them to use Air Bagan, it did not allow them to receive a settlement from the crash. It took lawyers, permission from the Treasury Department, and two years for the tourists to receive their payout.[30] Air Bagan would eventually suspend operations in 2015 because of necessary "mechanical maintenance," but it would finally fold altogether, at least partially due to the impact that sanctions had on the airline to secure parts and services to run safely.

Zaw Zaw, chairman of Max Myanmar Group of Companies, started his adult life as a student protester in the 1988 uprising but left for Japan in 1990. There, he gained work experience and amassed savings; he later returned to Myanmar and quickly built an empire valued at about $500 million annually. Max Myanmar Group of Companies is involved in construction, toll roads, hotels, tourism, gas stations, banking, and the Myanmar Football Federation. His regime connection was reportedly Senior General Than Shwe, though Zaw Zaw built relationships with other members of the SPDC, including Shwe Mann.[31]

Secretary of State John Kerry and his delegation ran afoul of the SDN List when they were assigned by Myanmar's Ministry of Foreign Affairs to stay at Zaw Zaw's Lake Garden Hotel Nay Pyi Taw in 2014 for the annual ASEAN Regional Forum. Despite being legal thanks to a special license, it was not good optics.[32]

Rounding out the top three was Steven Law, also known as Tun Myint Naing.[33] He was much less visible than the other two, and his reclusiveness, coupled with the legacy of his father Lo Hsing Han, or the "Godfather of Heroin," allowed for tall tales to be spun about the mysterious Steven Law. Steven Law got his start in a bakery business. He leapt from baking cakes to running one of Myanmar's largest construction businesses, Asia World. For many US policymakers, this leap was questionable, and many suspected that his father's drug money and regime connections made Asia World possible. The Drug Enforcement Agency (DEA) had successfully targeted Lo Hsing Han but never built a case against Steven Law and Asia World.

Asia World built the Yangon and Nay Pyi Taw airports, ports, hotels, hydropower plants, and roads. According to reports, Law's relationship with Senior General Than Shwe and his ability to speak Chinese and connect with major Chinese conglomerates helped build the Asia World empire.[34 and 35]

In 2015, trouble with Asia World erupted when the Myanmar port authorities changed the paperwork that would clear transactions and allow cargo in and out. This revealed that Asia World, then on the SDN List, owned the port and that therefore, any transactions should be blocked. Banks immediately halted all transactions, causing ships to drift in Yangon waters and cargo to pile up on the docks. US sanctions caused an unintended trade embargo as more than 80 percent of trade in and out of Myanmar went through that port. For six months, local and international businesses, the Myanmar government, and organizations trying to import items badgered the US government to do something. Under pressure, on December 7, the US issued General License 20 to allow for transactions at the port. This was a technical fix to an increasingly disastrous problem, but unfortunately, many in Congress saw it as a gift to Steven Law and Asia World. This once again highlighted the issue with balancing optics and the need to get things done to fix an unintended consequence: US policy often has to balance the need to look "tough" and exert pressure to change or deter behavior—the purpose of sanctions—while ensuring that the average person is unharmed.[36]

Other cronies dotted the landscape and caused unintended headaches. Win Aung, the chairman of the Union of Myanmar Federation of Chambers of Commerce and Industry (UMFCCI), was sanctioned, meaning that the organization's US counterpart, the US Chamber of Commerce, couldn't meet with him even though that would be their typical first port of call in entering any new market. Activists criticized Jose Fernandez, who was then the assistant secretary of state for economic and business affairs, for shaking hands with Win Aung at an event to promote business ties with the US.[37 and 38]

In many ways, it was easy to sanction these guys. They were ultrawealthy in a country that ranked at the bottom of nearly every development index. These guys helped the junta implement their economic and infrastructure agenda, often to the detriment of rural and ethnic communities. A lot of people hated the cronies, though it was unclear if it was because of their wealth or their connection to the military. Crony kids partied in Yangon, Singapore, and Bangkok clubs, went to top universities in the region, and posted photos of themselves in cars that cost more than the average Myanmar person would ever earn in their lifetime. It infuriated people.

It didn't seem like the cronies were changing their behavior or compelling sanctioned military leaders to either. But when Thein Sein came into government, the cronies saw an opening. They were sick of sanctions, even if they said otherwise, and wanted to take advantage of new investment opportunities with foreign businesses. They wanted to change their image, and without guidance on how to appeal to US policymakers to lift the sanctions, they took it into their own hands to decipher what to do. Some retired and focused on building a legacy through charitable work, leaving it to younger generations to guide the family business. Others promoted their charitable foundations and philanthropic endeavors as part and parcel of their private sector work. Many started to streamline their businesses, retooling sprawling business empires that relied on favors from the state, anticipating an end to sanctions and new competition from foreign brands.

Many thought currying favor with Aung San Suu Kyi would put them in the good graces of the US. Tay Za donated money to the NLD's health and education initiatives. Zaw Zaw also donated to the NLD and invited Aung San Suu Kyi to a football game (soccer to us Americans) in 2011 to see a match between Myanmar and Laos.[39] Some activists in Myanmar supported this outreach as long as it didn't influence policy or corrupt the NLD; it was good to get the cronies to think beyond the military.[40] For some of the cronies, they said that the political opening and reforms would give them a chance to be real businesses and conduct the type of investment they wanted to without being forced to support noncommercially viable projects like building hotels in Nay Pyi Taw or dropping cash into a general's pet project.

US businesses wanted sanctions gone too. Nearly two years on from the easing of the initial sanctions, the prophesied flood of Western investment was never fulfilled. Business compliance and due diligence teams would tie themselves in knots figuring out how to navigate Myanmar, determining in many cases that the risk wasn't worth it. With opaque organizational charts and serious questions over beneficial ownership, it was unclear who you were really doing business with. You could easily trip over the 50 percent rule and not even know it.

I left the government in December 2012 to start a consulting firm to encourage responsible and transparent investment into the country. But there were no investors going in because of sanctions. One way to aid nervous investors was to bring on board *the* expert on sanctions: Peter Kucik, a former senior sanctions advisor at OFAC. He had been working on Myanmar since 2007, as well as sanctions programs on Cuba and Libya. Peter brought an amazing amount of gravitas and knowledge to Inle; however, our professional experience and background didn't seem to mean much of anything to a lot of blue-ribbon law firms and top-tier companies. Their firm's reputation and their long legal career (none of it on Myanmar), meant they knew better than the actual people who wrote the policy and programs. We were sanctions-plained many times.

The US also saw an opportunity to address Myanmar's crony problem and break the patronage system that had plagued the economy, creating a unique,

Myanmar-specific policy to push for change and reward those who showed demonstrable and verifiable change with an SDN delisting. This could have consequences for other programs targeting tycoons elsewhere, creating a country- or circumstance-specific set of criteria that targeted the core issues and made the SDN List an even more effective tool. In June 2014, the new assistant secretary of state for DRL and former human rights advocate with the organization Human Rights Watch, Tom Malinowski, led the delisting policy efforts.

Tom had worked on the Myanmar issue for decades and claims he played the role in Washington's Burma policy origin story. While he was an undergraduate student in 1986, he backpacked through Asia and fell in love with the country. His first job out of school was working in Senator Patrick Moynihan's office in 1988. Burma was convulsing under its own summer of protests, but no one in DC cared. Through some confluence of fate, Tom partnered with Moynihan's legislative director, Andrew Samet, whose wife was the daughter of the last Shan Prince of Hsipaw, Kya Seng. Kya Seng studied at the Colorado School of Mines in Denver from 1949 to 1953 where he met his future wife, Inge Sargent. In a Hallmark movie twist, he revealed he was a prince, whisked Sargent to Shan State, and began a progressive rule that instituted poverty-alleviation and land-ownership programs and anti-corruption practices. Ne Win, who was then the army's commander-in- chief, became suspicious of him, recognizing the independence agreement with the British included a secession clause for Shan State that could be exercised within seven years of independence. Ne Win suspected Kya Seng would exercise that right, and soon, Kya Seng disappeared when Ne Win seized power in 1962. Unable to get answers from the government about her husband's whereabouts, Sargent returned to Austria in 1964 with their two young daughters. There was little love for the Myanmar military or Ne Win in Moynihan's office.[41]

Tom and Samet drafted a resolution condemning the violence in Burma and calling for democracy; the resolution passed by voice vote. A month later, Senator Moynihan received a photo of monks and students marching in the 88 Uprising with a sign saying "Thank you Senator Moynihan." Moynihan would go on to cut off aid to the military, persuade the State Department to downgrade diplomatic ties, and secure funding to bring Burmese students to the US to study. At that time, Senator McConnell grew interested in the issue and the torch was passed. And that's how US Burma policy was born according to Tom Malinowski.[42]

Nearly thirty years later, Tom was meeting the people who helped finance the junta's projects and fill their bank accounts. He explained to them that they must show to OFAC that they had severed business ties with the military, respected human rights, and ran a responsible and transparent business. He suggested SDNs could conduct a credible, independent audit of all business holdings and a social and environmental impact assessment of their operations. Suddenly, KMPG,

Deloitte, and other big auditing firms—along with law offices—were extremely busy, ready to file delisting petitions with OFAC.[43 and 44]

Malinowski found an eager audience, with many expressing a desire to transform their legacy and leave a better situation for their families. The US saw this as a chance to influence Myanmar's wealthiest citizens who had significant control over the economy. It could make Myanmar stand out in the region, its corporates leading the way on responsible business practices. Given that political change and having Aung San Suu Kyi in government once seemed unbelievable, why not believe the cronies could change as well?

Not everyone was optimistic. Congressman Steve Chabot (R-OH) thought delisting SDNs while the Myanmar government was persecuting the ethnic Rohingya was sending the wrong signal, even though the cronies weren't involved with or influencing those policies. This was a great example of how issues and policy solutions can get conflated; multiple crises can occur in a country, but the causes are not the same. Linking policy solutions for one issue shouldn't be connected to another. Holding up an SDN delisting because of the violence against the Rohingya did not make sense. However, Chabot went on to say, making more sense, "I do not support US companies partnering with these cronies in any way."[45]

Given Peter's background with OFAC, we caught the attention of SDNs and law firms to help with delisting cases. At first, I was extremely leery about this. I started Inle Advisory Group to promote responsible business. I did not want to be a crony whisperer. I was also afraid of what it would do to Inle's reputation. It was one thing to state our values and ethics, but one look at our prospective client list could suggest otherwise.

What convinced me was a few things. We knew what we were doing. It was (and still is) compelling to me that there is no shortcut or legal loophole that gets someone off the SDN List. One way or another, SDNs have to demonstrate to the US government that they no longer warrant sanctioning, and the US government has to agree. We were facilitating necessary discussions between the parties to ensure that the US goals for the individual SDNs were being met. This was also an opportunity to prove that Inle stood for responsible and transparent business, and if we could get the cronies to change their corporate governance, that would have an immediate and far-reaching impact on the economy and people's lives. We also were clear about the reputational risk we were taking in working with these guys. Any hint or whiff that we were being played, and our contract would be terminated immediately.

We got a special license from OFAC and worked with lawyers who worked under a general license to be able to legally work on SDN cases. Led by the lawyers shepherding the cases, we requested mountains of documentation—accounting, secret accounting, and whatever other paperwork was available. It was entirely possible we weren't privy to everything, but we'd push. We worked with auditing firms to go through paperwork and financial reports, put their affairs in order, and start implementing corporate governance policies and educating employees about them. Next was getting information into the public domain. Very few companies had websites, so there was no way to know what a company did, who was in charge, how to contact them, or how they were changing.

A more challenging issue was divesting from controversial partnerships. SDNs had to cut businesses ties with the military, which primarily had business interests through two military holding companies, the Union of Myanmar Economic Holdings Ltd. (UMEHL) and Myanmar Economic Corporation (MEC). UMEHL and MEC had at least 106 businesses and twenty-seven subsidiaries that were involved in various sectors, including telecommunications, construction, trade, agriculture, forestry and fishing, pharmaceuticals, mining, manufacturing, insurance, tourism, arts and entertainment, food and beverage, transportation, real estate, and banking. There were concerns from the SDNs about breaking contracts and possible legal—and perhaps retaliatory—ramifications. For most SDNs, the ties to the military were based on concessions, like land leases or licenses, not equity shares or investments. This might mean selling land or getting permission from the military to divest, meaning it was going to be a slow process.[46]

We had no idea what the pace of the delisting process would be, but we had confidence that if a solid case was put forward, an SDN had a shot at a fair review. Tom had emphasized that it was a legal process, not a political one. We expected it to be slow, but the process not only went at a glacial pace; it seemed to not be moving at all.

Nearly a year after Malinowski's initial meeting with the SDNs, the Department of the Treasury announced the first removal. Win Aung, the head of the UMFCCI, was now free to engage with US companies and business delegations starting in April 2015.[47] Three months later, the Treasury lifted sanctions on two dead generals and Tay Za's now ex-wife. Tay Za's ex-wife, Thida Zaw, was removed "because she no longer meets the criteria for which she was designated" once she was no longer his spouse. Lieutenant General Soe Win and Lieutenant General Maung Bo, who died in 2007 and 2009, respectively, were members of the SLORC and its successor organization, the SPDC. The US embassy offered no explanation for their removal, but some speculated it was to make life easier for folks also named Soe Win and Maung Bo who wanted to travel or use a credit card.[48]

With the flurry of delistings and a peaceful election and transfer of power, there was excitement in Myanmar that a major delisting of one of the top three cronies was on the horizon. Foreign investors were starting to investigate some of the possible delistees as potential business partners. We waited to see if there were any more delistings. And waited.

Removing Obstacles

With the NLD in power and a peace process underway, many of the underlying conditions that sparked the advent of US sanctions against Myanmar had been addressed. To many, it was ridiculous to have such punitive economic measures with Aung San Suu Kyi leading the country. But for others, sanctions were considered a tool for leverage to compel the military to continue reforms, push for constitutional amendments, protect human rights, and protect the fragile semidemocratic government. Human rights groups thought the US had moved too fast and too soon when, in their view, nothing had changed. There was active conflict, the military still maintained a stranglehold on politics and the economy, and the Rohingya issue threatened to get out of control. In their minds, sanctions were the best tool to maintain leverage to push for change and to punish the military and those that supported it.

Congress was grappling with how to move forward on policy as well, recognizing legislation needed to be updated. Members of the House Foreign Affairs Committee (HFAC) and the Senate Foreign Relations Committee (SFRC) were pleasantly surprised by the 2016 election outcome and conceded that having the NLD in power warranted a rethink on legislation. Like the executive branch, Congress wanted to find a way to be able to target the bad actors without harming the average Myanmar citizen. Some members felt it was more important to increase money toward USAID programming and support more high-level diplomatic engagement than to push for an easing of sanctions. Any further moves, particularly lifting sanctions, would have to be informed by what they heard directly from Aung San Suu Kyi.[49]

In May 2016, exactly four years to the day of President Obama's announcement of Derek as ambassador and Secretary Clinton's outlining of the details of the first easing of sanctions, OFAC announced the removal of seven state-owned enterprises and three state-owned banks from the SDN List. It also allowed trade to, from, and within Myanmar (permanently fixing the port issue); allowed transactions by US individuals residing there; and permitted most transactions involving all the currently sanctioned Myanmar financial institutions. This was to make life easier for those living in Myanmar, so, for example, if Americans working in Myanmar discovered their apartment was owned by a sanctioned individual, they wouldn't have to move or pay steep fines.

Adam Szubin, acting undersecretary for terrorism and financial intelligence and the former head of OFAC, remarked in the announcement, "Burma reached a historic milestone over the last year by holding competitive elections and peacefully transitioning to a democratically-elected government. Our actions today demonstrate our strong support for this political and economic progress while continuing to pressure designated persons in Burma to change their behavior. These steps will help to facilitate trade with non-sanctioned businesses and, in turn, help the people and Government of Burma achieve a more inclusive and prosperous future." The announcement noted that the entities removed from the SDN List were either organized and transparently managed under civilian control or no longer in existence.

The removals didn't fit in with the delisting process launched by Malinowski in 2014. It was more of a nod to the NLD; these state-owned enterprises were now under their control and ostensibly would be better run. Because of that, they wanted them delisted to invite outside investment and expertise to help reform the sector.

The Treasury also announced the addition to the SDN List of six companies owned by Steven Law and Asia World; these companies were already blocked by operation of law through the 50 percent rule, so this had more to do with providing clarity to help the private sector comply with US sanctions than it did with punishing Asia World.[50] The whole thing seemed like a nothing-burger, except to American apartment-dwellers.

Obama also renewed the underlying authorities for the Myanmar sanctions program, the International Emergency Economic Powers Act (IEEPA), in May 2016. Renewing IEEPA is a standard technical operation; all IEEPA sanctions programs, which span the globe, require annual renewal, and the Myanmar program needed to be renewed by May 20 in order to continue or else the SDN List for Myanmar would disappear altogether. But the stock IEEPA language caused confusion and misperception in Myanmar that it was a "reimposition," rather than a maintenance, of sanctions. IEEPA authorizes the president to declare a "national emergency" and impose economic and trade sanctions in response to "unusual and extraordinary" threats to the national security, foreign policy, or economy of the US. Most countries that have been targeted by sanctions barely acknowledge the annual IEEPA renewal, but Myanmar took it personally. US interlocutors tried to carefully explain what the renewal was and that it was not a big deal. These explanations never made a difference, and the Aung San Suu Kyi-led government was even more upset. To declare a Myanmar governed by the NLD as posing an unusual and extraordinary threat to US national security was awkward, but IEEPA was the only way to maintain the sanctions that remained. Leverage had to be kept.

The day of the IEEPA renewal and the sanctions delisting, Ben Rhodes provided remarks on the updated policy for the Center for a New American Security, a Washington, DC, think tank. The discussion garnered a lot of attention because of DC's fixation on Myanmar and a chance for businesses and activists to register their very divergent opinions on sanctions. It was not a friendly gathering; these events on Myanmar rarely were on a good day.[51]

Rhodes had a sit-down conversation with Kurt Campbell, the former State Department official who helped kick off the policy opening on Myanmar and for whom I'm sure activists still harbored hostile feelings from the initial sanctions-easing. Rhodes went through the steps the Treasury and the State Department took at the White House's direction, and the rationale behind them. The Obama administration wanted to help Myanmar modernize, grow its economy, and allow those living in the country—especially Americans working with NGOs, development institutions, and a variety of professions that contributed to the country's developing economy—to be able to do what they needed to do without worry. The Obama administration wanted to give the NLD government as many tools as it needed to enact its economic reforms and not have to go running back to the US when they inadvertently hit a sanctions hurdle no one expected. It took six months to fix the unintended trade embargo; with an election year in the US, there wouldn't be too much juice to act "quickly" if necessary. He ended his remarks by saying, "We want to make clear through today's announcements that we strongly support the increased, responsible involvement of responsible US business in Burma, which will bring international best practices, high standards, and new technologies to the Burmese economy."[52]

* * *

In September 2016, Aung San Suu Kyi traveled to the US for the UNGA and a visit to Washington. The NLD had been governing for six months now; with her visit, the buzz around a full sanctions-easing was now a loud roar.

Some in Congress felt that they were being left out of the conversations on sanctions; what was once a cooperative effort between the executive and legislative branches was perceived by Congress to now be a one-sided affair. Congress wanted to show its hand on Myanmar policy.[53] On September 13, Senators John McCain (R-AZ) and Ben Cardin (D-MD) introduced legislation to support Myanmar in its political and economic transition and push for further progress on human rights issues. In introducing the Burma Strategy Act of 2016, McCain stated, "After nearly 50 years of military rule, Burma has achieved a historic milestone with a democratic election and successful transition of power to a civilian-led government. This extraordinary development warrants reconsideration of US policy towards Burma, and this legislation seeks to usher in a new era of relations between our two countries that will support continued progress towards democracy, human rights and peace for the Burmese people." The Burma Strategy Act brought together relevant bits from other legislation and updated them to address the current state of the country, both the good and the bad. The act called for increased and expanded economic and humanitarian assistance, limited military-to-military engagement, the creation of a Burma-American development fund to provide incentives for building a transparent and responsible private sector and supporting small-hold farmers, the request for a gemstone strategy report to help support sector reforms, and the setup of benchmarks and guidelines for SDN delistings.[54]

Congressional staffers told me that activists and DRL were going to Capitol Hill, saying Obama was going to ruin everything by lifting sanctions if that is what he intended to do. There was a constant drumbeat of advocacy groups going to meet with bipartisan members of Congress. Several congressional members new to the Myanmar policy issue received their first briefings on the country from the Holocaust Museum and activists, all of whom were primarily focused on Rakhine State given the renewed violence. This was their first taste of Myanmar, and the anti-Rohingya violence shaped their mindset on Myanmar policy and would influence any short- and long-term steps. They wanted to punish the military as much as possible and were very much in the mindset of the policymakers who had been introduced to Burma in 1988.[55]

Congress wanted to maintain some sanctions and advocated to keep pressure on military industries, especially the two military holding companies, MEC and UMEHL. But for investors, MEC and UMEHL's ownership stakes were shrouded in secrecy and very unclear, making the possibility of tripping the SDN List quite high.[56 and 57 and 58]

The Burma Strategy Act of 2016 was in part a response to frustration about the lack of executive action and of being left out. One SFRC staffer remarked that it was "sad that undersecretaries and assistant secretaries are too scared to get a beatdown from a nothing Congressional staffer. Too bad they can't handle an uncomfortable half-hour meeting." To them, legislation should be a last resort, but they felt they were left with no choice but to act.[59 and 60]

But Aung San Suu Kyi still drove policy. On September 14, 2016, following meetings with Aung San Suu Kyi and a series of discussions, negotiations, and everything in between with her and her party, Obama announced that all remaining financial and trade sanctions were lifted, rendering key elements of the Burma Strategy Act moot. Obama terminated IEEPA, meaning all of the individuals and entities listed on the SDN List under the Burma Sanctions Program, the import ban on jade and rubies, and the dreaded reporting requirements, were gone. That didn't mean that everyone in Myanmar was fair investment game; there were still organizations and individuals that were sanctioned under the Drug Kingpin Act (like the UWSA and Yangon Airways) and North Korea programs.

President Obama also announced the restoration of Myanmar's Generalized System of Preferences (GSP) privileges, which had been revoked in 1989, effective November 13. Without GSP, products sourced in Myanmar were subject to duties of as high as 17 percent when imported to the US. This was good news for some of Myanmar's more competitive industries, like garments, textiles, fishery, and agriculture, and it perhaps gave hope to fledgling businesses that were looking to grow and partner with international companies.[61 and 62]

As Ben alluded to during his CNAS discussion, the idea here was that it was up to the NLD to determine its economic and political trajectory themselves; US foreign policy was no longer needed to be a tool to shape events on the ground. Obama felt the US would have more leverage and could exert more influence through enhanced business and diplomatic ties. A moderate easing would not have facilitated that type of engagement; in his view, more engagement, not less, would have more impact. The so-called leverage sanctions had was lost when the world started lifting theirs and moving in. The NLD highlighted actions already taken to reform problematic sectors and actors—it suspended permits for jade mining, temporarily banned logging, and postponed high-rise construction in Yangon until certain environmental and corporate standards were defined. The government of Myanmar would now exclusively guide investment undertaken in the country through the enactment of its own laws and policies.[63]

The subject of much intrigue was how much Aung San Suu Kyi knew about the details of the sanctions-lifting and whether or not she had been coerced into an all-or-nothing policy. There were diverging narratives on what she really wanted, but some of those narratives are likely colored by people's own views of what they wanted to happen.

DRL, especially Tom Malinowski, thought the sanctions-easing was a terrible mistake. He fought it and took a lot of flak from senior officials for fighting a lost cause. For Tom, the main reason the US imposed sanctions was in solidarity with Aung San Suu Kyi and the opposition. There were not too many senior officials who had a theory of a case beyond that. Sanctions were more than symbolic, and he believed that at some point, it was likely that there would be a new generation of military officers who would want a modern Myanmar and a prosperous economy, especially if they traveled around ASEAN and saw how modern Singapore and Thailand were. Part of the leverage angle was that if they wanted those things, they'd have to convince Aung San Suu Kyi, who would in turn, convince the US. Aung San Suu Kyi would have tools at her disposal to urge the military to change, and when it seemed credible to her, the US would lift sanctions. By 2016, Tom felt that some at high levels in the State Department and at the "Ben level" at the NSC—whoever that was to Tom beyond Ben (and something Ben disputes as being solely his policy)—moved policy in a different direction, not the step-by-step/action-for-action approach Clinton had kicked off in 2011.

Tom also preferred a one-on-one-off approach to the SDN List. If you removed a name, you had to add a name. To me, one-on-one-off doesn't work; the point of sanctions is that it works to deter people from behaving in a certain way so you successfully get the list to zero. You don't go searching for someone to put on just because you take someone off.[64 and 65]

For EAP and folks at the "Ben level," sanctions felt right and morally sound, but they weren't having any impact on the challenges the US wanted the government and military to address. The purpose of sanctions was to encourage the transition to democracy and support Aung San Suu Kyi; those purposes were fulfilled. Ambassador Scot Marciel was sending messages to Washington about the sentiments on the ground, what the new NLD government needed to accomplish their goals, and how the US could help. People in Myanmar were feeling quite positive after the election, but sanctions were becoming a dark cloud for the NLD and more of a hindrance, not leverage, for further economic and political reforms. The US Treasury removals so far had had little effect, probably because the people were dead or divorcees. Sanctions also became a binary issue, and Myanmar was always an asterisk with banks; no US bank wanted to open a branch in country, and they were extremely leery of providing services. Your account could still be frozen if you checked it online in Myanmar, and it happened to me more than once.

Marciel had lengthy conversations with Aung San Suu Kyi on what she wanted to do, especially on the economy and balancing her relationship with the military. A full sanctions-lifting wasn't a slam dunk for her or the most definitive yes, but she agreed (and reiterated several times) that lifting sanctions was better.[66]

During her trip to the US, Aung San Suu Kyi was being asked about her views on sanctions by everyone. One congressional staff member who attended a meeting disputes that Aung San Suu Kyi was confused about whether sanctions should stay on and was "pretty clear" that she wanted them off. Another staffer confirmed that Aung San Suu Kyi was clear she wanted things lifted and that she could work with changing the military and improving the economy though the country's own laws. She was clear on what she wanted lifted. She was concerned about military enterprises and wanted the military out of business but felt she could do that through legal means and increased foreign direct investment. She was going to look for Myanmar strategies to solve Myanmar problems.[67]

This culminated in a tense scene between Tom and State Department officials at a US Chamber of Commerce/US-ASEAN Business Council dinner on September 15, which was being put on for Aung San Suu Kyi. I was invited to the dinner and was in a general celebratory mood. Apparently, my former government colleagues were not.

According to an article in *Politico* by Nahal Toosi, "The Genocide the US Didn't See Coming," Tom allegedly told Aung San Suu Kyi, after the new sanctions policy had been announced mind you, that she didn't need to accept the administration's full lifting of sanctions and that there was a way to calibrate and keep some restrictions; she grew confused by Tom's insistence, which did not correspond with her earlier discussions with the White House, State Department leaders, and some members of Congress. Marciel then joined the conversation and there were "words." To EAP, DRL pulled the thirteenth-hour antics. For DRL, EAP went through back channels and got their way. But there was no turning back policy. It was time for a new set of dictates for a new situation.[68]

Patrick Murphy, who was then the deputy assistant secretary of state for Southeast Asia and Multilateral Affairs, was not surprised at the Rashomon effect. Having worked with Aung San Suu Kyi over the years, he understood that she could be cryptic. She's never been one to declare anything black or white. The other truism is more about her audience than the woman herself; those that have engaged with Aung San Suu Kyi often hear what they want to hear. Bearing this in mind, it was as clear as it could be to many that she thought sanctions had run their course and that it was time to help the new Myanmar, which was being dragged down by desperate economic needs. But given the way that the sanctions programs were structured, she could not get the calibration on sanctions to the degree she wanted.[69]

I also think sanctions had run their course, and if punitive economic measures were to continue, the US would have to wholly impose a new set of criteria and policy tailored to the circumstances and not simply offer a retread of the last twenty-five years. Sanctions were most useful during the 2011–2012 period in pushing for further reform; the US could show the universe of options to Thein Sein and his cohort and go on a step-by-step/action-for-action approach. The delisting process, in my view, could have had greater success and been a model for other countries. There were several cronies who were actively participating in the process and making the changes to meet US requirements. Whether their heart was in it or not didn't matter; they were becoming more transparent, implementing policies critical to good corporate governance, and they were keenly interested in abiding by rule of law frameworks that would allow them to work with US companies and investors.

But I guess the more critical question here was this: Was it all or nothing? The answer is yes. The IEEPA renewal, a technicality to renew the underlying authorities to maintain the Burma sanctions program, was emotional for the country. Despite ad nauseam explanations that it was a technicality and allowed the economic restrictions to remain, it was viewed as a reimposition of sanctions every year. No other country felt this way—just Myanmar. If the US was to keep any part of the Burma sanctions program, in order to include MEC and UMEHL on the SDN List, you had to have IEEPA in place. Only recently has a new sanctions program been implemented that could capture those problematic entities on which Congress and Aung San Suu Kyi were focused; the Global Magnitsky Act would be later used to sanction military officers and divisions tied to the 2016 and 2017 violence against the Rohingya, but at that time, it did not have the language or utility in place to do what Aung San Suu Kyi and many of the supporters of targeting MEC and UMEHL wanted to be able to do. It was geared primarily toward Russia and was not yet a global program like the Drug Kingpin Act. Well, you say, come up with a new sanctions program for Burma! That would require IEEPA. No IEEPA, no sanctions. You have IEEPA, and then you have a very disturbed and upset country.

There were discussions that sanctions could have prevented the Rohingya violence, and renewed discussions that it could have prevented the February 2021 coup. That's doubtful in that sanctions programs could not effectively target the industries in which the military is significantly involved, primarily jade and logging. The US would have to convince China and some ASEAN countries to get on board with sanctions to squeeze the junta; this would be next to impossible. In the end, the military does not care what the sanctions do to the country as they can survive with or without Western investment. It may not be ideal, but this is a cabal that is used to surviving and being a pariah.

But what isn't discussed is what would have happened if the US had lifted sanctions wholesale in 2012 to allow for the so-called flood of investment. Maybe there would have been less incentive to undertake a coup because the potential loss would have been too much. We'll never know, and it's even more doubtful that if the military does decide to hand back power, its most prominent critics will allow for such thinking in rolling back the new set of sanctions imposed following the violence against the Rohingya and the February 2021 coup.

7

INVESTMENT

A LEAP OF FAITH

I had decided to leave government to start my own consulting firm to help investors do business transparently and responsibly in Myanmar. I wrote my last analytic piece, cleaned out my desk, and prepared for my new life as a businesswoman. On December 7, 2012, my last day at the CIA, I decided I would take the long way out of the building and walk through the lobby, past the wall of stars for my fallen colleagues and over the seal of the CIA. Unfortunately for me, Acting Director Mike Morrell was hosting the annual holiday party for senior staff, and the front lobby was blocked. I got completely lost trying to find my way out as I hadn't been in that part of the building for a while, but once I located an exit thirty minutes later, I left the CIA for what would be the last time.

Though it seemed like a good idea to leave my government job at the time, I went into a bit of a panic once I was home. My colleagues and friends, who understand my calculated, impulsive nature, tried to offer support. During my time as a graduate school student and in government, I had gotten to know Derek Mitchell, the new US ambassador to Myanmar. Our conversations would range from Asia policy matters to a number of non-Asia things, like *30 Rock*. I was often compared to the main character of Liz Lemon for many reasons, most likely because I wear glasses and like cheese. I recapped an episode for Derek and told him about one where the character Kenneth—a naive, cheerful, and television-obsessed NBC page—gave a pep talk to his mentor, Tracy Jordan, the star of *30 Rock*'s show within a show, *TGS*. When Tracy, who often messes up phrases, thinks he's going to die at the hands of an old nemesis, Kenneth tells him, "Aren't you the man who told me to live every week like it's Shark Week and that nothing's impossible except dinosaurs? Don't give up on life, sir." To which Tracy responds, "The manatee has now become the Mento." During one particularly difficult week on Burma policy, I provided this recap and reminded Derek to live every week like it's Shark Week and that nothing was impossible. Before he left for Myanmar and I had hinted that I might start a consulting firm, he had left me a pack of Mentos.

I was now the Mento.

On January 7, 2013, I filed the paperwork to form Inle Advisory Group, LLC. I chose the name Inle for the lake in Shan State because it represented the importance of sustainably modernizing the country while preserving what made the country unique. My tagline, "Uniting Myanmar's Heritage with its Brightest Future," was also Inle's ethos. My company's logo featured the famed fisherman who stood at the front of the boat and used his leg to row, keeping his hands free to cast fishing nets and navigate the murky waters from the tangle of vines from floating gardens in the lake. Like the leg rower, Inle would use its unparalleled knowledge and experience to navigate the challenges of this frontier economy. The symbolism was off the charts. With my company name, logo, articles of organization, and a snazzy website, I was officially out of government, on my own, and running a business.

My great leap forward was met with derision. Some of my former colleagues considered me a sellout and thought I was cashing in on my knowledge of the region. Media outlets like the *Guardian* and *Foreign Policy* wrote pieces on the government revolving door and how former administration officials were raking in the cash by using their contacts and former policymaking savvy to forge new business opportunities. Let me tell you, there's not a lot of cash in pushing for responsible investment in one of the world's most closed-off markets. It was a Sisyphean task I had laid out for myself.[12]

After being called out, I planned my first trip to Myanmar. I would soon find out how much the country was changing since its initial opening in 2011. It was amazing to witness and doubly hard to navigate, especially on my own.

"If your business doesn't require water or electricity, you can be very successful here"

Myanmar had it all and was an incredible draw for anyone who had any sense of opportunity. It was located in one of the most strategic locations, sitting between China and India. The country had gems, gas, old growth teak forests, minerals, and agriculture opportunities. The country was the size of Texas and had a population of fifty-five million, many of which were under thirty and hungry for work and access to Western brands. But as an astute Burmese friend reminded me, Myanmar has always been geo-strategically located and has always had everything. What good did it do for the country then, and what's the difference now?

The thrill of seeing a newly emerging country (like Cuba for America) sparked a flood of visitors. Tour groups flocked to the Shwedagon Pagoda and local markets, and both tourists and curious businesspersons filled once empty hotels. Travel companies that struggled to persuade clients to visit Myanmar were now deluged with bookings; travel agencies reported a 90 percent increase in the number of Myanmar-bound tourists between the first quarter of 2011 and the first quarter of 2012. Yangon received 554,531 foreign visitors in 2012, up 54.31 percent from 2011. Nearly 36,500 came from the United States.[3]

Booking a hotel was a challenge. I couldn't book online (no websites; they couldn't take credit cards) and when I could get through on the phone, the connection was so bad that I assumed my reservation never made it into the system. When I would arrive, I was often told the rooms were all booked up or I was quoted an astronomical price due to the demand and lack of supply. Myanmar had less than 35,000 hotels and guest rooms in the entire country—8,000 of which were in Yangon—and only 20 percent of those rooms reached "international standards." When I was able to secure a hotel room, I was shocked at how bustling the lobbies were and how I had to share a breakfast table with five or six travelers; government officials who traveled before Secretary Clinton's trip would have had the whole dining room to themselves.[4]

Now that tourists were coming to Myanmar, the hotel managers had to kick out long-term residents who were using rooms for office space, including the UN, the World Health Organization, and other NGOs. Office space was practically nonexistent. Colliers, a real estate service organization, estimated that in 2012 and 2013, Yangon had a total of 667,000 square feet of office space. By comparison, a single building in Bangkok, the Empire Tower, has more than twice that amount. Office space cost up to USD $100 per square meter, more than Singapore and four times the fees in Bangkok and Hanoi.[5]

If you could secure an office or building outside of a hotel, you likely ran into crony or military ownership, presenting sanctions or optics issues. UNICEF was criticized for paying USD $87,000 per month to rent its office headquarters in Yangon from the family of a retired military official.[6] Also, most everything at this time had to be paid in cash: hotels, airfare, and rent. For rent, that meant the entire year up front, in cash.

The office space costs and shortages extended to living space as well. Yangon's shortage of serviced apartments pushed the price of a three-bedroom property from USD $2,000 to USD $6,500 a month, twice the price of similar property in Bangkok. Some 800-square-foot studios went for USD $5,000, making New York prices seem reasonable. Some companies chose to rent houses and villas in lieu of office space, similar to what UNICEF did, but that rent skyrocketed from USD $4,000 per month to USD $25,000.[7 and 8]

Tales of apartment hunting could range from disturbing to harrowing. One friend looked at three apartments in one day. The first housed a hoarder who was still living there; the landlord insisted they would be out and the place would be cleaned in just a few days. The second had a few inches of standing water throughout the apartment. The last place had blood spatter (and not betel nut, which can resemble blood) on the walls. She decided to call it a day and start again another time.

If your office or apartment had uninterrupted electricity or access to a decent generator, you were in great luck. Power generation was a huge issue in Myanmar, and frequent power cuts and blackouts plagued Yangon and Mandalay. Myanmar had an electrification rate of 31 percent, meaning only one-third of the country had access to a somewhat functioning grid. Less than 16 percent of rural villages were connected to a grid and used fire at night to read, study, and generally live their life. Even for those with access to power, supply was intermittent; wealthier districts got an average of six hours of power per day, and poorer districts only one. Generators roared all day. The country had plenty of energy resources but sold most of it off to neighboring China and Thailand. Myanmar has hydropower and natural gas, and its rivers are able to produce more than 100,000 megawatts of power. Proven gas reserves were estimated at 20.11 trillion cubic feet in 2012 and coal reserves at around 489 million tons. Electrification was a major drag on business development, especially for the manufacturing sector and any business that used refrigerators, computers, lights, or stoves. As one Japanese businessman told me, if your business doesn't require water or electricity, you could be very successful here.[9 and 10]

Myanmar was also—and still is—cash-based. Most places didn't take credit cards and there were no ATMs in 2012 and just a few dozen in 2013. Using ATMs was a huge risk. Your bank could freeze your account because they had not caught up with sanctions changes, the ATM could eat your card, or the power could go out and you'd lose your card. Myanmar accepted US dollars and generally preferred to be paid in such; foreign travelers to Myanmar had to request the crispest hundred-dollar bills from their home banks and take piles with them to the country. Before 2011, if a bill had a "C" or "F" in the serial number, it couldn't be used because obviously, "C" and "F" stood for "counterfeit" and "fake." Even in 2013, when I began traveling there for business, it remained the case that if there was the tiniest crease, the smallest of tears, or a hint of a pen mark, the bill would be rejected. There were times I ironed dollars out of desperation to pay a hotel bill or feed myself.

Communications were also a problem at the beginning of my consulting days. The telecom industry was still operating under the India Telegraph Act of 1886. Cell phones also didn't really exist, and even if you had a cell phone, who would you call? No one had a phone that worked! Myanmar Post and Telecommunications had a monopoly on the telecom game, and SIM cards costs hundreds, if not thousands, of dollars. Aside from the expense, there were very few cell towers in the country. Less than 10 percent of the Myanmar people had access to mobile technology, and mostly everything was still done on landlines. There were small desks with a landline set up on city and village streets with an "operator" who acted as a pay phone for folks needing to make a call. Many of the apartment buildings also shared a phone; people would wait for several minutes, if not longer, waiting for someone to pick up and hoping it was the person they were trying to reach.

Communication technology also impacted the way people were able to get information. Newspapers were heavily censored, and outside magazines and newspapers would hit stands or mailboxes weeks after publication so the censors had time to rip out pages or black out sentences that could undermine the junta. Until the telecom boom in 2013, internet was still lacking. You couldn't use Gmail or Hotmail or access most websites, especially foreign news sites. Prior to the political opening, Freedom House, an organization dedicated to expanding democracy, political freedom, and human rights globally, ranked Myanmar's internet policies as the world's second-most repressive, surpassed only by Iran's and "tied" with China and Vietnam. Those who defied them faced severe penalties, including torture and lengthy prison sentences. In 2013, Myanmar had around 400,000 internet users, about 0.8 percent of the population, and most of them were in the country's largest cities of Yangon and Mandalay. There were about five internet service providers, but the cost to get online was about $600 per month, a price too steep for the average person.[11]

The state of communications would change at a breakneck pace when the Thein Sein administration put out a competitive tender for telecommunication services in 2013. The government awarded licenses to Norway's Telenor and Qatar's Ooredoo in 2014. SIM card prices dropped to less than USD $2, and cheap smartphones made mobile technology accessible. By June 2017, 90 percent of the country had a phone and multiple SIM cards.[12]

Though telecom was a bright spot for Myanmar, traveling was less so. International and local media outlets called the safety record for the 2012 travel season "grim" with at least four "incidents." I should note I'm terrified of flying, so every time I went on one of these trips, I'd be a complete wreck. In Myanmar, the danger wasn't just in the sky but coming from the sky; a poor motorbike rider was hit and killed by a plane that missed the runway.[13]

Traffic became a growing menace. After Secretary Clinton's trip in 2011, the Thein Sein administration began lifting restrictions on car imports. Previously, only senior officials and cronies who had military patrons were lucky to get import licenses, meaning only the most well-off and well-connected could get new cars.

Now the streets of Yangon were full of cars, some left-hand drive, some right-hand drive. Streets with three painted lanes could soon squish in six lanes of cars, battling each other to get ahead, honking all the while; I could easily reach out to the car next to me without effort. Buses, left- or right-hand drive, would dump out passengers in the middle of busy streets. Driving at night came with its own horrors, as most drivers drove with their headlights off to "save gas" or took yaba—a mix of methamphetamines and caffeine—or drank alcohol to stay awake.[14]

If you got into a car accident, your medical treatment could be hair-raising. Once the region's best location for medical care, Myanmar now ranked among the world's worst, made appallingly clear during the COVID-19 pandemic. The junta spent a paltry sum on health care, providing less than 3 percent of its budget for health and education, and it showed. The country had the highest mortality rate from snake bites; child and maternal health were a joke; water and mosquito-borne illnesses could easily kill you; and you best not get cancer.[15] I once got my hand slammed in a taxi door. The following morning, it was the size of a multicolored baseball mitt. I went to a clinic where the doctor poked at my hand, compared it to the other one, and gave me some colorful pills. No X-rays, no icing, no wrapping, nothing. I asked about the X-ray and was told that my hand didn't make a crinkly sound, so it probably wasn't broken. That night as I lay down to sleep, my hand made a crinkly sound.

There's No Where to Go but Up

Despite all the challenges, there were some good things happening too that could attract the businesses Myanmar wanted and needed. For the first time, the World Bank did a "Doing Business" report, meaning that the government was taking measurable efforts on reforms and regulations and was qualified to have economic indicators evaluated. The low ranking centered on issues like electricity, water, internet, capacity issues, and costs of starting and running a business. The country was listed 157 out of 177 countries on the Transparency International's Corruption Perceptions Index, tied with Burundi and Zimbabwe and only ahead of the Sudans, Afghanistan, Haiti, North Korea, Cambodia, and a few others. Myanmar ranked near the bottom of nearly every development and economic indicator, but the government took a positive view, saying there was nowhere to go but up.[16 and 17]

The government pushed through economic reforms, including a managed float of the Myanmar kyat in 2012, granting the central bank operational independence in July 2013, enacting a new anti-corruption law in September 2013, and granting licenses to thirteen foreign banks in 2014. Myanmar's economic growth rate was under 6 percent in 2011 but increased to 8 percent in 2012. The

Thein Sein administration also drafted and passed a new Foreign Investment Law, easing restrictions and opening sectors once off-limits to foreign businesses. The government also took steps to improve transparency in the mining and oil sectors through the publication of reports under the global organization promoting best standards, the Extractive Industries Transparency Initiative (EITI).[18] Joining EITI was a key demand made by the US, and Myanmar's joining was seen as a positive step to reform its notorious fossil fuels sector.

Investors began to show up—first a trickle in 2013, and then a babbling brook in 2014. Japan went all in, both with development assistance and investment. Major conglomerates and automotive companies set up shop quickly.[19] German and French companies started testing the market. Carlsberg signed a strategic partnership agreement with Myanmar Golden Star Breweries and announced plans to build a production facility. Heineken followed suit three months later by entering into a joint venture with Alliance Brewery Company.[20] Unilever also made plans to open a factory.[21] Soon, brand-name hotels would pop up, relieving the glut: Novotel, Best Western, Melia, Pan Pacific, Wyndam, and boutique hotels.

The Yangon skyline was changing quickly. Shopping malls, office buildings, and high-rise condos rose up amidst the construction cranes dotting the landscape. Old colonial buildings and teak structures were torn down to make way for new concrete and glass buildings, though historian Thant Myint-U and his Yangon Heritage Trust were able to convince government authorities and developers to consider saving old buildings. Some businesses repurposed old buildings downtown. Zaw Zaw's Aya Bank headquarters occupied the historic Rowe and Co. building, constructed in 1910 and referred to as the "Harrods of the East."[22] They maintained the outside architecture and the original elevators but with a sign in many languages that said "Do not use." They loved having the old elevator but didn't want to take a chance of sending an employee plummeting to the basement. The Japanese-inspired restaurant, Gekko, sat in the Sofaer Building, built by the Baghdad-born, Yangon-educated, Jewish brothers, Isaac and Meyer Sofaer, in 1906. The building once housed a *Reuters* telegram office and shops selling a variety of goods—German beer, Scotch, Egyptian cigars, and English confections.[23]

The US Chamber of Commerce was looking at Myanmar for its members; prior to 2012, it didn't waste efforts to press the US government on policy changes since there seemed to be little appetite in Congress or subsequent administrations to allow any type of investment. The conversation changed early in 2012, and the Chamber of Commerce was getting hints from government officials, both in the executive and legislative branches, that it would be good for businesses to start pressuring the government to ease sanctions. US investors found for the first time since 1997 that they were "pushing on an open door." There was still concern that the business community would be vilified due to ongoing human rights issues, but it wasn't the case. It was a "uniquely welcoming" set of circumstances.[24]

The first Chamber of Commerce visit to Myanmar took place in mid-2012, after the first announcement of the ease of some sanctions. The country seemed like a hornet's nest of issues; most of the major businesses, land, office space, and potential investment opportunities were linked to cronies on the SDN List. The team met with the US embassy and later drove up to Nay Pyi Taw to meet with government officials on how to strategize market entry on the infamous "Death Highway," the road from Yangon to Mandalay that was not built to proper road code, was full of blind spots, often had motorbikes driving the wrong way, and had cattle and people randomly crossing it. After these discussions, they decided it was time for the business community to see it for themselves. The first official business delegation took place in July 2012. The US-ASEAN Business Council, an organization that supports investment in Southeast Asia, also concluded its first trade mission to Myanmar two days after sanctions were lifted. By the next year, interest was so high the Chamber of Commerce had to turn people away. Everyone was excited; this was an untapped, big market. There were challenges, but Vietnam had been extremely challenging two decades ago and it was the darling of Southeast Asian investment now. Myanmar's issues, however, would soon be discovered to be quite different and a lot more difficult to deal with. The Myanmar government and local business community began to get frustrated by the risk aversion, calling the Western investment approach the "Four Ls": look, listen, learn, and leave (and sometimes a fifth "L" for laugh). For US investors, it was hard to comprehend just how far behind the country was thanks to more than five decades of brutal military rule, years of civil war, and two decades of sanctions.[25]

Some of the largest and most well-known businesses took the leap. GE agreed through its local dealer to provide X-ray machines for cardiology and topography to two private hospitals in Myanmar.[26] GE also signed a contract with Myanmar National Airways to support the airline's upgrade and expansion by providing fuel-efficient engines for six Boeing 737-800 and four Boeing 737MAX 8 aircraft.[27]

Pepsi signed an agreement with a local firm to distribute its products and looked into constructing a production facility, putting physical stakes in the country for the first time since it divested in 1997.[28] Coca-Cola began bottling in Myanmar for the first time since its operations were nationalized in 1965, bringing along with it Ball Corporation to do the bottling. At the time of this writing, the only markets in the world that are Coca-Cola-free are North Korea and Cuba.

The Gap began sourcing from the country. KFC opening in 2016 caused a frenzy, with lines forming around blocks for a taste of its famous fried chicken. Other chains like Swensons, Burger King, and Krispy Kreme opened. ATMs were in all of the malls and on street corners. MasterCard and Visa had processed more than US $260 million in payments, and thousands of merchants, including hotels and some restaurants, accepted credit cards. Now we could chow down on Western comfort food and withdraw cash or use credit cards to pay for our medevac flights to Bangkok to put in stents.[29 and 30 and 31]

Google chairman Eric Schmidt visited in March 2013, and soon Google Maps included directions in the Burmese language. Hilton made plans to build a hotel downtown to bring its brand to tourists looking for familiar names. Ford opened a full-service showroom and service center in Yangon. Ford's Asia and Pacific managing director said that entering Myanmar was part of the company's "aggressive expansion" in the Asia-Pacific region.[32]

Despite these initial market entries, many companies, especially from the US, wanted Aung San Suu Kyi's blessing. They felt it was an important insurance policy from future sanctions actions—many companies constantly feared that sanctions could be reimposed at any moment—or "naming and shaming" from US government officials and activists. One client told me I couldn't leave Myanmar until I secured her go-ahead for their investment.

Reforms were continuing, but things were still slow. For Myanmar, there was an understanding among the reformers about the need to change the way of doing things. But the bureaucracy was still operating under fear and, in some cases, complacency and malaise. In the junta days, just a few short years ago, you could be severely punished for thinking outside the box or coming up with ideas that could potentially open the junta up to outside threats to sovereignty (real or perceived) or that would fundamentally undermine their grip on power.

There were still reminders of very deeply rooted issues in the country. On my last trip of my first year in business, Myanmar was rocked by bombings. Though not uncommon, this shattered the euphoria around the country's opening. In the span of a week in October 2013, bombs went off at a guesthouse, a bus stop, in a truck, and in restaurants in Yangon and in Bago, killing two and hurting several others. Then a bomb went off in a hotel room at the Traders Hotel, now known as the Sule Shangri-La Hotel, in downtown Yangon, badly wounding an American tourist and showering the streets below with glass. Soon after the bomb went off at the Traders, other devices exploded at a pagoda and in the parking lot of a hotel in Sagaing Division. These were a lot of incidents for one week.

The police detained a group of ethnic Karen businessmen from the mining industry, who they alleged planned the blasts to scare off foreign investors to Karen State. At least one of those detained allegedly had ties to the KNU, but the KNU, still in the middle of peace talks said, "We do not know anything about these bombings. We don't know who did it and we also do not have any evidence to provide. It is not our members who have done this."[33 and 34]

I stayed away from big markets and large gatherings, noticing immediately that all of the major hotels set up metal detectors and searched under vehicles entering hotel grounds. In unfortunate timing, October was also the Thadingyut festival, the Festival of Lights marking the end of Buddhist lent, so there were celebrations aplenty. In addition to lighting candles, people were setting off fireworks. Having the night air punctuated with booms and crackles further frayed the nerves.

A Mixed Bag

The NLD won the election in 2015 and took the government reins in March 2016. For businesses, this meant a huge reputational hurdle was removed. But challenges remained, including the NLD's capacity to formulate and implement economic policy and ongoing access to finance issues, and to update decrepit, outdated legal frameworks and basic things like contract and investment laws that made it extremely difficult for companies to enter the market. The NLD had no experience in governing and often viewed business with suspicion, seeing them as more a predatory enterprise than a beneficial boon to the country.

Unfortunately, 2016 would be the peak year for interest in US investment in Myanmar. It was just too hard to make a case that this market was worth it. The combination of capacity, low or delayed returns on investment, due diligence costs, risks associated with sanctions, and reputational harm was too great. Each day, the headlines focused on stories about landslides killing people at jade mines, violence against the Rohingya, conflict in the ethnic states, and corruption at all levels. It was hardly a good sell.

For Inle Advisory Group, we had our own successes and failures and questioned what we were doing often. We helped transform local companies, professionalizing their philanthropic efforts and getting them comfortable with outreach to supporters and critics alike to share their transformation stories and get advice on how to take it further. We helped with big-ticket deals in the telecommunications and insurance sector, and we also helped smaller NGOs connect with sources of funding to maintain operations. But we also failed to get financing for a small renewable energy project, leaving villagers who subsisted on fire for light at night to be left waiting for who knows how long for electricity. We also planned trips for clients that went completely south, where requested government meetings never materialized or the bridge between what the Myanmar market could absorb versus what the company wanted to give was too wide.

Our client engagement brought us on some incredible adventures and provided us with learning experiences, particularly on how hard it would be to transform certain industries and push for change in the country. In 2016, we worked with the American Gem Trade Association (AGTA) to lead a scoping mission, along with the Jewelers of America (JA) and the Gemological Institute of America (GIA), to better understand the ruby industry and reestablish responsible and transparent trade between the US and Myanmar. AGTA led similar reform efforts in Tanzania to help stop the sales of tanzanite from financing terrorism and thought Myanmar would be a worthy effort.

This was the kind of work we set out to do; tackle an issue through drawing on experienced practitioners and a wide range of stakeholders. We reached out to folks from all walks of the ruby-industry life, including in the US, Europe, Myanmar, Sri Lanka, and the other gemstone-producing regions. We spoke with several State Department offices, the Organization for Economic Cooperation and Development (OECD),[35] which wrote the gold standard on due diligence guidance on responsible supply chains and conflict minerals. We met with congressional staffers and members to talk about the trip and Congress's views on transforming the gemstone industry. We also spoke with Global Witness, the London-based organization that wrote the bombshell report on Myanmar's jade industry in 2015, to get their insights and assessments. We met with Myanmar government officials, gemstone traders and miners, jewelers, the international and local civil society, and nongovernment organizations, trying to help implement labor and environmental standards to a millennia-old business.

We traveled to gemstone markets, emporiums, and museums, checking out the economics and the trail from mine to market for rubies, sapphires, spinel, apatite, scapolite, moonstone, zircon, garnet, iolite, peridot, amber, jade, and amethyst gemstones. Then we got to experience gemstones in their natural habitat: Mogok, the Shangri-La for gemologists. There are only two roads to get there, and you needed to secure a permit and a guide. Our guide, Ma Thiri,[36] whose family had been in the ruby mining and jewelry business for a couple of centuries, took us on the "fastest" road to Mogok, which was about 130 miles and ninety-nine hairpin turns.

As we drove out of Mandalay and headed toward the road to Mogok, mining activity alongside the road increased dramatically. The leaves of trees were covered in dust, and huge trucks carting large gray stones joined us on the road. The road eventually leads to the Myanmar-China border, the destination for most of these materials. There were several requests to stop for photos until one of the drivers asked if I could inform the delegation that we shouldn't stop until we got to Mogok because of roaming armed groups that might shoot us.

Mogok resembles a beautiful town in the Alps; the air is cool, and the landscape is completely different from Yangon. All of the roads are winding and dotted along the way with people selling piles of rocks speckled with bits of gems, illegal artisanal mines drilled into the sides of mountains, and the occasional monastery or pagoda.

We went to visit ruby, sapphire, and peridot mines and told our guide that we didn't want to give prior warning of our visit to the mine owners to prevent opportunities to clean up any safety hazards or shoo child laborers away. We were greeted at the first mine by an entire village who performed a traditional dance and showered us with snacks. We trekked to a peridot mine, definitely not giving warning, that had been operating for twenty years. Unlike sapphires and rubies, peridot was found in softer rock, and the shaft walls had to be supported by wooden beams; these beams have to be replaced every three to five years due to degradation and water damage. These beams had been replaced a decade ago. The peridot mines are also pretty wet, so water continually dripped, making the nearly vertical mine very slippery. Half the team easily shimmied their way down, but Peter and I, as well as another team member, took a pass. Thinking we were safer outside the mine, we noticed a pile of dynamite sticks next to a lit cigarette and a boiling teapot over an open firepit. Our trip mate picked up the already assembled dynamite to move it away from the cigarette while Peter and I booked it toward the car.

During the trip, we had dinner at one of the mine owner's houses, Ko Shwe.[37] He was operating a small mine in his backyard, and he told me that at one time, you had to get a mining permit to dig a toilet because the land was so rich; any digging could unearth precious gems. Ma Thiri told us of an uncle who had purchased former dictator Ne Win's house in Mogok. Since this was the Valley of the Rubies, surely Ne Win had inside information that the house sat atop great riches. Ma Thiri went to visit her uncle one day to find the floorboards ripped up and him sitting in a six-foot hole in the dining room. She couldn't believe he was actually serious about this but somewhat flippantly asked if had found anything. He replied, "Only skeletons."

Our AGTA, JA, and GIA colleagues shared their experiences in Africa and Sri Lanka and with Myanmar government agents, miners, and traders, offering recommendations, lessons learned, and case studies. Aside from the DIY dynamite shacks, there was real potential to work with nonmilitary or non-EAO connected miners who were contributing to their communities and wanted to transform their industries.

However, our initial success ran into the buzz saw of bureaucracy and military abuse. Like most things that happen in Myanmar, the government was slow to implement recommendations from the AGTA and other global organizations. When they were finally making some progress in Parliament, the Rohingya crisis erupted, spooking any would-be investors and technical advisors from investing or helping. The miners, scientists, and organizations we met got frustrated both with the government on slow policy and with the international community's decision to withhold investment or technical assistance because of the violence targeting the

Rohingya. I tried to explain to them the seriousness of the human rights issues and how it impacted all areas of Myanmar. They saw the problems in front of them and thought they were finally getting help after decades of flailing. What they couldn't connect was what the Rohingya had to do with them.

8

THE ROHINGYA

EVERYTHING OLD IS NEW AGAIN

In January 2017, Ko Ni, the NLD legal advisor and the mastermind behind the state counsellor bill that allowed Aung San Suu Kyi to circumvent Article 59(f)—which banned her from the presidency—and run the government, walked out of the Yangon International Airport after attending a senior leadership program in Indonesia. He picked up his tiny grandson who came to meet him at the airport and waited outside for his car to arrive. A man walked up behind Ko Ni and shot him in the head. A taxi driver ran after the shooter and was also shot dead.[1]

Ko Ni had been receiving death threats for months. Aside from the state counsellor's bill, he pushed to reduce the military's role in government and he was also a Muslim, the cherry on top for Buddhists nationalists. In the weeks following his murder, three former military officers were accused by police of organizing his death by a hired gunman.[2]

The US was extremely concerned. This was a top NLD figure and a Muslim as well. The US embassy looked into the case, and though they did not issue an official report, embassy spokesperson Aryani Manring said the embassy consulted "many actors" about the murder, but "the killing itself and problematic elements of the resulting trial, which has continued for over a year, raise serious questions about who was behind the murder and whether they will face accountability."[3]

Aung San Suu Kyi's conduct following his death shocked everyone. This man made her political position possible. Ko Ni believed in Aung San Suu Kyi and thought she would be the one to finally expel the military from power. She did not attend his funeral, offer condolences, or speak of his assassination until a memorial service one month later. Ko Ni's son said, "People were quite unhappy about her absence the day of the funeral, as well as keeping too quiet." Others were more forgiving and sought to find a reason behind her reticence, suggesting she feared for her own life. Regardless, Myanmar's Muslim population was devastated by her lack of empathy and felt, perhaps, that she was not going to save them from the military's guns.[4]

The Enduring Problem of Ethnicity and Identity

Ethnicity in Myanmar drives politics, conflict, and identity but is one of the most fluid and hard-to-define concepts in the country. Ethnicities can incorporate language, customs, locations, clothing and textiles, politics, and food. You can be many ethnicities or one. It's often celebrated and fiercely protected; however, when it comes to the Rohingya, things get quite complicated and very nasty.

I do not give an exhaustive history on Rakhine State or the country's sectarian problems in this book. Historian Thant Myint-U addresses these themes more thoroughly in his book, *The Hidden History of Burma: Race, Capitalism, and the Crisis of Democracy in the Twenty-First Century*. Martin Smith, my go-to on most things, captured the earlier struggles in his book, *Burma: Insurgency and the Politics of Ethnicity*. Francis Wade, Azeem Ibrahim, Anthony Ware, and Costa Laoutides, and two organizations, BRAC and UN High Commission on Refugees (UNHCR), have books, documents, and reports on the issue for those interested in delving deeper.

The ethnic identity of the Rohingya who call Myanmar home evolved over centuries from a mixed migration of Muslims into the Arakan, now Rakhine, region. The term "Rohingya" came from their own Bengali-related language that meant "of Rohang," their name for Arakan. The ethnic Buddhist Arakan, who had been defeated by the ethnic Bamar kingdom in 1784, viewed everyone as an outsider and considered the Muslim Arakans and Rohingya as outsiders as well. This sentiment only grew during World War II, when the Japanese supported and armed the Arakan Buddhists, and the British did the same for the Muslim populations. After the war, Rakhine State fell into deep poverty, leaving each side with wartime memories of fighting each other and a fight over scraps.[5]

Ne Win came into power and hated the Rohingya (and the Chinese and Indians) so much that he led the first purge against them in 1977 and 1978—code-named Operation Dragon King—that sent 200,000 Rohingya fleeing into Bangladesh. The International Committee of the Red Cross and the Bangladesh government supplied emergency relief but were quickly overwhelmed. The Bangladesh government requested assistance from the UN, which built thirteen refugee camps along the border. Almost immediately upon the refugees' arrival, Bangladesh wanted to discuss repatriation. This became a repetitive vicious cycle, one that would play out for decades to come. Bangladeshi authorities complained of the economic and social burden of hosting refugees, and Burma only agreed to repatriation if the Rohingya could provide residency and other legal documents.[6] and 7

Another purge took place in 1992 under the auspices of targeting the EAO, the Rohingya Solidarity Organization, which led to another 200,000 refugees fleeing to Bangladesh. Attacks occurred again in 2001–2002, 2008–2009, 2012, and 2016. During the 2008–2009 purge, Rohingya refugees took to the seas to escape. Several boats washed up on Thai shores where they were met by Thai Internal Security Operations Command (ISOC) officers. ISOC promptly beat them and pushed them back to sea with very little food or water. This was not the first time this happened, but this was the first time ISOC got caught. A shocked, beach-going tourist using a camera phone filmed the whole spectacle and uploaded it onto the internet.[8] The US said it was "very aware of the situation" and that it was "one of unfortunately many very serious human rights problems." The plight of the Rohingya was included in discussions with the SPDC on treatment of ethnic nationalities, and the US pointed out that "sometimes that treatment is different [with the] Rohingya."[9]

The Rohingya situation for those in Yangon or Mandalay seemed like a faraway problem. But when the international community grew more vocal and discussed reimposing economic and diplomatic restrictions, ethnic Bamar Buddhists began to pay attention. They started believing conspiracy theories, including that Muslims were aiming to displace and replace Buddhists and/or that Muslims were all terrorists. They also believed that swarms of illegal immigrants were sweeping over the Bangladesh border into Myanmar; this is why they insisted on calling them Bengalis and not Rohingya. Using the term "Rohingya" meant they were trying to carve out their own identity to claim rights and privileges in a country where they didn't belong. This was the first step in pursuing their own state or autonomous region.

What once was infrequent—but horrific—violence became the disturbing norm. On June 3, 2012, long simmering tensions between Arakan Buddhists and Rohingya Muslim communities boiled over. A local incident ignited widespread conflict in four districts in Rakhine State and displaced an estimated 61,000 people. USAID dispatched advisors to assess the humanitarian and security situation; measure progress, if any, on the Myanmar government's response; and provide $850,000 to UNICEF for water, sanitation, and hygiene support. The UN and the INGOs providing assistance to affected areas were finding that they were not welcome. Staff reported finding stickers saying "No UN/INGOs" on office doors and homes, and Arakan Buddhists were wearing T-shirts with inflammatory statements about aid workers. The Buddhist community didn't want the NGOs to help the Rohingya, who they saw as taking their resources and receiving preferential treatment from the aid community when the entire region was rife with poverty and development issues. Even Myanmar government officials providing assistance were harassed. In July 2012, Thein Sein bowed to pressure from Arakan Buddhists and told the UN High Commission on Refugees (UNHCR) that he would not recognize the Rohingya as citizens and was contemplating deporting them to a third country or to UNHCR refugee camps.[10]

In September 2012, Secretary Clinton asked Joe Yun from EAP and Dan Baer from DRL to travel with Derek to Rakhine State and Bangladesh to get an on-the-ground perspective. She wanted to see if there was space for the US to help stem the violence or put programming in place to promote tolerance.[11] After the trip, Joe and other State Department officials pitched the idea of an international conference to gin up pledges for assistance, to find locations to send refugees, and to come up with creative programming to target other short- to medium-term issues. There were a lot of discussions, but in the end, nothing came of it. It was too big of an idea and too difficult to get the buy-in and attention of US officials who were about to leave government by the end of 2012. There was also no political will anywhere—not in the Organization of Islamic Countries (OIC), ASEAN, the EU, or Japan. No one cared enough in 2012, and the pledging conference was dead in the water.[12]

The violence grew worse. On October 1, 2012, ethnic Rohingya living in Bangladesh's Cox's Bazar lit Buddhist temples and houses on fire in retaliation for a picture of a burned Quran on a Buddhist man's Facebook page. More than 150 people were arrested in connection with the violence, and authorities instituted a curfew. Several protests erupted in Myanmar and throughout the region, including in Bangladesh and Thailand, in response to the response. Five hundred ethnic Arakan Buddhist women protested in Rakhine State against the government's decision to allow the OIC to open an aid office there. The Thein Sein government signed an MOU in early August, following the earlier communal clashes, to bring humanitarian aid and assistance to both Muslim and Buddhist communities. The number of protesters grew to tens of thousands, and once again bending to the will of the people, Thein Sein said he would not allow an OIC office to open.[13] It was an extremely disappointing move and hard for the US to explain the difference concerning when to adhere to the will of the people—like in the case of the Myitsone Dam—and when to consider the greater good and take risks that were unpopular.

Violence would continue through October and November 2012, forcing the police and military to deploy to Rakhine State to protect both ethnic Arakan and Rohingya from mob violence and bring in disaster relief and supplies.

Aung San Suu Kyi started taking heat for her ambivalence to the issue. In an interview with the Indian news outlet NDTV in November 2012, she said she completely condemned the violence that was taking place and wanted to work on reconciliation between the communities. When asked about the citizenship issue, she danced around the topic and said that the violence must be addressed first and then the citizenship law and immigration policy had to be looked into, saying, "There's a lot of illegal crossing of the border still going on that they have got to put a stop to, otherwise there will not be an end to the problem, because Bangladesh will say all these people have come over from Burma and the Burmese say all these people have come over from Bangladesh. And where is the proof either way?"[14]

The Face of Buddhist Terror

By 2013, the idea that Buddhism in Myanmar was not all loving-kindness began to take hold. In July 2013, the cover of *Time* featured controversial Buddhist nationalist monk, U Wirathu, and labeled him the "Face of Buddhist Terror." Wirathu had been spewing anti-Muslim rhetoric for years; in 2003, Wirathu was sentenced to twenty-five years in jail for inciting anti-Muslim hatred but was released in 2012 in a general amnesty.[15]

Wirathu was a charismatic speaker and had a huge following on social media thanks to Myanmar's newfound digital connectivity. Wirathu was a member of the sangha, the Buddhist clergy, and as a respected member of the Buddhist community, his words and status had impact. Wirathu led a group called 969, a "grassroots" Buddhist nationalist movement organized as a nonviolent response to the strain from "foreign" influence on Buddhist society. As with many things in Myanmar, there was a numerology-based logic for the group's name. In an article for *The Diplomat*, Mong Palatino breaks down the meaning behind the numbers. Muslims represent the phrase "bismillah-ir-rahman-ir-rahim," or "In the Name of Allah, the Compassionate and Merciful," with the number 786. To 969, 786 is evidence of a Muslim plot to conquer Myanmar in the twenty-first century because seven plus eight plus six is equal to twenty-one (but, as a budding numerologist, if you go the requisite step further, you add the two and one and get three). The number 969 is intended to be 786's cosmological opposite, representing the "three jewels": the nine attributes of the Buddha, the six attributes of his teachings, and the nine attributes of the sangha, or monastic order.[16] Thus, 969 was on a cosmological mission from Buddha to save Myanmar from the Muslims. Wirathu's fiery rhetoric gave life to the paranoid and xenophobic attitudes that few expressed out loud. Many Buddhists, particularly in Rakhine State, felt they were under siege by Muslims, and Wirathu spoke directly to them.[17]

In 2014, Ma Ba Tha, or the Association for the Protection of Race and Religion, was started by Wirathu as well. It came out of the 969 movement, and its members gave vitriolic speeches filled with slurs and incitements to violence. In 2017, the state-backed Buddhist cleric organization, Ma Ha Na, declared Ma Ba Tha an unlawful organization.[18]

The military seemingly supported 969 and Ma Ba Tha and their calls for Buddhist justice. Min Aung Hlaing, the commander in chief of the Tatmadaw and the future 2021 coup leader, donated to U Wirathu. The government seemed to support them too. Thein Sein, a devout Buddhist, aimed to push through a set of four laws supported by Buddhist nationalists, the so-called "Race and Religion Laws," before his administration ended in March 2016. The four laws included the Religious Conversion Bill governing conversions to other faiths; the Buddhist Women's Special Marriage Bill that regulated the marriage of Buddhist women with men from other religions; the Population Control Healthcare Bill that established a thirty-six-month "birth spacing" interval for women between childbirths; and the Monogamy Bill that would criminalize extramarital relations and polygamy. Christians would get caught up in this too, but these laws targeted perceptions and misconceptions about Muslims.[19]

Yanghee Lee, the UN Special Rapporteur on Human Rights, immediately condemned these laws and pled with the government to dismiss them. Buddhist nationalists in turn condemned Lee, with Wirathu saying, "We have already made public the Race Protection Law, but this bitch, without studying it, kept on complaining about how it is against our human rights, just because some loud-mouthed women say so. Can this bitch really be from a respectable background? Don't assume you are a respectable person, just because you have a position in the UN. In our country, you are just a whore."[20] Exactly the type of language you'd expect from a Buddhist monk.

Many devout Buddhists opposed 969 and Ma Ba Tha, finding their own ways to undermine their malevolence by seeking legal action, preaching tolerance, and practicing acts of kindness towards Muslims. The NLD filed official complaints against Ma Ba Tha for illegal election activities. Min Ko Naing, one of the leaders of the 88 Generation Students, condemned the 969 movement, and other prominent monks spoke out against these nationalist monks, especially Wirathu, saying they did not represent Buddhist beliefs and practices and urged fellow Buddhists to spur their teachings.[21]

The Rohingya issue was a regional one too. In 2015, a crackdown on human trafficking in Thailand led traffickers to abandon thousands of mostly Rohingya Muslims and Bangladeshis adrift at sea, with thousands of them washing ashore in Indonesia and elsewhere.[22] Thailand disliked the Rohingya as much as Myanmar did, and the Muslim-majority Indonesia and Malaysia barely tolerated refugees washing up on their beaches unless it helped to make a domestic political point. Unsurprisingly, a regional summit, which was held a few weeks later to address the issue, failed to yield results, with Myanmar becoming defensive and ASEAN member states reluctant to shoulder the burden of resettling the refugees. Commander in Chief Min Aung Hlaing told Tony Blinken, the US deputy secretary of state who had traveled to Myanmar to urge more progress on the Rohingya and other democracy issues, that most boat people were posing as Rohingya from

Myanmar in the hope of receiving assistance from UNHCR or that the Rohingya were exaggerating their stories in order to seek asylum elsewhere, like in the US.[23]

In August 2016, Aung San Suu Kyi invited former UN Secretary-General Kofi Annan to lead a high-level commission to investigate the root causes of the issues in Rakhine State and come up with recommendations to solve them, a move that was praised by the international policymaking and human rights community and viewed as an effort to take the situation seriously. Aung San Suu Kyi told the commission to be bold in their recommendations.[24]

Just two months later, in October 2016, several hundred local Muslim men, armed mostly with kitchen knives, sticks, and about thirty firearms, launched simultaneous attacks on three police posts in townships in Rakhine State. Nine police officers were killed, and the attackers ran off with dozens of firearms and more than 10,000 rounds of ammunition. The attacks marked a major escalation of violence in Rakhine by the oppressed and beleaguered Muslims. It showed a level of organization and planning not seen by ethnic Rohingya in years. Unfortunately for the broader Rohingya population, this fed into the narrative that the Rohingya were terrorists, a label they had fought for years to avoid.

Behind the attack was a group calling itself Harakah al-Yaqin (HaY, or "Faith Movement" in Arabic), which was later renamed the Arakan Rohingya Salvation Army (ARSA). ARSA was established in 2012 by Abu Ammar Jununi, who had been born to a Rohingya immigrant father and Pakistani mother in Karachi. After the violence against the Rohingya in 2012, Abu Ammar Jununi gathered a few dozen Rohingya and started ARSA. ARSA began to recruit others with an aim to take territory and be part of the peace process.[25]

A year after its formation, on August 24, 2017, the Kofi Annan-led advisory commission on Rakhine State released its long-awaited report. The report was the outcome of more than 150 consultations and meetings held throughout Rakhine State, Yangon, Nay Pyi Taw, Indonesia, Thailand, Bangladesh, and Geneva. At the press conference, Annan stated, "Unless concerted action—led by the government and aided by all sectors of the government and society—is taken soon, we risk the return of another cycle of violence and radicalization, which will further deepen the chronic poverty that afflicts Rakhine State."[26]

The report, which did not use the terms "Rohingya" or "Bengali" per Aung San Suu Kyi's guidance, included eighty-eight recommendations for all levels of government, religious and community leaders, and the people of Rakhine to implement. These recommendations covered equitable economic development and access to basic services for all communities; a transparent citizenship verification and a safe, dignified repatriation process; freedom of movement; full humanitarian access to affected areas; support for community development initiatives and political participation; support of inter-communal dialogue; access to justice; and the reform of the security services.

Also highlighted was a request to review and update the controversial 1982 Citizenship Law, a law that incorporated the worst of former leader Ne Win's most xenophobic tendencies and was seen as one of the key causes for the tenuousness of living as a Rohingya in Myanmar. The list of accepted ethnicities for citizenship in the law totaled 135, which Ne Win considered as having settled in Myanmar before 1824, the year of the first British annexation. At the Citizenship Law's release, the British embassy cabled back to the Foreign Office that the law was "blatantly discriminatory on racial grounds." The Rohingya were not included.[27] and 28

Aung San Suu Kyi promised the full implementation of the eighty-eight recommendations listed in the report.

Two weeks before the Annan commission's report release, I met with the *Reuters* bureau chief, Antoni Slodkowski, for dinner in Yangon. Toward the end of dinner, he received a text saying that troops were mobilizing to Rakhine State's largest city of Sittwe. We both thought that odd. Apparently, the 33rd and 99th Light Infantry Divisions (LID) were sent to Rakhine State to provide "increased protection" for Buddhists who were concerned about attacks from ARSA.

Hours after Annan turned in his report, ARSA staged a coordinated attack on thirty police posts and an army base in Rakhine State, killing twelve security officials. A small number of minimally trained leaders had some arms, a significant number of untrained villagers used sticks and knives, and some attackers had improvised explosive devices. A few hours later, ARSA entered a small Hindu village and rounded up its occupants, killing most and abducting the rest. They also attacked other Buddhist villages, and Facebook lit up with rumors and videos. Annan immediately condemned the violence, saying, "no cause can justify such brutality and senseless killing."[29]

What happened next would shock the world.

According to the UN Fact-Finding Mission investigative report issued in 2018, the Tatmadaw responded with a brutal and disproportionate response. Within hours, the military launched "clearance operations" to eliminate the "terrorist threat" by ARSA, targeting Rohingya communities in hundreds of villages across northern Maungdaw, Buthidaung, and Rathedaung townships in Rakhine State. The operations continued for more than two months, despite the government claiming the mission had been accomplished by the first week of September. Satellite imagery and eyewitness accounts showed that more than 40 percent of all villages in northern Rakhine State were partially or totally destroyed. The report's case studies and media footage all told the same story. For example, in the township of Tula Toli, the military set fire to homes and shot villagers escaping to the hills, resulting in one hundred people dead or injured. The military rounded up women and girls in their homes, took their jewelry and money, beat, raped, and stabbed them, and locked them in their houses to die in fires set by officers. Children and babies were killed in the most horrific ways.[30]

Wa Lone and Kyaw Soe Oo, two *Reuters* reporters, uncovered similar stories in the village of Inn Dinn. There, ten Rohingya Muslim men, who the military claimed were terrorists, dug their own graves, had their hands bound, and were shot or hacked to death by the military and Buddhist villagers. None of Inn Din's 6,000 Rohingya remained in the village as of October 2017. Police officers agreed to meet Wa Lone and Kyaw Soe Oo for the story and passed them information to confirm their research. The officers noted that operations in Inn Din were led by the army's 33rd LID and supported by the paramilitary 8th Security Police Battalion.[31]

Wa Lone and Kyaw Soe Oo were arrested in December 2017 for violating the colonial era Official Secrets Act "for possessing important and secret government documents related to Rakhine state and security forces" and that the information had been "illegally acquired with the intention to share it with foreign media."[32] In talking to people who worked with Wa Lone and were aware of the details of the arrest, the whole thing seemed like a setup. The journalists had gotten too close and were arrested for doing their job.

In the end, 725,000 Rohingya fled to Bangladesh in the largest and fastest refugee movement since World War II.

The world reacted immediately. The US initially condemned ARSA's attacks on the security forces and called on the Myanmar government to prevent further violence and "bring those responsible for the attacks to justice . . . in a way that is consistent with the rule of law, protects and respects human rights and fundamental freedoms, demonstrates transparency, and avoids inflaming a tense situation." Soon after, the US then condemned the military for its disproportionate response.

Aung San Suu Kyi had been planning a trip to the White House in August 2017 but had postponed it so she could be in Myanmar for the release of the Kofi Annan report. That trip was now shelved indefinitely. The Trump NSC, like their predecessors, went into interagency meeting overdrive, with at least two sub-policy coordination committee (PCC) meetings per week.[33] It seemed that every government office wanted to attend the PCCs, filling the largest secure conference room in the Eisenhower Executive Office Building with dozens of people from all different government agencies who were beaming in on twelve secure video conference screens.[34]

The US government was largely split on what to do. Some were calling for blood while others pushed for a more realpolitik approach. Sam Brownback, the Ambassador-at-Large for International Religious Freedom, wanted to call the atrocities "genocide" immediately, cut diplomatic ties completely, and sanction "the shit out of" Myanmar. UN Ambassador Nikki Haley and Vice President Pence also wanted to call it genocide. The other side was concerned that if the US did that, the democratic experiment would be over and efforts to work on other long-standing and critical issues would be lost. The Myanmar embassy in DC pleaded with the State Department to not cut ties and to continue to work with them.[35]

The outcome of these very emotional and intense meetings led to an NSC-level government strategy on Myanmar, the only country-specific strategy for Southeast Asia. National Security Advisor H. R. McMaster, NSC Senior Director for Asia Matt Pottinger, and the US embassy in Yangon went through rounds of interagency edits and input to accomplish two objectives: (1) to mitigate the immediate crisis in Rakhine State and in Bangladesh's refugee camps and (2) to support Myanmar's continued political transition and economic development. The strategy focused on several pillars. The first was the broadest but also the most urgent, using the kitchen sink of policy tools to address the violence, ease ethnic tensions, provide aid, and push for humanitarian access for NGOs, the UN, and donors to reach impacted communities. The other pillars included promoting civil society and supporting the next generation of government leaders and civic voices, promoting economic development, addressing possible terrorism concerns, and getting Myanmar to cut military trade ties to North Korea, and reform and professionalize the armed forces. The last pillar would be the hardest to pursue and the most limited; it would be impossible to gain broad support in Congress or at the State Department to help reform a military that was being accused of war crimes, but it was also necessary to try to reform the military so that it would stop doing these things.[36]

In October 2017, Simon Henshaw, the acting assistant secretary of state for population, refugees, and migration, led a delegation with officials from DRL, EAP, and the Bureau of South and Central Asian Affairs to Myanmar and Bangladesh. Henshaw met with the Myanmar government and pushed for greater humanitarian and media access, guaranteed human rights, and a credible path to citizenship for the Rohingya population. The Myanmar government gave the delegation an earful, saying they were only paying attention to the Rohingya and not ARSA, which had perpetrated the original attacks. The delegation also went to the refugee camps in Bangladesh's Cox's Bazar.[37] In an interview with NPR, Henshaw stated, "I've been to a lot of camps, and I've never quite seen something like this . . . dried muddy terrain covered with makeshift shelters with people in them as far as you could see."[38]

That same month, Secretary of State Tillerson traveled to Myanmar to discuss US support for democratization and the Rakhine State issue. He met separately with Aung San Suu Kyi and Senior General Min Aung Hlaing and pushed for the protection of local populations, unhindered humanitarian and media access, a credible investigation of abuses, accountability for those who were responsible for abuses, and the implementation of the recommendations of the Kofi Annan commission report. Tillerson called for a credible investigation into reports of human rights abuses against the Rohingya, saying, "In all my meetings, I have called on the Myanmar civilian government to lead a full and effective independent investigation and for the military to facilitate full access and cooperation." He also said it was the duty of the military to help the government to meet commitments to ensure the safety and security of all people in Rakhine State. After the meeting, Min Aung Hlaing posted to his Facebook page that he had explained to Tillerson the "true situation in Rakhine," the reasons why Muslims fled, how the military was working with the government to deliver aid, and the progress that had been made for a repatriation process with Bangladesh. I'm sure Min Aung Hlaing's "true version" didn't line up with Tillerson's briefing notes on the situation.[39 and 40]

H. R. McMaster also spoke with and eventually met with his Myanmar counterpart, U Thaung Tun. He explained the new NSC strategy and stated that Myanmar had to do something, say something, to stem the bleeding from the Rohingya situation. The US was not going to be able to work on anything else until the Myanmar government began to effectively address the situation.[41]

By November 2017, the Trump administration was feeling the heat on perceived inaction (i.e., not pursuing sanctions) on the Rohingya issue. There was significant pressure to sanction the military and for the administration to state publicly that the violence constituted ethnic cleansing and/or genocide. In late November 2017, Secretary Tillerson slammed Myanmar's military and local vigilantes for carrying out "horrendous atrocities" that caused "tremendous suffering . . . . After a careful and thorough analysis of available facts, it is clear that the situation in northern Rakhine state constitutes ethnic cleansing against the Rohingya. Those responsible for these atrocities must be held accountable." He called for an independent investigation into the violence. Unlike terms such as "crimes against humanity" and "genocide," the "ethnic cleansing" label does not automatically trigger domestic or international legal actions. As a senior State Department official told reporters after the announcement, "It is a descriptive term and it carries with it, again, the sense of urgency. It does not require any new obligations, but it does emphasize our concern about the situation."[42]

The Trump administration allocated nearly $500 million for humanitarian assistance in Bangladesh and Rakhine State, and in December, to the likely relief of Congress and activists, it sanctioned Major General Maung Maung Soe, the army officer who had been in charge of western command troops in Rakhine, under the US Global Magnitsky Act.[43] The original Magnitsky Act, formally known as the Russia and Moldova Jackson-Vanik Repeal and Sergei Magnitsky Rule of Law Accountability Act of 2012, was a bipartisan bill passed by Congress and signed into law by President Obama in December 2012 to punish Russian officials responsible for the 2009 death of Russian tax lawyer, Sergei Magnitsky, in a Moscow prison. It was expanded upon and passed in December 2016 as a new global tool to target an entire spectrum of individuals and entities that committed human rights abuses and corrupt acts.[44] Maung Maung Soe had been sanctioned that day along with individuals from Pakistan, the Gambia, Serbia, Sudan, and Ukraine.

In August 2018, OFAC took action and added to the SDN List four military and border guard police (BGP) commanders, as well as two military units, for their involvement in ethnic cleansing in Rakhine, Kachin, and Shan States. This included military commanders Aung Kyaw Zaw, Khin Maung Soe, Khin Hlaing; BGP commander Thura San Lwin; and the 33rd LID and the 99th LID.[45] More than a year later, in December 2019, OFAC added the military's top brass to the SDN List because of their role in perpetrating "serious human rights abuse against members of ethnic minority groups across Burma, including those in the northern Rakhine, Kachin and Shan States, among others. . . . The United States prioritizes the protection of fundamental freedoms and human rights as a key part of our vision for a free and open Indo-Pacific, recognizing them as integral to US foreign policy and national security interests and in line with US values. Such human rights abuse undermines the ability to realize the vision for a free and open Indo-Pacific that we share with ASEAN and other Indo-Pacific partners." Commander in Chief Min Aung Hlaing; Deputy Commander in Chief Soe Win; the leader of the 99th LID, Than Oo; and the leader of the 33rd LID, Aung Aung, were officially held accountable by the US for their actions.[46]

Congress added to the policy mix too. The House of Representatives in September 2018 introduced H. Res. 1091 with the actual title of "Expressing the sense of the House of Representatives that atrocities committed against the Rohingya by the Burmese military and security forces since August 2017 constitute crimes against humanity and genocide and calling on the Government of Burma to release Burmese journalists Wa Lone and Kyaw Soe Oo sentenced to seven years imprisonment after investigating attacks against civilians by the Burmese military and security forces, and for other purposes," which stated, "the atrocities committed against the Rohingya by the Burmese military and security forces since August 2017 constitute crimes against humanity and genocide."[47] The resolution was not binding, but it expressed what the House wanted to see. In December 2018, Congress passed the Asia Reassurance Initiative Act of

2018, which prohibited funding for the International Military Education and Training (IMET) and Foreign Military Financing (FMF) Programs in Myanmar for fiscal years 2019 through 2023.[48] The House and Senate tried to reintroduce the McCain-Cardin Burma Strategy Act and attach sanctions provisions in the annual National Defense Authorization Act, but Senator McConnell stymied these efforts. He saw them as counterproductive and the path to least resistance in terms of policymaking. To him, it would limit Aung San Suu Kyi's ability to work with the military to change the 2008 constitution and solidify democratic gains. He thought her former allies in Congress were too hostile to her and suggested she had powers she did not. She didn't have control over the military, and she walked a tenuous line to either push for reforms and greater freedoms or find herself and her colleagues in jail again and irrelevant.[49 and 50] This assessment seemed prescient when the military put her under house arrest in February 2021.

The Fall of an Icon

Myanmar, regional neighbors, and global governments came no closer to securing protection for the Rohingya after sanctions, summits, or debates. In December 2017, following the Kofi Annan report and in the wake of the atrocities, Aung San Suu Kyi set up an independent advisory board to implement the recommendations in the report. The board was chaired by Dr. Surakiart Sathirathai, a Thai politician and former president of the Asian Peace and Reconciliation Council, and it included: former South African Defense Minister Roelof Meyer; British doctor and politician Lord Darzi of Denham; the Speaker of the Swedish Parliament Urban Ahlin ; Chairman of Myanmar National Human Rights Commission U Win Mra; member of the Myanmar National Human Rights Commission U Khin Maung Lay; former United Nations Assistant Secretary-General U Tun Myat; former Ambassador and Myanmar Representative to the ASEAN Inter-Governmental Commission on Human Rights U Hla Myint; and parliamentary member of the Health and Sport Development Committee Dr. Daw Khin Nyo, .

Bill Richardson, a former US governor, joined the board but quit a month later in January 2018, issuing a scorcher of a statement. He called the board a pro-government "cheerleading squad," slammed the board's lack of sincerity and commitment to handling their responsibilities, and deplored the absence of Aung San Suu Kyi's moral leadership. He slammed Dr. Surakiart Sathirathai, saying he "parroted the dangerous and untrue notion that international NGOs employ radicals and that humanitarian agencies are providing material support to [Arakan Rohingya Solidarity Army] ARSA" and that his avoidance of the "real issues at the risk of confronting our Myanmar hosts, led to an agenda devoid of any meaningful engagement with the local communities in Rakhine whose people the Advisory Board is meant to serve."[51] In an interview, he said of his likely now former friend, Aung San Suu Kyi, "She has developed an arrogance of power. I've known her a long time and am fond of her, but she basically is unwilling to listen to bad news, and I don't want to be part of a whitewash."[52]

Two days later, Aung San Suu Kyi issued a press release on the state counsellor website, which has gone dark since the February 2021 coup, stating, "In the course of the discussions in Nay Pyi Taw on 22 January, it became evident that the intent of Governor Bill Richardson, a member of the board, was not to provide advice based on the recommendations of the Advisory Commission on Rakhine State chaired by Dr. Kofi Annan but to pursue his own agenda. In view of the difference of opinion that developed, the government decided that his continued participation on the Board would not be in the best interest of all concerned."

Back in Washington—despite efforts to broaden the Myanmar policy scope to include the many pressing issues beyond Rakhine State—Congress, human rights groups, the international community, and some in the Trump administration remained solely fixated on the Rohingya crisis. Of key concern was the safety of refugees in Cox's Bazar. The refugee camps were overcrowded, with the average usable space at 10.7 square meters per person, much less than the recommended international standard of forty-five square meters per person, contributing to increasing levels of communicable diseases, community tensions, and domestic and sexual violence. Schooling was sparse, putting Rohingya children further behind their peers. Bangladesh's patience was wearing thin as the medium- to long-term needs were overwhelming.[53]

In September 2018, the independent UN Fact-Finding Mission (FFM) on Myanmar released its final report, determining that the actions of Myanmar's security forces in Kachin, Rakhine, and Shan States possibly constituted genocide, crimes against humanity, and war crimes. It recommended the UN Security Council "refer the situation to the International Criminal Court or create an ad hoc international criminal tribunal." The report also included a hefty list of criticisms and recommendations for nearly everyone: the Myanmar government, foreign governments, businesses, Facebook, and multilateral institutions like the UN.[54]

The State Department was also undertaking its own investigation and tasked investigators with collecting survivor testimonies and including data and reporting gathered by other government agencies. This report would assess whether the Tatmadaw's actions constituted genocide, and it would include a policy game plan to address the issue and look to alleviate the immediate suffering of the Rohingya. An internal debate around declaring the violence as genocide ensued; a declaration would result in a series of automatic punitive steps such as cutting military-to-military programs and cutting aid for certain programs or augmenting them for victims. But it could have a strong psychological impact on the Tatmadaw, as being labeled a purveyor of genocide would severely strike at their pride. Some thought it would snap some sense into them and spook partners and allies from working with them. Others thought it might shut down all lines of communication, put Aung San Suu Kyi in an impossible position to further necessary political reforms, and plunge the country back into full-on military rule. Secretary of State Pompeo was to issue the statement on the one-year anniversary of the attacks. In August, however, *Politico* published an article based on the leaked Pompeo remarks and notes on the internal debate.[55]

Notoriously sensitive to leaks, the Trump administration was irate. The *Politico* piece drove the State Department to delay the report and policy rollout. Pompeo issued a tweet, stating the US would continue to hold accountable those responsible for the "abhorrent ethnic cleansing" of the Rohingya.[56] The State Department quietly released the findings of its own study at the end of September 2018, concluding, "the vast majority of Rohingya refugees experienced or directly witnessed extreme violence and the destruction of their homes," and the refugees "identified the Burmese military as a perpetrator in most cases." It also stated "that the recent violence in northern Rakhine State was extreme, large-scale, widespread, and seemingly geared toward both terrorizing the population and driving out the Rohingya residents," and, "the scope and scale of the military's operations indicate they were well-planned and coordinated." The hope for stronger action from the State Department faded.[57 and 58]

Vice President Pence was highly critical of Aung San Suu Kyi and the NLD government. In a conversation with her on the sidelines of the East Asia Summit in November 2018, he slammed the military for its persecution of the Rohingya and wanted to hear from her that those responsible would be held accountable. He told her in front of the press, "The violence and persecution by military and vigilantes that resulted in driving 700,000 Rohingya to Bangladesh is without excuse. I am anxious to hear the progress that you are making of holding those accountable who are responsible for the violence that displaced so many hundreds of thousands and created such suffering, including the loss of life." The Lady snapped back with, "Of course people have different points of view but the point is that you should exchange these views and try to understand each other better. In a way we can say that we understand our country better than any other country does and I'm sure you will say the same of yours, that you understand your country better than anybody else."[59]

In private, Pence pushed for the release of *Reuters* journalists Wa Lone and Kyaw Soe Oo. A few weeks prior, the reporters were convicted of violating the 1923 Official Secrets Act and sentenced to seven years in prison. In December 2018, *Time* magazine chose "The Guardians and the War on Truth," a group of journalists who have been targeted for their work, as Person of the Year. One cover featured the wives of Wa Lone and Kyaw Soe Oo, holding their photos.[60] Pence stated, "In America, we believe in our democratic institutions and ideals, including a free and independent press." David Nakamura from the *Washington Post* asked for my comments on the meeting, which came around the time Trump called the press the "enemy of the people." I was quoted as saying, "It's hypocritical. What happened to the *Reuters* journalists is terrible. Jim Acosta is not in jail—is that where the difference is? If I were the Myanmar government or Aung San Suu Kyi, I would throw it back in Pence's face."[61] One of my former coworkers emailed me, saying, "Was that sarcasm I hear in your quote in the *Washington Post* article?" Sarcasm certainly, frustration definitely. Wa Lone and Kyaw Soe Oo were freed in a general amnesty in May 2019 after more than five hundred days in prison.

A Pariah Once More

International courts got involved—the same courts the US sanctioned in September 2020[62]—on remedying the Rohingya crisis. In September 2018, the International Criminal Court (ICC) ruled that it could prosecute Myanmar for alleged crimes against humanity against the Rohingya. Myanmar is not a signatory to the ICC, but the court argued that the institution could still take action because even though the initial violence took place in Myanmar, the crime would not have been completed until the refugees entered Bangladesh, which is a party to the Rome Statute that governs the court. The ICC could go after Myanmar for crimes of mass deportation.[63]

In November 2019, the Gambia submitted a forty-six-page application to the UN's International Court of Justice (ICJ), alleging that Myanmar murdered, raped, and destroyed Rohingya communities. The Gambia operated under an ICJ rule allowing member states to bring actions against other member states over disputes alleging breaches of international law. For the Gambia, they alleged Myanmar violated the 1948 convention on the prevention and punishment of the crime of genocide. During the proceedings, Aung San Suu Kyi travelled to The Hague to defend Myanmar, a move that shocked the international community but inspired the Myanmar people, who swelled with pride that Mother Suu was defending them. It was a great political move and played incredibly well at the local level but not at the global one. Hours before the ICJ ruling in January 2020, Aung San Suu Kyi published an op-ed in the *Financial Times*, once again urging the court to allow Myanmar to handle this domestically and saying that the Gambia's case against Myanmar was "precariously dependent on statements by refugees in camps in Bangladesh" who "may have provided inaccurate or exaggerated information" and that the court lacked "substantiated facts."[64]

Despite Myanmar's full-court, public relations press, the ICJ issued their ruling on January 23, 2020. It instituted four provisional measures compelling

Myanmar (1) to prevent the killing, the causing of serious bodily or mental harm, the deliberate infliction of abuses and limitations on quality of life, or measures to prevent births among the Rohingya population; (2) to prevent security forces from committing crimes against humanity or genocide; (3) to prevent the destruction and ensure the preservation of evidence related to allegations; and (4) to submit a report to the court within four months and every six months thereafter until the ICJ rendered its final decision on the case.[65] Myanmar issued its first report in May 2020; however, the contents of it will remain confidential unless the court deems they should be publicly available.[66]

The international court systems weren't done with Myanmar yet. In November 2019, the Burmese Rohingya Organization UK filed a petition with the federal appeals court in Argentina to open an investigation into the role of Myanmar's civilian and military leaders in committing genocide and crimes against humanity against the Rohingya. Under the principle of universal jurisdiction, such crimes can be investigated anywhere in the world regardless of where they were committed, a key factor the UNFFM highlighted and hoped some government would do. The Argentine court could pursue a broader set of charges than the ICC and the ICJ; in June 2020, the court in Buenos Aires overturned a previous decision not to pursue a case against State Counsellor Aung San Suu Kyi and senior officers in the Myanmar military, meaning they were open for prosecution.[67]

The Platform for Disinformation

Despite US sanctions and court cases, one aspect the international community collectively wanted to resolve on the Rohingya issue was the spread of misinformation and racist rhetoric on Facebook. Facebook was the de facto internet for Myanmar; it was used as a messenger app, a market, a browser, and a way to share stories, gossip, and updates.

The trouble began in 2014 when the telecommunications companies moved in and brought the country online. SIM card prices dropped and brought the internet to the masses. Given its popularity, most phones came with Facebook preloaded. For many, whatever was on the internet had to be true. This country didn't have the tools to discern which information was false or real, and there was no clearinghouse for fact-based content or flags to denote propaganda or hate speech. As we would discover, this issue was not limited to Myanmar, but the country was the canary in the coal mine.

The first sign of trouble occurred in June 2014 after the Buddhist nationalist monk, U Wirathu, circulated a report on his Facebook page of an alleged rape of a Buddhist woman by a Muslim tea shop owner, calling for a harsh government response to "jihadist Muslims." The city of Mandalay erupted in violence, leaving two people dead and more than a dozen injured. The government tried to contact

Facebook to remove the posts, but they couldn't reach anyone. President Thein Sein called for a curfew and temporarily blocked access to Facebook in Mandalay. Five people, including a woman who admitted she had been paid to make the false rape claim, were eventually sentenced to twenty-one years in prison for their roles in starting the riots.[68 and 69]

Reporter Tim McLaughlin detailed Facebook's role in Myanmar for *Wired*, showing the missed opportunities and the general negligence by the tech giant. Facebook had been warned repeatedly by NGOs and local tech start-ups of the troubling things they were seeing, but the company's response was haphazard and slow. Following the Mandalay troubles, representatives from Google and Facebook, Myanmar government officials, and the Asia Foundation, a nonprofit international development organization, convened a panel discussion on the recent violence and allowed Facebook a chance to share its plans to combat hate speech. Facebook pledged to speed up the translation of the sites' user guidelines and code of conduct into Burmese and would look to users to flag offensive posts. This meant a reliance on both native speakers (Facebook had one Burmese-language speaker who was based in . . . Dublin) and volunteers to find disturbing posts in a sea of social media content. The Burmese-language community standards were launched fourteen months after the discussion.[70]

In 2015, Facebook partnered with local tech civil society groups to create digital stickers on the messenger platform to counter hate speech and promote online inclusion. The company also worked on an initiative to "empower people in Myanmar to share positive messages online" and offer local education on fake news. Most of the groups found the efforts "toothless."[71]

In April 2018, Mark Zuckerberg appeared in front of Congress and, among other topics, discussed the role of Facebook in Myanmar. Senator Patrick Leahy (D-VT), referring to the UNFFM investigation blaming Facebook for the Rohingya's ills, said, "You know, six months ago, I asked your general counsel about Facebook's role as a breeding ground for hate speech against Rohingya refugees. . . . You say you use A.I. to find this. . . . It calls for the death of a Muslim journalist. Now, that threat went straight through your detection systems, it spread very quickly, and then it took attempt after attempt after attempt, and the involvement of civil society groups, to get you to remove it. Why couldn't it be removed within 24 hours?" Zuckerberg responded, saying that Facebook was hiring dozens of Burmese-language content reviewers, working with civil society to identify those responsible for stirring violence and hateful rhetoric, and establishing a team to make product changes in Myanmar and other countries in similar situations to prevent this from happening.[72] For critics, Facebook still failed to take full responsibility and continued to be too slow.

Four months after the hearing, *Reuters* looked into the impact of the company's proposed changes. The site was still filled with disturbing posts that had been up for days. Some called the Rohingya and other Muslims groups awful things and called for them to be "exterminated." Facebook used tools to monitor hate speech and outsourced monitoring to Accenture, who then hired Burmese speakers outside of the country, but it wasn't working. *Reuters* highlighted the difficulties of flagging offensive posts by having so few Burmese-language speakers, which was further compounded by automated systems that could not reliably interpret Burmese script. For example, one post said, "Kill all the kalars that you see in Myanmar; none of them should be left alive."[73] Facebook's translation: "I shouldn't have a rainbow in Myanmar."[74]

Facebook did take some important steps. In February 2018, the platform banned U Wirathu. In late August, hours after UN investigators released their FFM report, Facebook removed Myanmar's senior-most military officials, including Min Aung Hlaing and other military or Buddhist nationalist-associated organizations. Facebook also hired BSR, a global nonprofit organization, to undertake a human rights impact assessment of the company's presence in Myanmar and come up with an action plan and recommendations to mitigate Facebook's role in promoting violence and ways to prevent it.[75 and 76]

But Facebook's past involvement in spreading hate-filled messages and disinformation would not be forgotten. The Gambia not only went after Myanmar, but it targeted Facebook too. In June 2020, the Gambia filed a request in the US to order Facebook to divulge information, including "all documents and communications produced, drafted, or published" from accounts linked to the military that were shut down and private communications that may be relevant to their case against Myanmar. Two months later, Facebook huffed at the request as being too broad—that it violated the Stored Communications Act and then asked for "special unbounded access" to private accounts.[77]

Facebook faced congressional hearings, mentions in global reports, and criticism from NGOs for its role in spreading disinformation and contributing to the violence targeting the Rohingya. Yet, the hard work wasn't done and soon, even the West would be inundated with misinformation that would lead to violence and conspiracy theories becoming mainstream. It seems no lessons were learned.

A Preventable Genocide?

The 2017 violence rekindled the debate on the 2016 sanctions-lifting. Many felt that if sanctions hadn't been lifted, Min Aung Hlaing would have ordered his troops to spare the Rohingya because he feared being sanctioned. I find this argument completely ridiculous.

Sanctions can be effective, but they are limited in what they can do, especially in a case like this. Sanctions freeze bank accounts and cut targets off from the international financial system, but most of the military's senior leadership didn't hold accounts, and if they did, the countries that held them weren't about to freeze them or make them known to US authorities. Even going after MEC and UMEHL wouldn't make much difference financially to the military. Most of the industries MEC and UMEHL were in didn't link up to international markets or hold much importance for Western consumers; for example, jade mining made tons of money for the military, but most of the consumers were from China. It was highly unlikely that the PRC would sanction Myanmar jade.

Could the US compel change? The system of self-funding through the MEC and UMEHL model is an outlier today, but not too long ago, Thailand, Indonesia, Vietnam, and China had similar models. Could we not target those streams through different policy maneuvers? How could we convince Myanmar to pursue similar methods to unwind these conglomerates as it had occurred in those countries?

Psychologically, sanctions would have an impact, but it would wear off quickly. The military had been considered pariahs and had been sanctioned for so long that it would be easy to go back to their old ways. One possible leverage point was if SDNs wanted their children and grandchildren to travel and study in the US. However, they made do with sending their kids to Singapore, Japan, or elsewhere. Myanmar always had a way to get by and they had proved it time and time again.

Perversely, at the time, the SDN designation could have had a morale-boosting effect. Rallies filled Yangon streets, cheering on the military and jeering UN and US officials for their condemnatory statements. The military's actions were popular, including among some prodemocracy activists, former political prisoners, and people who had been trained in human rights and civil society work. To be sanctioned for acting against the Rohingya was almost a badge of honor. After the February 2021 coup, however, most of Myanmar celebrates the military being sanctioned, but it is not because of their treatment of the Rohingya.

There are also accusations that the US didn't see the genocide coming. But what kind of tools can one use to prevent the eradication of an entire people?

There were dozens of acronymic interagency meetings—IPCs, PCCs, DCs—during the Clinton, Bush, Obama, Trump, and now Biden years. Our officials in the field were busy raising the issue as well. In 2012, representatives from the US, Australia, and the UK traveled to Rakhine State and came away with the impression that it was a ticking time bomb. Derek, who joined those trips and visited Rakhine ten times during his tenure as ambassador, raised the Rohingya issue and shared his observations gleaned from his trips in countless meetings with Thein Sein and other senior Myanmar officials. He found it was not a core issue for most, including ASEAN, an organization that was often uncomfortable around coordinated initiatives against any one country.[78]

Ambassador Marciel found the same reception. Like Derek, he raised the issue with Thein Sein and his key advisor, Soe Thane. President Obama raised it in his meetings. Deputy Secretary of State Tony Blinken raised it. Ben Rhodes felt he talked about Rakhine State ad nauseam with the Myanmar government. Samantha Power, Mike Posner, and Tom Malinowski raised the issue. Ben knew they all succeeded in making enough noise so Myanmar knew it was of importance to the US.[79 and 80]

As Aung San Suu Kyi also got the full-court press, she finally said it should be left to Myanmar to figure this out and she didn't want to be told what to do. Myanmar officials were inundated with advice and armchair foreign policymaking from afar; everybody knew what the problem was, but no one in the country did anything to fix it.

In April 2012, the White House stood up the Atrocities Prevention Board (APB), an interagency committee consisting of officials from the NSC; the Departments of State, Defense, Justice, and the Treasury; USAID; and the US intelligence community. The board was originally chaired by Samantha Power and later her successor at the NSC, Steve Pomper, and it met to assess the long-term risks of atrocities around the world.

Two months after its launch, the Rohingya were attacked, and human rights groups started coming in to see what the APB could do. This was the exact situation that the APB was set up for. For Power and Pomper, the APB was created to reject the thinking that any issue was too big or too complicated for the US to tackle. The board held interagency meetings—including beaming in Derek via video conference from Yangon—and discussed how to make policy and engage effectively. They sought ways to organize the diplomatic community, to get information on what was happening, to ensure accountability, and to formulate an appropriate foreign policy and humanitarian assistance tool kit. Though progress seemed to be taking place on paper, the APB found that bureaucratic victories don't translate into real-world victories.[81]

There was growing fatigue from work on Libya and Syria, and several senior officials were leaving government at the end of Obama's first term. Myanmar mattered and got attention, but it wasn't a top priority, and there were competing pursuits. One thing the APB knew it had to confront was that human ugliness was deep on this issue, and there was no political champion, like a Rohingya Aung San Suu Kyi, to help change local minds. There had to be political will on the Myanmar side to make things happen. That never came to fruition.[82 and 83]

There were other things to be considered, like the R2P that was nearly invoked during Cyclone Nargis, but it was unlikely that would get the votes in the UN necessary to go ahead.

Most of the attention of what went wrong was centered on one woman: Aung San Suu Kyi. Without her, Myanmar probably wouldn't have sustained the type of attention it had. Aung San Suu Kyi was critical to US policy, and everyone took their cues from her, even if they disagreed with her. She was an overwhelming power and mesmerized policymakers through the years who saw her as an otherworldly presence. But she was also a useful partner to those who wanted to change policy; she could help drive the middle, and if she wanted something, it would be done.

These views on Aung San Suu Kyi got complicated when she was in power. Her silence on the Rohingya crisis and her defense of the military's actions were disturbing. Also of concern were the growing number of political prisoners and the arrests of activists and journalists, including Wa Lone and Kyaw Soe Oo, who were convicted under the same laws that had put her and her colleagues behind bars. Many of the NGOs that had supported her (and made money off of her cause) quickly fled. In turn, they lost her ear to influence, and she closed herself off from their advice. I would note she is quite stubborn, so she probably would not have listened to their advice anyway. Once the darling of the West, she was now a villain. Celebrities like Bono and Bob Geldof condemned her actions. Bono had once been her number one fan. I attended a U2 concert in 2009, and when they played the song "Walk On," Bono announced that it was dedicated to Aung San Suu Kyi and urged everyone to put on their Lady masks, available for download and printing on the U2 website. Her face was literally everywhere. There were calls for the Nobel rules to be changed so that her prize could be withdrawn. Oxford University tore down her portrait.

Senator McConnell was very clear that he still supported and admired her. She decided to be a part of the government and took responsibility—or as much responsibility as she could to get under this "bizarre constitution which is laughable by any Western standards"—to do the tough stuff. Aung San Suu Kyi had been pragmatically trying to move in a direction toward genuine representative democracy that would not include the military in government, and she knew she couldn't get to where she wanted to go without that relationship. McConnell was disappointed that those who claimed to support her for all those years failed to recognize those challenges, expecting more of her than she, or anyone in that country, could ever achieve.[84]

Secretary Clinton recognized the issue with balancing the country's most powerful institution and trying to push through more difficult reforms. For the most part, Aung San Suu Kyi was on the outside, pulling all the levers she could.

She may have a powerful voice, but it may not be as powerful where it counts as we think.[85]

On the Rohingya issue, she should get some credit for taking early steps, like calling for the Annan commission and discussions on the path to citizenship. She clearly understood that it was a major issue, but she was also surrounded by people, including the military, who did not like the Rohingya. Questions remain: Did she believe the military's account of their response? Was she in a position to stand up to them? Or did she truly not care? I give her the benefit of the doubt that she truly did not see the depth of the situation, blinded by being on the constant defensive. It's also clear now that she could not stand up to the military.

Aung San Suu Kyi is an exceptional human being with talent, intelligence, and drive, but she was dealt a weak hand and had little experience in governing. To attribute every shortcoming in the country to her is ridiculous. Some of the blame can be laid on the rest of us. Maybe none of us knew her at all or only heard what we wanted to hear from a caged bird. We were too busy telling the story of a woman who couldn't speak for herself for twenty-five years. Once she could, we didn't like what we heard.

In the end, we all failed the Rohingya.

Ultimately, it is and will be up to the Myanmar government and people to create the conditions necessary to build safe, tolerant communities for all ethnicities, whenever that time will be once the military passes from the political scene. The international community must help provide tools, but it can't do it for them.

BEYOND RANGOON

They began to burn the poets
When the smoke of burned books could
No longer choke the lungs heavy with dissent.

—Ko Khet Thi

I came late to Rangoon
Everything was already there:
a city of blood,
dreams and gold . . .

—Pablo Neruda

Each time I travel to Myanmar, I assume it's my last trip. Somewhere in the back of my mind, I'm either waiting for the other shoe to drop from the military or for something in my life that will change significantly so that Myanmar is no longer a part of it. In February 2021, it would turn out to be the former.

Once the NLD secured another landslide win in the 2020 election, the party began to discuss constitutional reform to chip away at the military's hold on political power. The military started claiming the results were illegitimate and needed to be investigated. The complaints sounded eerily similar to what was being tossed around in the US after the November 2020 election. In late January 2021, the military claimed it had found eight million cases of election fraud.[1]

In the early hours of February 1, 2021, allegedly at an astrologically auspicious time, the Tatmadaw rounded up key figures in the civilian government, including Aung San Suu Kyi and President Win Myint, and placed them under house arrest or in jail. Commander in Chief Min Aung Hlaing sacked the president and got the military-appointed vice president to declare a state of emergency. The military was back in control of the government, less than ten years since the opening. Soon, union- and regional-level ministers, well-known political activists, poets, protestors, and average citizens were arrested, filling Myanmar's prisons with thousands of political prisoners as the COVID-19 pandemic started to burn through the country. Ministry positions were filled, some with people who had previously been considered as progressive technocrats, critical interlocutors, honest brokers, and friends. It was a punch in the gut.

The junta murdered hundreds by early July 2021.[2] The army shut off the internet, shot protestors, strafed ethnic areas with aerial assaults, and beat and tortured those arrested to death. It opened fire on urban streets, and wanton violence and stray bullets killed small children and innocent bystanders. Hundreds of thousands of protestors flooded the streets, becoming known as the Civil Disobedience Movement (CDM). A general strike was called, and people walked off their jobs, bringing the economy to a standstill. The banking system and the broader economy teetered on a cliff's edge, and health and public medical services were strained, if not shut down altogether in many areas, exacerbating the impact of the pandemic. Banks were short on cash, and lines to withdraw money stretched for blocks; the junta threatened to nationalize the banks if they didn't get their affairs in order.

Similar to 1988, democratic revolutionaries also fled to the border. Since the coup, new armed resistance groups formed and the peace process was thrown in disarray. Beauty queens, models, and average citizens ran to the Thailand-Myanmar border and began to train to fight the military, creating the People's Defense Force. On April 16, elected parliamentarians, activists, and ethnic representatives formed the government-in-exile, the National Unity Government (NUG). In what was a small silver lining in all this, the NUG took an incredible step of issuing a statement that recognized the Rohingya, promised to repeal the 1982 Citizenship Law, sought justice for the military's crimes and human rights abuses, and hoped to find a way to safely repatriate refugees.[3]

It is hard to express just how bad the situation in Myanmar is. On the violence alone, my social media feeds were full of dead bodies, weeping families, and horrifying images. The junta starved citizens of oxygen and denied proper medical care to treat COVID-19. Death by any means.

My friends and colleagues swapped information to confirm who was safe and who wasn't and to serve as a listening board for our Myanmar friends inside and out of the country to hear their anguish, fears, and hope. The economy is a wreck, and the country is quickly sprinting toward becoming a failed state. The complexities and challenges are well beyond the capabilities for Min Aung Hlaing to control. A burning animosity that had been building toward the military since

1962 is now an uncontrollable inferno. Building on the legacy of his military predecessors, Min Aung Hlaing will be Myanmar's ruin.

It seems clear that Min Aung Hlaing did not understand the full scope of the consequences of his actions, how visceral the hate for the military was, or how much the country wanted to move beyond the patronage system and cycles of poverty. In the early days of the coup, there may have been time for a face-saving move to put the military back in the barracks, but it's too late now. Min Aung Hlaing was seemingly clueless about how fragile Myanmar's economic situation was but also how much the country had changed in the decade since the SPDC was in control. Myanmar's economy was not strong or stable enough to maintain such shocks as its neighbor, Thailand, had successfully been doing throughout its many coups. Min Aung Hlaing also did not calculate the massive response from the country's citizens, particularly its tech-savvy and devastatingly creative Generation Z cohort, with protests reaching every corner of Myanmar.

The CDM has called on the international community to intervene and use R2P. The UN has issued some harsh statements, but the likelihood of the UN invoking R2P is overwhelmingly slim, and any binding punitive actions within the Human Rights Council or UN Security Council are unlikely to happen with Russia—which has upped its military sales and outreach after the coup—and the PRC as voting members.

ASEAN action has been a mixed bag. ASEAN rightfully earned plaudits for orchestrating a meeting in late April 2021 that resulted in a five-point consensus, which included an immediate cessation of violence, dialogue to finding a peaceful solution, the allowance of an ASEAN special envoy to facilitate this dialogue with all stakeholders, safe passage of humanitarian aid, and a visit by the special envoy to the country.[4] However, there was no mention of political prisoners or recognition of the 2020 election winners. The group also proposed watering down a UN General Assembly draft resolution on Myanmar, including removing a call for an arms embargo on the country.[5] By June 2021 (and the time of this writing), the junta had made no progress on the consensus, ASEAN had not selected an envoy, and a frustrated ASEAN turned to the PRC to help urge Myanmar to cooperate.[6]

The Myanmar coup was the first major foreign policy crisis of Biden's presidency, and the administration wasted no time in reacting. Key figures present at the opening—Kurt Campbell, Jake Sullivan—were now there at the close.

Speaking from Washington, DC, less than a month after a physical attack on American democracy, President Biden issued a press release on the Myanmar situation stating, "In a democracy, force should never seek to overrule the will of the people or attempt to erase the outcome of a credible election."[7] Ten days after the coup, President Biden issued Executive Order 14014, setting a framework for

US sanctions. In the ensuing months, the US targeted members of the military and coup government and rebuilt the SDN List that had dwindled down to only narcotics traffickers and friends of North Korea. USAID and other US agencies immediately halted any direct government assistance and programs, and an interagency committee was established to review assistance and engagements to ensure no US government funds supported the coup government or military.[8]

Months later, it seems like US-Myanmar relations are where they were when I first started working on the issue in 2008. The US government was back to issuing calls for the unconditional release of Aung San Suu Kyi and thousands of political prisoners, demanding the military recognize the election results from a flawed but credible election, and asking the coup government to respect human rights. Some of the names and the years were different—2020 instead of 1990. It made me wonder: Will we be in the same place in 2040 as we were in 2010? Asking for the release of thousands of political prisoners? Providing lists of names to a regime? Working with ailing and aging prodemocracy activists who just want the freedom to live their lives? Demanding for the parliamentarians elected in 2020 to finally take their seats? It is a depressing thought.

Though things seem quite bleak, we've been here before, meaning we should have decades of lessons learned and ways to build off the smallest of silver linings to create an even stronger foundation for the people of Myanmar and their future. There's only so much the US can control and influence at the moment, but there are ways that government action and assistance can be retooled and reconfigured to better match today's situation and prepare for when it's time for the people to take back power.

I will remind you that these views are solely my own. They do not represent US government views or policies. Just mine.

Most of the work should focus on breaking down existential issues to their most basic building blocks, like settling on the definitions of what "democracy" and "equity" mean for Myanmar. Since the opening in 2011, Myanmar has struggled with what democracy means for the country and how it should manifest itself. Foreign governments, donors, multilateral institutions, and NGOs have deployed democracy promotion programs since 1988 to varying degrees of success. One key aspect for long-term success is ensuring programs are inclusive of diverse political voices and not funded disparately, which will help create a shared vision within Myanmar with all stakeholders. Government assistance and programming agents must continuously evaluate their role, educate themselves on the history, stakeholders, and grievances, and aim for objectivity to ensure they are playing the most appropriate and effective role for those they seek to help. We need to think outside the box of experiences in other countries and contour our programs to the unique set of circumstances there and everywhere. Does it mean the right to vote and have democratically elected officials take office? A disciplined democracy with a mix of military and civilian representatives? A representative government that includes all ethnicities and religions? Is it whatever the military government wasn't? A civilian-led, majority Buddhist Burman government? What does universal human rights mean? Does it include all ethnicities, including the Rohingya? This should be the first set of questions donors, governments, and NGOs ask.

There already seems to be movement on the Myanmar side in this direction; the CDM and the country's dissidents are going beyond seeing the NLD as the sole beacon for democracy, and the NUG seems to have built a bigger tent for political participation—something past political movements did not do, including U Nu and Aung San Suu Kyi—allowing for discussion of ethnic representation, a solution to Rohingya citizenship and safe repatriation, and an addressing of the peace process. Convening a productive dialogue at some point will have to include the military and their outsized role in the country's political, economic, and social fabric.

Along the same lines, a nationwide discourse on the meaning of equity is critical not only to Myanmar's democratic development but is also one that has compelling significance for the peace process. What does equity mean for the diverse set of actors in Myanmar that includes but goes beyond the NLD, military, and EAOs? Is it power-sharing, access to natural resource wealth, individual freedoms? Myanmar must determine, through comprehensive outreach to communities, and transparent and clear discourse, what this concept of equity is and means for the whole of Myanmar. There will be disagreements, which traditionally have contributed to a zero-sum mentality and lack of compromise, but this is necessary to both the peace process and the chipping away of the fractious nature of politics. For international governments and donors, assistance, both through aid dollars and engagement through dialogue and meetings, should focus on this question of equity and get to the details of what this means for Myanmar. Capacity-building on negotiations, consensus, and compromise is critical to get beyond the typical zero-sum mentality and will be paramount for future political discourse and nation-building once—and hopefully it will be soon—Commander in Chief Min Aung Hlaing sees the light and takes his soldiers back to the barracks.

Also seminal to Myanmar's future is what leadership looks like in Myanmar, particularly once Aung San Suu Kyi inevitably passes from the scene. The top-down, hierarchical way of operating is not just military practice but also strong in the NLD and other political parties as well, leaving little room for building a deep bench for upcoming leaders and capable technocrats. With the advent of the NUG, Myanmar has a chance to get beyond personality politics and patron-client relationships and start discussing the structural side of creating leaders, organizing political parties, and building institutions that can outlive icons. This is a critical exercise too for Myanmar's most marginalized communities that need to find ways to effectively organize and engender positive changes.

Finally, there is the question of what to do with the military. This is a question best answered by the people who have suffered the most from their rule. The international community has to provide the means and resources to ensure an objective, safe, and comprehensive solution. That also includes a discussion on the international community's behalf about military-to-military engagement and how to professionalize the institution.

This will be one of the most challenging aspects and will require a comprehensive truth and reconciliation component, which defines the Tatmadaw's role and finds ways to ensure they stay in the barracks. Thankfully, Myanmar does not have to create this process from scratch as there are global examples and lessons learned, both good and bad, including from South Africa, Chile, Germany, Indonesia, Iraq, and several others.

To influence an entity, person, or institution, one has to know what it values, fears, and desires. Some of that is pretty clear with the Tatmadaw—protecting the country's sovereignty from outside actors, bringing the EAOs to heel, and keeping the country from disintegrating. Over decades in power, that mission has been warped so that the military is essentially creating the circumstances for those things to occur rather than protecting the country from them. I am not advocating for establishing ties with the military and Min Aung Hlaing now, especially while they are killing people and refuting any commitments it's agreed to with ASEAN. But when we are at a place where there is an opportunity to have a discussion, likely when Min Aung Hlaing is no longer on the scene, military-to-military ties need not be a third rail. We cannot ignore and isolate the country's most outsized and powerful institution and hope that it goes along with what we want.

When the time is right, there's a range of options that can be offered that should be seen as a long-term investment in promoting and protecting human rights and Myanmar's most vulnerable communities who are caught in the crossfire of conflict. Deciding to work with the military or other security forces, like the police or even customs officials, doesn't go from nothing to making them better killers. There is a universe of options that can primarily focus on promoting human rights before we even talk about joint exercises and weapons sales. Being more proactive about demonstrating why it's important to be under civilian control and demonstrating how it's done is critical. But it also doesn't help if the government that controls it is incompetent; this was the case when Ne Win took control in 1958. The U Nu government was in a stalemate and failed to give Ne Win and the military direction and support on the anti-government and EAO conflicts; frustrated with the government's inability to do much of anything (among several reasons), he took control. Working with the civilian government on how to best manage a military, including on unsexy but important stuff like budgets and pension reform, would be crucial. Even working with the military on rewriting their field manuals would perhaps chip away at the seventy-plus years of the "four cuts" strategy, borne out of a legacy of guerrilla warfare and counterinsurgency campaigns, and provide more on soldier codes of conduct, peace negotiations, security, and humanitarian assistance. The military is not a monolith. For many soldiers, this is the only option for upward mobility in society, one of the few options for a career with skills-building and a steady income. It's a chance to protect your country and build something. Not all members of the Tatmadaw are hardened killers, and it would behoove policymakers and human rights organizations that are interested in making a significant impact through the country's most powerful institution to commit to finding avenues to reach changemakers and change mindsets. We've worked with every group in the country except the military. That must change.

In the meantime, there are options to compel this military with things they really fear. Now that the US no longer sanctions ICC judges, we are in a better position to support the Gambia's case against the military on the Rohingya violence or begin a new process related to the coup. The US and partners can also support no-fly zones, primarily to protect ethnic areas from being strafed by the country's MiGs. Or we could rattle the saber a bit; perhaps a float-by by the Seventh Fleet or a visit by Sylvester "Rambo" Stallone to the border. Let's get creative.

In the meantime, we need to look to our past engagement during the country's darkest times to see what worked for the people and helped it open after 2011.

I asked each interviewee for this book what the US does well in terms of foreign policy and assistance programs. At the macro-level, US programs have a significant impact on long-term issues. For example, there are still former political prisoners, not just from Myanmar, who thank the US for helping them, for standing up for their freedom, and for ensuring they were never forgotten.

Another example is the way the US is able to marshal resources and engage with allies and partners to tackle difficult issues head-on, especially on public health pre-2020. President George W. Bush launched the President's Emergency Plan for AIDS Relief (PEPFAR), which has saved millions of lives worldwide by treating and preventing the spread of HIV/AIDS, as well as malaria and tuberculosis. Myanmar has been a lucky recipient of PEPFAR engagement, and there's been a significant drop in cases in the past five years in the three diseases—a great achievement. COVID-19 and pandemic preparedness is a worthy cause and should be beyond who is in power. Myanmar is suffering greatly from lack of health care; this is one area where the US and its partners can convene good work.

What several interviewees also told me was that the US still has space and operates where the PRC doesn't; the US actively works with civil society, builds capacity, provides space for political actors, and works on programs, including agriculture, education, water, and health, at the most local levels. We can still work with the people of Myanmar, though it's decidedly harder, but these programs can be a lifeline to a stable livelihood and basic income in the midst of an economic and political crisis.

It was some of our smaller ticket projects and programs that had the most impact. The US could shell out billions of dollars on initiatives, but our exchange and leadership-building programs cost very little and have lasting impact. The Young Southeast Asian Leaders Initiative (YSEALI), a program launched during the Obama administration and continued under the Trump and Biden administrations, builds leadership capabilities of youth in the Southeast Asia region and promotes cross-border cooperation to solve regional and global challenges. Thousands of young alumni from across Southeast Asia, including Myanmar, have participated in the program and have traveled to the US, nurturing connections and fostering an appreciation for the US that is worth its weight in gold. Plus, these alumni are making a real difference; participants have engaged in efforts to address climate change, raise awareness of COVID-19, eliminate plastic waste, launch agribusinesses, and have other pivotal impacts in their communities and beyond.

The American Center in Yangon is another highlight. This center was an outlet for activists and average Myanmar citizens who wanted a place to read, study, and debate in peace during the worst of the junta times. At the American Center, visitors had access to computers, books, English lessons, movies, and other resources. It was invaluable during military rule, and it is still an important resource for Myanmar students, activists, and for folks who just want to check their email. This place will be even more important as the days get darker.

For the development community, donors certainly had their hands full in determining which priorities to tackle first—poverty, malnutrition, communicable and noncommunicable diseases, education, and mental health—all while ensuring money doesn't get into the hands of the military. While donors' hearts are often in the right place, the grant process and implementation often are not. The Request for Proposal (RFP) process is onerous, costs organizations tons of money, requires extremely strict auditing and finance procedures (understandable given the organization will spend taxpayer money), and the decision-making process takes an inordinate amount of time, rendering the needs and means to address urgent issues unmet. The process effectively rules out small NGOs and other organizations that may have a better sense of what is needed on the ground and tilts in favor to those that can write grants really well and have deep pockets to finance the grant-writing process. Given the coup, small NGOs and local organizations may be the only option to implement important programs, but they certainly don't have the resources to participate in the RFP process.

RFPs usually result in a race to the bottom. Donors typically award the lowest dollar number bid, meaning you often get what you pay for. Donors must reform the request process, both by maintaining the due diligence process to be able to effectively account for funds spent and the effectiveness of the program implementation and by allowing for new players to be able to compete.

Policymakers must also be flexible, valuing expertise and experience and looking beyond a feel-good project. Perhaps the reason Myanmar policy was able to evolve the way it did and register successes in 2011 and 2012 was that the right people were in place on all sides at the right time. While it partly relied on luck and serendipity, it also reflected the strategy of valuing expertise and experience and encouraging collaboration and not competition.

For sanctions policy, a program must have a defined end point and steps toward a delisting or program wind-down that are clear, achievable, and flexible enough to take into account change, particularly if a policy was put in place decades earlier. The Myanmar of 1988 was not the same as the Myanmar of 2012 or 2016. Who knows what Myanmar will be in a few years? The whole purpose of sanctions is to change and deter behavior. A government's success metric should be that their policy tool kit was deployed so successfully, sanctions are no longer needed.

For human rights groups, please give credit where credit is due, acknowledge and encourage the progress that happens, and create plausible pathways to achieve human rights protections. I've had so many conversations with government officials, conglomerates, and even small businesses that are looking to implement transformative measures but that feel they will be criticized if they don't go far enough. If they enact something and it's not done perfectly, they get criticized and piled on for other things. I'm not asking to accept the mediocre; I'm asking for a recognition on where folks are trying, an acceptance of an achievable phased approach, and a provision of technical assistance or resources when needed. This will be critical when we see the days where the military rolls back its control, or is forced to.

My advice to businesses has changed dramatically since I first drafted this book. For those that choose to stay in the country, protect your workers. Offer a safe place, an income, and access to resources, including mental health services. Myanmar's economy for its citizens shouldn't go off a cliff and leave the average person destitute, and most businesses that are there are the lifeline to thousands of families. Businesses may be in a position to maintain a level of professional capacity and technical expertise, preparing for a democratic future that will hopefully return soon. Though there is likely pressure from the military to kiss the ring or adhere to laws that will compromise companies' (particularly US companies') ability to adhere to international laws and standards, businesses must find space to maintain good corporate governance and ensure their businesses, of course, do not flout international laws and sanctions programs.

Ultimately, the best way the US government can lead in Myanmar is to be an example of democracy. We were indoctrinated with the idea of John Winthrop's evangelical concept of America: "For we must consider that we shall be as a city upon a hill. The eyes of all people are upon us." To do that, we must embrace and protect the democratic process, hold credible elections and recognize the results, hold our leaders accountable, rally the support and cooperation of our partners and allies, face and address hard truths on race and inequality, ensure our foreign policy and national security policies incorporate these issues, hire staff that support such policies and reflect the true diversity of America, and prize, above all, e pluribus unum: out of many one.

The US has been severely tested on these merits and should hardly receive a passing grade. At the time of this writing, a commission to investigate the events of January 6 that were a direct threat to our democracy have been blocked by Senate Republicans. Senator Mitch McConnell, who has sought to provide Aung San Suu Kyi with every bit of leverage to preserve and solidify democratic gains, opposed the bill to create a commission into the insurrection.[9] It should not go unnoticed that Myanmar's prodemocracy champion is now on trial because the military saw her government as a threat to their power and attempted to label the 2020 election as flawed and fraudulent. It is not a big stretch to assess that Min Aung Hlaing saw what was happening in the US and was being championed by the country's forty-fifth president and his supporters. How could he not get away with the same?

Further adding the growing list of disturbing anti-democratic sentiments emerging from former US government officials, Michael Flynn, the former national security advisor to Donald Trump, during a May 2021 QAnon conference responded to a question from an audience participant who asked why something like what happened in Myanmar couldn't happen in the US. Flynn agreed that it should.[10] Flynn denied he made these comments, but the exchange was captured on video. As George Orwell wrote in *1984*, "The party told you to reject the evidence of your eyes and ears. It was their final, most essential command." Flynn told us to reject what we saw on video once he realized how problematic his statements were. What message does all this send to Myanmar? It was unclear which country was headed more quickly toward Orwell's dystopian vision—the US or Myanmar.

Only if we can be the example can we be a good model for Myanmar. We have to be.

* * *

For those of us who have traveled within our own borders or overseas, some places leave a greater impression than others. That has been Myanmar for me. One quote by the late Anthony Bourdain encapsulates my ongoing experience: "Travel isn't always pretty. It isn't always comfortable. Sometimes it hurts, it even breaks your heart. But that's okay. The journey changes you; it should change you. It leaves marks on your memory, on your consciousness, on your heart, and on your body. You take something with you. Hopefully, you leave something good behind."

Myanmar has challenged and enlightened me in ways I never expected. It's broken my heart over and over, but there have been moments and experiences that have had such a positive impact on me and have made me grow in ways I am forever grateful for. The good story of Myanmar is not over yet, and I hope I will one day have another chance to go there and leave something good behind.

NOTES

Preliminary Notes

[1] The name has been changed to protect Ko Thura's identity.

[2] Steinberg, David, *Burma/Myanmar: What Everyone Needs to Know*, Oxford University Press, 2010, p. xx–xxi.

[3] Selth, Andrew, "Burma's Armed Forces: Power Without Glory," Eastbridge, 2001, p. xxix–xxxi.

[4] Selth, Andrew, "More name games in Burma/Myanmar," Lowy Institute, *The Interpreter*, August 10, 2016, https://www.lowyinstitute.org/the-interpreter/more-name-games-burmamyanmar.

Prologue

[1] Kennard, Matt and Claire Provost, "Burma's bizarre capital: a super-sized slice of post-apocalypse suburbia," *The Guardian*, March 19, 2015, https://www.theguardian.com/cities/2015/mar/19/burmas-capital-naypyidaw-post-apocalypse-suburbia-highways-wifi.

[2] Romey, Kristin, "First Dinosaur Tail Found Preserved in Amber," *National Geographic*, December 8, 2016, https://news.nationalgeographic.com/2016/12/feathered-dinosaur-tail-amber-theropod-myanmar-burma-cretaceous/.

[3] "Headhunting Days over for Burma's 'Wild Wa,'" *Reuters*, September 9, 2007, https://www.reuters.com/article/idUSBKK83023.

Chapter 1

[1] Interview with Rena Pederson.

[2] Interview with US government official with knowledge of the First Lady's work on Burma.

[3] Steinberg, David, *Burma/Myanmar: What Everyone Needs to Know*, Oxford University Press, 2010, p. 9

[4] "U.S. to restore full diplomatic ties with Burma," CBS News, January 13, 2012, https://www.cbsnews.com/news/us-to-restore-full-diplomatic-ties-with-burma/.

[5] Pedrosa, Veronica, "Myanmar's 'seat of kings,'" *Al Jazeera*, November 20, 2006, https://web.archive.org/web/20061123141200/http://english.aljazeera.net/NR/exeres/80733C47-7F1C-45EB-BB8E-805DB15BFE67.htm.

[6] Interview with Samantha Carl-Yoder.

[7] Tun Lwin, *Nargis and I: I feel pain, even though I was hit by a flower*, n.p., 2015, chapter 43.

[8] https://www.nasa.gov/topics/earth/features/nargis_floods.html.

[9] Interview with Samantha Carl-Yoder.

[10] Cobra Gold, first held in 1982, is a joint theater security cooperation (JTSC) exercise cosponsored by Thailand and the US and conducted annually in the Kingdom of Thailand. Cobra Gold is one of the largest theater security cooperation exercises in the Asia-Pacific region and includes several exercises on nonlethal activities, such as humanitarian assistance and disaster relief. Globalsecurity.org, "Cobra Gold," https://www.globalsecurity.org/military/ops/cobra-gold.htm.

[11] H. R. 4286—To award a congressional gold medal to Daw Aung San Suu Kyi in recognition of her courageous and unwavering commitment to peace, nonviolence, human rights, and democracy in Burma, 110th Congress, 2007–2008, https://www.congress.gov/bill/110th-congress/house-bill/4286/cosponsors?searchResultViewType=expanded.

[12] Blocking Property and Prohibiting Certain Transactions Related to Burma, Federal Register, May 2, 2008, https://www.federalregister.gov/documents/2008/05/02/08-1215/blocking-property-and-prohibiting-certain-transactions-related-to-burma.

[13] S. Res.554—A resolution expressing the Sense of the Senate on humanitarian assistance to Burma after Cyclone Nargis, 110th Congress, 2007–2008, https://www.congress.gov/bill/110th-congress/senate-resolution/554?s=1&r=75.

[14] Interviews with Wunna Maung Lwin and Soe Thane.

[15] Interview with Toe Naing Mann.

[16] Interview with Toe Naing Mann.

[17] Min Lwin, "Burmese Navy Decimated in Cyclone, *The Irrawaddy*, May 12, 2008.

[18] Larkin, Emma, *No Bad News for the King*, Penguin, 2011, p. 8–9.

[19] Interviews with Samantha Carl-Yoder.

[20] Interview with a US official with knowledge of the situation.

[21] Interviews with Toe Naing Mann.

[22] Interview with Soe Thane.

[23] Interview with Samantha Carl-Yoder.

[24] "First C-130 crew provides humanitarian assistance to Burma," US Air Force, May 12, 2008, http://www.af.mil/News/Article-Display/Article/123597/first-c-130-crew-provides-humanitarian-assistance-to-burma/.

[25] Interview with Admiral Timothy Keating.

[26] Interview with Admiral Timothy Keating.

[27] "No need for chocolate bars, survivors can eat frogs," *The Daily Star* via AFP, May 31, 2008, https://www.thedailystar.net/news-detail-39023?amp.

[28] "U.S. Navy Ships to Leave Myanmar Without Delivering Aid," PBS News Hour, June 4, 2008, https://www.pbs.org/newshour/world/asia-jan-june08-myanmar_06-04.

[29] Karl, Jonathan, Kirit Radia, and Luis Martinez, "Adm. Keating: 'We're Anxious to Help,'" ABC News, January 8, 2009, https://abcnews.go.com/International/story?id=4866922&page=1.

[30] Kyaw Le Win, "The tide was like a monster: Ten years after Nargis, Delta remains vulnerable," *Frontier Magazine*, May 2, 2018, https://frontiermyanmar.net/en/the-tide-was-like-a-monster-ten-years-after-nargis-delta-remains-vulnerable.

[31] *New Light of Myanmar*, Volume XVI, Number 18, May 6, 2008; Volume XVI, Number 19, May 7, 2008.

[32] The NDSC included the president, the two vice presidents, the Speakers of both houses of Parliament, the commander in chief (CINC), the deputy CINC, and the ministers of defense, home affairs, border affairs, and foreign affairs.

[33] Myanmar's Constitution of 2008, https://www.constituteproject.org/constitution/Myanmar_2008.pdf?lang=en.

[34] Stanford, Peter, "The pain of Aung San Suu Kyi's sons parted from their mother for 25 years," *The Telegraph*, June 12, 2012, https://www.telegraph.co.uk/women/mother-tongue/9349279/The-pain-of-Aung-Sun-Suu-Kyis-sons-parted-from-their-mother-for-25-years.html.

[35] Aung Zaw, "Will Suu Kyi Give Up 59(F)?" *The Irrawaddy*, February 20, 2016, https://www.irrawaddy.com/news/burma/will-suu-kyi-give-up-59f.html.

[36] *New Light of Myanmar*, Referendum Announcement, "Commission for Holding Referendum Issues Announcement No 10/2008."

[37] "Burma 'approves new constitution,'" BBC, May 15, 2008, http://news.bbc.co.uk/2/hi/asia-pacific/7402105.stm.

[38] "Myanmar formally announces ratification of new constitution draft," *People's Daily Online*, May 30, 2008, http://en.people.cn/90001/90777/90851/6421254.html.

[39] "World sends help for tsunami victims," CNN, January 1, 2005, https://www.cnn.com/2004/WORLD/asiapcf/12/29/quake.aid/.

[40] Cosgrave, John and John Telford, "The international humanitarian system and the 2004 Indian Ocean earthquake and tsunamis," 2007, https://onlinelibrary.wiley.com/doi/pdf/10.1111/j.1467-7717.2007.00337.x.

[41] "Response to cyclone in Myanmar 'unacceptably slow'—Ban Ki-moon," United Nations, May 12, 2008, https://news.un.org/en/story/2008/05/259002-response-cyclone-myanmar-unacceptably-slow-ban-ki-moon.

[42] Magnusson, Anna and Morten B. Pedersen, "A Good Office? Twenty Years of UN Mediation in Myanmar," 2012, p. 9, https://www.ipinst.org/wp-content/uploads/2012/11/pdfs_ipi_ebook_good_offices.pdf.

[43] In contrast to an envoy, a special rapporteur's mandate it is to conduct fact-finding missions to "examine, monitor, advise and publicly report" on human rights.

[44] "Yozo Yokota Resigns," *Reuters*, June 29, 1996, https://www.burmalibrary.org/reg.burma/archives/199606/msg00373.html.

[45] "Questions of the Violation of Human Rights and Fundamental Freedom, In Any Part of the World, With Particular Reference to Colonial and Other Dependent Countries and Territories," UN Economic and Security Council, January 12, 1995, http://hrlibrary.umn.edu/commission/country51/65.htm.

[46] Magnusson, Anna and Morten B. Pedersen, "A Good Office? Twenty Years of UN Mediation in Myanmar," 2012, p. 6, https://www.ipinst.org/wp-content/uploads/2012/11/pdfs_ipi_ebook_good_offices.pdf.

[47] Larkin, Emma, *No Bad News for the King*, Penguin, 2011, p. 63–64.

[48] Magnusson, Anna and Morten B. Pedersen, "A Good Office? Twenty Years of UN Mediation in Myanmar," 2012, p. 50–73.

[49] Crossette, Barbara, "Vijay Nambiar, UN Envoy, Untangles the Problems Plaguing Myanmar," May 19, 2014, https://www.passblue.com/2014/05/19/vijay-nambiar-un-envoy-untangles-the-problems-plaguing-myanmar/.

[50] "The Failed UN Mission in Myanmar," *The Irrawaddy*, June 16, 2017, https://www.irrawaddy.com/opinion/editorial/the-failed-un-mission-in-myanmar.html.

[51] "Ms. Noeleen Heyzer of Singapore - Special Envoy on Myanmar," United Nations, October 25, 2021, https://www.un.org/sg/en/node/260300.

[52] Magnusson, Anna and Morten B. Pedersen, "A Good Office? Twenty Years of UN Mediation in Myanmar," 2012, p. 5–7, https://www.ipinst.org/wp-content/uploads/2012/11/pdfs_ipi_ebook_good_offices.pdf.

[53] Cohen, Roberta, "The Burma Cycle and the Responsibility to Protect," The Brookings Institute, July 21, 2008, https://www.brookings.edu/on-the-record/the-burma-cyclone-and-the-responsibility-to-protect/.

[54] ASIL Conference, Open Plenary Sessions, "Military Intervention and the International Law of Peace," March 29, 2012, https://legal.un.org/ola/media/info_from_lc/POB%20at%20ASIL%20Annual%20Meeting%202012.pdf.

[55] "Surin Pitsuwan dies at 68," *Bangkok Post*, November 30, 2017, https://www.bangkokpost.com/news/general/1369695/surin-pitsuwan-dies-at-68.

[56] Larkin, Emma, *No Bad News for the King*, Penguin, 2011, p. 74

[57] Creach, Yves-Kim and Lilianne Fan, "ASEAN's role in the Cyclone Nargis response: implications, lessons and opportunities," *Humanitarian Practice Network*, December 2008, https://odihpn.org/magazine/asean%c2%92s-role-in-the-cyclone-nargis-response-implications-lessons-and-opportunities/.

[58] Creach, Yves-Kim and Lilianne Fan, "ASEAN's role in the Cyclone Nargis response: implications, lessons, and opportunities," December 2008, *Humanitarian Practice Network*, December 2008, https://odihpn.org/magazine/asean%c2%92s-role-in-the-cyclone-nargis-response-implications-lessons-and-opportunities/.

[59] Larkin, Emma, *No Bad News for the King*, Penguin, 2011, p.194–95, 201.

[60] Interview with Shari Villarosa.

[61] Macan-Markar, Marwaan, "Burma: Donor View Civil Society in New Light after Nargis," *Inter Press Service*, May 1, 2010, http://www.ipsnews.net/2010/05/burma-donors-view-civil-society-in-new-light-after-nargis/.

[62] Krembzow, Jakob, "A bigger say for local NGOs," *Frontier Myanmar*, September 12, 2016, https://frontiermyanmar.net/en/a-bigger-say-for-local-ngos.

[63] "The Role of CSOs in Myanmar's Transition from Military Rule to Democracy," Partnership for Transparency, https://ptfund.org/the-role-of-csos-in-myanmars-transition-from-military-rule-to-democracy/.

Chapter 2

[1] "Myanmar sentences 14 dissidents to 65-year sentences," *New York Times*, November 8, 2011, https://www.nytimes.com/2008/11/11/world/asia/11iht-myanmar.1.17714485.html

[2] "Border Guard Scheme," *Myanmar Peace Monitor*, http://www.mmpeacemonitor.org/background/border-guard-force.

[3] *Civil and Military Gazette,* December 10, 1886 edition, http://www.kiplingsociety.co.uk/rg_webb_burma.htm.

[4] Smith, Martin, *Burma: Insurgency and the Politics of Ethnicity*, Zed, 1991, p. 78–79.

[5] Kachin Development Networking Group, "Valley of Darkness: Gold Mining and Militarization in Burma's Hugawng Valley," 2007, http://www.burma.no/documents/ValleyofDarkness.pdf.

[6] Steinberg, David, *Burma/Myanmar: What Everyone Need to Know*, Oxford University Press, 2010, p.43–44.

[7] Inside Asia, "Politics of Opium," September–October 1985.

[8] Clymer, Kenton, *A Delicate Relationship: The United States and Burma/Myanmar Since 1945*, Cornell University Press, 2015, p. 63.

[9] Ibid., p. 85–100.

[10] Fuller, Thomas, "Lo Hsin Han, Myanmar Drug Kingpin, Dies at 80," *New York Times*, July 8, 2013, https://www.nytimes.com/2013/07/09/world/asia/lo-hsing-han-wealthy-trafficker-from-myanmar-dies-at-80.html?mcubz=1.

[11] Lintner, Bertil, "Asia's drug 'kingpin' more Hollywood than reality," *Asia Times*, December 1, 2019, https://asiatimes.com/2019/12/asias-drug-kingpin-more-hollywood-than-reality/.

[12] Paluch, Gabrielle, "The Female Warlord Who Had C.I.A. Connections and Opium Routes," *New York Times*, July 21, 2017, https://www.nytimes.com/2017/07/21/world/asia/burmese-warlord-olive-yang.html.

[13] Smith, Martin, "Politics of Opium: Burma's Shan Rebel Groups," Inside Asia, September–October 1985.

[14] House Select Committee on Narcotics Abuse and Control, "Asian Heroin Trafficking," 101st Congress, 1st Session (1989), 96.

[15] Interview with John Whalen.

[16] Letter, Secretary-General Sai Lek to Mrs. Nancy Reagan.

[17] "Burma's Dangerous Herbicide," *The Nation*, April 14, 1986.

[18] Letter, Carlton E. Turner to Edith Mirante, October 30, 1986, ID #453341 (1), CO0025, WHORM: Subject File, Ronald Reagan Library.

[19] UNODC, "Organized crime syndicates are targeting Southeast Asia to expand operations: UNODC," July 18, 2019, https://www.unodc.org/southeastasiaandpacific/en/2019/07/transnational-organised-crime-southeast-asia-report-launch/story.html#:~:text=%22Organized%20crime%20groups%20are%20generating,UNODC%20Regional%20Representative%2C%20Jeremy%20Douglas.

[20] International Crisis Group, "Fire and Ice: Conflict and Drugs in Myanmar's Shan State," January 8, 2019, https://www.crisisgroup.org/asia/south-east-asia/myanmar/299-fire-and-ice-conflict-and-drugs-myanmars-shan-state.

[21] Duangdee, Vijitra, "Chemicals in, Meth Out in Asia's Booming Golden Triangle Drug Trade," Voice of America, May 31, 2021, https://www.voanews.com/east-asia-pacific/chemicals-meth-out-asias-booming-golden-triangle-drug-trade.

[22] Smith, Martin, *Burma: Insurgency and the Politics of Ethnicity*, Zed, 1991, p. 377–379.

[23] Wai Moe, "More Chinese flee Burma as Kokang remain stranded in China," *The Irrawaddy* via UN OCHA, September 4, 2009, https://reliefweb.int/report/myanmar/more-chinese-flee-burma-kokang-remain-stranded-china.

[24] "General Min Aung Hlaing," ALTSEAN, https://web.archive.org/web/20110731003910/http://www.altsean.org/Research/Regime%20Watch/Executive/CIC.php.

[25] Wai Moe, "Myanmar: Border Guard Force plan leads to end of ceasefire," *The Irrawaddy* via UN OCHA, August 31, 2009, https://reliefweb.int/report/myanmar/myanmar-border-guard-force-plan-leads-end-ceasefire.

[26] Interview with John Whalen.

[27] Interview with Dr. Kurt Campbell.

[28] Transnational Institute, Myanmar Policy Briefing, "Beyond Panglong: Myanmar's National Peace and Reform Dilemma," September 21, 2017.

[29] Steinberg, David, *Burma/Myanmar: What Everyone Needs to Know*, Oxford University Press, 2010, p. 175.

[30] Interview with US official with knowledge of State Department and USAID programs.

[31] "From Burma to Thailand: Refugee Flows and U.S. Policy," Congressional Research Service, November 21, 2003, https://www.everycrsreport.com/files/20031121_RS21648_e635da76449ef09efa65440f6dbe11b661f13119.pdf.

[32] USAID Fact Sheet, "USAID Assistance to Burma from 2008–2012," USAID, https://www.usaid.gov/sites/default/files/documents/1861/USAID_Burma_assistance_2008-2012_fact_sheet.pdf.

[33] Interview with US official with knowledge of State Department and USAID programs.

[34] Institute for Security and Development Policy, "Myanmar's Nationwide Ceasefire Agreement," October 2015, https://isdp.eu/content/uploads/publications/2015-isdp-backgrounder-myanmar-nca.pdf.

[35] Transnational Institute, "Ending Burma's Conflict Cycle? Prospects for Ethnic Peace," Burma Policy Briefing, Nr 8, February 2012, https://www.tni.org/files/download/bpb8.pdf.

[36] Ibid.

[37] Mathieson, David Scott, "One Flew Over the Pigeon's Nest," *The Irrawaddy*, May 11, 2020, https://www.irrawaddy.com/culture/books/one-flew-pigeons-nest.html.

[38] Brooks, Xan, "Rambo" *The Guardian*, February 21, 2008, https://www.theguardian.com/film/2008/feb/22/actionandadventure.

[39] Bell, Thomas, "Banned Rambo film hot property in Burma," *The Telegraph*, February 18, 2008, https://www.telegraph.co.uk/news/uknews/1579082/Banned-Rambo-film-hot-property-in-Burma.html.

[40] "Fw: ceasefire and prisoners," US Department of State, Case No. F-2014-20439, Doc No. C05787937, Date: 10/30/2015.

[41] "Re:Burma developments/prisoner release update" US Department of State, Case No. F-2014-20439, Doc No. C05787950.

[42] https://www.usaid.gov/political-transition-initiatives/burma.

[43] https://www.usaid.gov/sites/default/files/documents/1861/USAID_Burma_peace_fact_sheet.pdf.

[44] Thant Myint-U, *The Hidden History of Burma*, W. W. Norton, 2019, p. 175.

[45] Brookings Institute, "China's Intervention in the Myanmar-Kachin Peace Talks," https://www.brookings.edu/articles/chinas-intervention-in-the-myanmar-kachin-peace-talks/.

[46] Thant Myint-U, *The Hidden History of Burma*, W. W. Norton, 2019, p. 170–71.

[47] Nazaryan, Arthur, "With less foreign aid, Thai clinic struggles to serve migrants and refugees from Myanmar," *PRI/The World*, January 21, 2020, https://www.pri.org/stories/2020-01-21/less-foreign-aid-thai-clinic-struggles-serve-migrants-and-refugees-myanmar.

[48] Interview with US government official with familiarity of US assistance programs.

[49] Thant Myint-U, *The Hidden History of Burma*, W. W. Norton, 2019, p. 179.

[50] "Explainer: The insurgents plunging Myanmar's Rakhine back into chaos," *Reuters*, January 15, 2019, https://www.reuters.com/article/us-myanmar-rakhine-explainer-idUSKCN1P90KZ.

[51] "Chin Party Condemns Abuses by Burma Army, Arakan Army," *The Irrawaddy*, July 5, 2016, https://www.irrawaddy.com/news/burma/chin-party-condemns-abuses-by-burma-army-arakan-army.html.

[52] Transnational Institute, Myanmar Policy Briefing, "Beyond Panglong: Myanmar's National Peace and Reform Dilemma," September 21, 2017.

[53] The signatories were: All Burma Students' Democratic Front, Arakan Liberation Party, Chin National Front, Democratic Karen Benevolent Army, Karen National Liberation Army-Peace Council, Karen National Union, Pa-O National Liberation Organization and Shan State Army-South.

[54] US State Department, "Signing of the Nationwide Ceasefire Agreement in Burma," October 15, 2015, https://2009-2017.state.gov/r/pa/prs/ps/2015/10/248222.htm.

[55] Institute for Security and Development Policy, "Myanmar's Nationwide Ceasefire Agreement," October 2015, https://isdp.eu/content/uploads/publications/2015-isdp-backgrounder-myanmar-nca.pdf https://isdp.eu/content/uploads/publications/2015-isdp-backgrounder-myanmar-nca.pdf.

[56] Radio Free Asia, "Myanmar Signs Historic Cease-Fire Deal With Eight Ethnic Armies," October 15, 2015, https://www.rfa.org/english/news/myanmar/deal-10152015175051.html.

[57] Hnin Yadana Zaw, "Myanmar's Suu Kyi says peace process will be government's priority," *Reuters*, January 4, 2016, https://www.reuters.com/article/us-myanmar-politics/myanmars-suu-kyi-says-peace-process-will-be-governments-priority-idUSKBN0UI0GX20160104.

[58] Transnational Institute, "Beyond Panglong: Myanmar's National Peace and Reform Dilemma," Myanmar Policy Briefing, September 21, 2017.

[59] https://www.aljazeera.com/news/2019/03/ethnic-minorities-myanmar-protest-aung-san-statues-190328013321078.html.

[60] Interview with Ambassador Kelley Currie.

[61] Transnational Institute, "Beyond Panglong: Myanmar's National Peace and Reform Dilemma," Myanmar Policy Briefing, September 21, 2017.

[62] "Rebooting Myanmar's Stalled Peace Process," International Crisis Group, Report N. 308, June 19, 2020, https://www.crisisgroup.org/asia/south-east-asia/myanmar/308-rebooting-myanmars-stalled-peace-process.

[63] "Who We Are," Joint Peace Fund, https://www.jointpeacefund.org/en/who-we-are.

[64] Interview with US official with familiarly of US assistance programs.

Chapter 3

[1] US Department of State, Case No. F-2014-22125, Doc No. C05762006, Date: 08/11/2016, "BURMA AND NORTH KOREA RE-ESTABLISH DIPLOMATIC RELATIONS."

[2] Haberman, Clyde, "Bomb Kills 19, Including 6 Key Koreans," *New York Times*, October 10, 1983, https://www.nytimes.com/1983/10/10/world/bomb-kills-19-including-6-key-koreans.html.

[3] Choe, Sang-hun, "Forgotten Killer Among the Korean 'Erased,'" *New York Times*, November 23, 2013, https://www.nytimes.com/2013/11/24/world/asia/forgotten-killer-among-the-korean-erased.html.

[4] "IAEA: Syria tried to build nuclear reactor," *YNet news.com* via *AP*, April 28, 2011, https://www.ynetnews.com/articles/0,7340,L-4062001,00.html.

[5] Farrell, Stephen, "Israel admits bombing suspected Syrian nuclear reactor in 2007, warns Iran," *Reuters*, March 20, 2018, https://www.reuters.com/article/us-israel-syria-nuclear/israel-formally-acknowledges-destroying-suspected-syrian-reactor-in-2007-idUSKBN1GX09K.

[6] McDonald, Hamish, "Revealed: Burma's nuclear bombshell," *Sydney Morning Herald*, August 1, 2009, http://www.smh.com.au/world/revealed-burmax2019s-nuclear-bombshell-20090731-e4fw.html.

[7] "Burma's nuclear secrets," *Sydney Morning Herald*, August 1, 2009, http://www.smh.com.au/world/burmax2019s-nuclear-secrets-20090731-e4fv.html.

[8] The Myanmar side included Lt. Gen. Myint Hlaing (anti-air defense chief), Maj. General Hla Htay Win (training), Maj. General Khin Aung Myint (Air Force), Maj. General Thein Htay (vice chief of staff, ordnance), Maj. Gen. Mya Win (munitions), Brig. Gen. Hla Myint (tanks), Brig. Gen. Kyaw Nyunt (military communications), Brig. Gen. Nyan Tun (engineering), and staff officers.

[9] "From Foes to Friends: Military Trip Rekindles Burma-North Korean Relations," *The Irrawaddy*, April 19, 2017, https://www.irrawaddy.com/from-the-archive/foes-friends-military-trip-rekindles-burma-north-korean-relations.html.

[10] "Burma, North Korea Said To Expand Military Ties," *RFA*, July 2, 2009, https://www.rfa.org/english/news/myanmar/nkorea-07012009231914.html.

[11] Tarrant, Bill, "Is Myanmar joining nuclear club with North Korea aid?" *Reuters*, August 11, 2009, https://www.reuters.com/article/us-myanmar-nuclear-northkorea-analysis-idUSTRE57A1W920090811.

[12] Kyaw Zaw Moe, "Skepticism over North Korean Ship's Mission," *The Irrawaddy*, May 24, 2007, http://www2.irrawaddy.com/opinion_story.php?art_id=7266.

[13] Wan, William and Craig Whitlock, "North Korean ship turned back by U.S. Navy," *The Washington Post*, June 13, 2011, https://www.washingtonpost.com/national/national-security/north-korean-ship-turned-back-by-us-navy/2011/06/13/AG7wxLTH_story.html?utm_term=.b9cec5d9c730.

[14] "Report to the Security Council from the Panel of Experts established Pursuant to Resolution 1874," 2009,

https://fas.org/irp/eprint/scr1874.pdf.

[15] David Albright, Paul Brannan, Robert Kelley, and Andrea Scheel Stricker, Institute for Science and International Security, "Burma: A Nuclear Wannabe, Suspicious Links to North Korea and High-Tech Procurements to Enigmatic Facilities" January 28, 2010.

[16] Kelley, Robert E. and Ali Fowle, "Nuclear Related Activities in Burma," *Democratic Voice of Burma*, June 21, 2010, https://democracyforburma.wordpress.com/2010/06/21/nuclear-related-activities-in-burma-may-2010-robert-e-kelley1-ali-fowle2/.

[17] Lintner, Bertil, "Burma's Nuclear Temptation," Yale University, December 3, 2008, https://archive-yaleglobal.yale.edu/content/burmas-nuclear-temptation.

[18] http://www.burmalibrary.org/docs09/NLM2010-06-12.pdf.

[19] David Albright, Paul Brannan, Robert Kelley, and Andrea Scheel Stricker, Institute for Science and International Security, "Burma: A Nuclear Wannabe, Suspicious Links to North Korea and High-Tech Procurements to Enigmatic Facilities," January 28, 2010.

[20] Lewis, Jeffrey, "Does Burma Still Have Nuclear Dreams?" *Foreign Policy*, November 16, 2012, https://foreignpolicy.com/2012/11/16/does-burma-still-have-nuclear-dreams/amp/.

[21] Kelley, Robert E. and Ali Fowle, "Nuclear Related Activities in Burma," *Democratic Voice of Burma*, June 21, 2010, https://democracyforburma.wordpress.com/2010/06/21/nuclear-related-activities-in-burma-may-2010-robert-e-kelley1-ali-fowle2/.

[22] Saw Yan Naing, "Shwe Mann Denies Nuclear Program," *The Irrawaddy*, December 7, 2011, https://www2.irrawaddy.com/article.php?art_id=22616.

[23] "Myanmar says it's ready to sign nuclear agreement," *USA Today* via *AP*, November 12, 2012, https://www.usatoday.com/story/news/world/2012/11/21/myanmar-nuclear-agreement/1719285/.

[24] Work, Clint, "Is Myanmar Serious About Enforcing Sanctions on North Korea?" *The Diplomat*, October 27, 2017, https://thediplomat.com/2017/10/is-myanmar-serious-about-enforcing-sanctions-on-north-korea/.

[25] Sun, Yun, "China and Myanmar's Peace Process," US Institute for Peace, March 2017.

[26] Steinberg, David, *Burma/Myanmar: What Everyone Needs to Know*, Oxford University Press, 2010, p.121.

[27] Ibid., p. 21, 43–44, 49.

[28] Sun, Yun "China and Myanmar's Peace Process," US Institute for Peace, March 2017.

[29] Interview with Ambassador Derek Mitchell.

[30] "Jade: Myanmar's "Big State Secret," *Global Witness*, October 23, 2015, https://www.globalwitness.org/en/campaigns/oil-gas-and-mining/myanmarjade/.

[31] "Dramatic moment landslide engulfs Jade mine in Myanmar killing 113," *Evening Standard*, July 2, 2020, https://www.youtube.com/watch?v=9qm0i26a6RU.

[32] Chau, Thompson and Kyaw She Htet, "Chinese tech firm claims digital plans for Mong La SEZ," *Myanmar Times*, February 24, 2019, https://www.mmtimes.com/news/chinese-tech-firm-claims-digital-plans-mong-la-sez.html.

[33] Vrieze, Paul, "Inside Mong La, the Myanmar Town Where You Can Buy Drugs, Sex, and Endangered Animals," *Vice*, December 14, 2015, https://www.vice.com/en_us/article/avyq3g/inside-mong-la-the-myanmar-town-where-you-can-buy-drugs-sex-and-endangered-animals.

[34] Chau, Thompson and Kyaw She Htet, "Chinese tech firm claims digital plans for Mong La SEZ," *Myanmar Times*, February 24, 2019, https://www.mmtimes.com/news/chinese-tech-firm-claims-digital-plans-mong-la-sez.html.

[35] Nan Lwin, "Mongla Official Denies Chinese Firm Permitted to Set Up Autonomous Digital Economic Zone," *The Irrawaddy*, February 20, 2019, https://www.irrawaddy.com/news/burma/mongla-official-denies-chinese-firm-permitted-set-autonomous-digital-economic-zone.html.

[36] "YONGBANG SEZ: Mongla, cryptocurrency and sovereignty," BNI Multimedia Group, March 1, 2019, https://www.bnionline.net/en/news/yongbang-sez-mongla-cryptocurrency-and-sovereignty.

[37] Naw Betty Han, "Kayin Border Guard Force celebrates ninth anniversary," *Frontier*, August 20, 2019, https://www.frontiermyanmar.net/en/kayin-border-guard-force-celebrates-ninth-anniversary/.

[38] Tower, Jason and Priscilla Clapp, "Myanmar: Transnational Networks Plan Digital Dodge in Casino Enclaves," US Institute for Peace, July 23, 2020, https://www.usip.org/publications/2020/07/myanmar-transnational-networks-plan-digital-dodge-casino-enclaves.

[39] Ibid.

[40] Nan Lwin, "Myanmar, China Sign Dozens of Deals on BRI Projects, Cooperation During Xi's Visit," *The Irrawaddy*, January 18, 2020, https://www.irrawaddy.com/news/burma/myanmar-china-sign-dozens-deals-bri-projects-cooperation-xis-visit.html.

[41] Lintner, Bertil, "Myanmar a perfect fit on China's Belt and Road," *Asia Times*, January 27, 2020, https://asiatimes.com/2020/01/myanmar-a-perfect-fit-on-chinas-belt-and-road/.

[42] K. Yhome, "The BRI and Myanmar's China Debate," Observer Research Foundation, July 11, 2018, https://www.orfonline.org/expert-speak/bri-myanmar-china-debate/.

[43] Abi-Habib, Maria, "How China Got Sri Lanka to Cough Up a Port," *New York Times*, June 25, 2018, https://www.nytimes.com/2018/06/25/world/asia/china-sri-lanka-port.html.

[44] Sun, Yun, "Slower, smaller, cheaper: the reality of the China-Myanmar Economic Corridor," *Frontier*, September 26, 2019, https://www.frontiermyanmar.net/en/slower-smaller-cheaper-the-reality-of-the-china-myanmar-economic-corridor/.

[45] Sibley, George N. "How the Erosion of Sovereignty Elsewhere Impacts Myanmar at Home," US Embassy Yangon, July 18, 2020, https://mm.usembassy.gov/how-the-erosion-of-sovereignty-elsewhere-impacts-myanmar-at-home/.

[46] "Spokesperson of the Chinese Embassy in Myanmar Refutes the False Argument by the Chargé d'Affaires of the U.S. Embassy in Myanmar," PRC Embassy Yangon, July 18, 2020, http://mm.china-embassy.org/eng/sgxw/t1798794.htm.

[47] Runde, Daniel F. and Romina Bandura, "The BUILD Act Has Passed: What's Next?" Center for Strategic and International Studies, October 12, 2018, https://www.csis.org/analysis/build-act-has-passed-whats-next.

[48] "S.2736 - Asia Reassurance Initiative Act of 2018," 115th Congress, December 31, 2018 https://www.congress.gov/bill/115th-congress/senate-bill/2736/text

[49] "S. 2736 Asia Reassurance Initiative Act of 2018," US Congress, https://www.congress.gov/115/bills/s2736/BILLS-115s2736enr.xml.

Chapter 4

[1] Steinberg, David, *Burma/Myanmar: What Everyone Needs to Know*, Oxford University Press, 2010, p. 77, 99

[2] An LDC status allows countries to write off their debt to creditor governments and receive interest-free overseas aid in areas such as health, education, social welfare, and development. There have been forty-four countries on the list, and only four have "graduated." The current Myanmar government aims to "graduate" by 2021 at the earliest.

[3] Williams Jr., Nick B. "Commerce Snarled as Burma Rules Much of Its Currency Worthless," *The Los Angeles Times*, September 12, 1987, http://articles.latimes.com/1987-09-12/news/mn-1980_1_worthless-currency.

[4] Smith, Martin, *Burma: Insurgency and the Politics of Ethnicity*, Zed, 1991, p. 25–26.

[5] Ibid., p. 1–4.

[6] Meixler, Eli. "How a Failed Democracy Uprising Set the Stage for Myanmar's Future," *Time*, August 8, 2018, http://time.com/5360637/myanmar-8888-uprising-30-anniversary-democracy/

[7] Smith, Martin, *Burma: Insurgency and the Politics of Ethnicity*, Zed, 1991, p. 4–6.

[8] Ibid., p. 9.

[9] "Suu Kyi Pays Tribute to Her Mother," *The Irrawaddy*, December 10, 2010, http://www2.irrawaddy.com/article.php?art_id=20420.

[10] Aung San Suu Kyi, *Freedom from Fear*, Penguin, 1991, p. xvii.

[11] Ibid., p. 192–98.

[12] Smith, Martin, *Burma: Insurgency and the Politics of Ethnicity*, Zed, 1991, p. 8.

[13] Ibid., p. 10, 16, 408.

[14] Martin, Michael, "U.S. Sanctions on Burma: Issues for the 113th Congress," Congressional Research Service, January 11, 2013, https://fas.org/sgp/crs/row/R42939.pdf.

[15] Selth, Andrew, *Burma's Armed Forces: Power Without Glory*, Eastbridge, 2001, p. 266.

[16] Smith, Martin, *Burma: Insurgency and the Politics of Ethnicity*, Zed, 1991, p. 21, 23.

[17] Steinberg, David, *Burma/Myanmar: What Everyone Needs to Know*, Oxford University Press, 2010, p. 90–93.

[18] "Democracy and Discontent: The 2010 Elections in Myanmar," The Australian Institute of International Affairs, 2010, http://www.internationalaffairs.org.au/wp-content/uploads/2014/01/democracy-and-discontent-the-2010-elections-in-myanmar.pdf.

[19] Clapp, Priscilla, "Burma's Long Road to Democracy," The US Institute of Peace, November 2007, https://wayback.archive-it.org/3453/20150904051732/http://www.usip. org/sites/default/files/sr193.pdf.

[20] Selth, Andrew, *Burma's Armed Forces: Power Without Glory*, Eastbridge, 2001, p. 253, 267

[21] Interview with Priscilla Clapp.

[22] "The Myanmar Elections," Briefing 105, International Crisis Group, May 27, 2010, https://www.crisisgroup.org/asia/south-east-asia/myanmar/myanmar-elections.

[23] Interview with Ambassador Scot Marciel.

[24] Interview with Ambassador Larry Dinger.

[25] Interview with Dr. Kurt Campbell.

[26] "Purposes and Principles of U.S. Engagement in Burma," Remarks by Kurt Campbell, US Department of State, May 10, 2010, https://2009-2017.state.gov/p/eap/rls/ rm/2010/05/141669.htm.

[27] "Burma: Military Resignations Confirmed; USDA Registers as Political Party," US Department of State, Case No. F-2014-22125, Doc No. C05762226, https://foia.state.gov/ Search/results.aspx?searchText=burma%3A+military+resignations+confirmed&beginDat e=&endDate=&publishedBeginDate=&publishedEndDate=&caseNumber=F-2014-22125.

[28] Interview with Toe Naing Mann.

[29] "Democracy and Discontent: The 2010 Elections in Myanmar," The Australian Institute of International Affairs, 2010, http://www.internationalaffairs.org.au/wp-content/ uploads/2014/01/democracy-and-discontent-the-2010-elections-in-myanmar.pdf.

[30] "Burma: Election Results are in, and the Winner is . . ." US Department of State, Case No. F-2014-22126, Doc No. C05762186, https://www.foia.state.gov/Search/results.aspx?se archText=*&beginDate=20101101&endDate=20101130&publishedBeginDate=&publishe dEndDate=&caseNumber=F-2014-22125.

[31] "Statement by President Obama on Burma's November 7 Elections," The White House, November 7, 2010, https://obamawhitehouse.archives.gov/the-press-office/2010/11/07/ statement-president-obama-burmas-november-7-elections.

[32] "Burma's Elections," US Department of State, November 7, 2010, https://2009-2017.state. gov/secretary/20092013clinton/rm/2010/11/150517.htm.

[33] "Release of Aung San Suu Kyi," US Department of State, November 13, 2010, https://2009-2017.state.gov/secretary/20092013clinton/rm/2010/11/150872.htm.

[34] Davies, Jack, "Aung San Suu Kyi release brings joy, tears—and new hope for Burma," The Guardian, November 13, 2010, https://www.theguardian.com/world/2010/nov/13/burma-aung-san-suu-kyi-released.

[35] Interview with Ambassador Larry Dinger.

[36] US Department of State, "Burma: Some signs—though inconsistent—of a Changing Media Environment," FOIA, Case No. F-2014-22713, Doc. No. C05740789, 2/23/2017.

[37] Osnos, Evan, "The Burmese Spring," New Yorker, August 6, 2012, https://www. newyorker.com/magazine/2012/08/06/the-burmese-spring.

[38] Wai Moe, "Suu Kyi, Thein Sein Hold First Talks," The Irrawaddy, August 19, 2011, http://www2.irrawaddy.com/article.php?art_id=21927.

[39] Wai Moe, "Suu Kyi 'Satisfied' with Thein Sein Talks," *The Irrawaddy*, August 20, 2011, http://www2.irrawaddy.com/article.php?art_id=21932.

[40] Interview with Ambassador Derek Mitchell.

[41] Hinshelwood, Colin, "Advance Voters Cry Foul," *The Irrawaddy*, March 30, 2012, https://www.irrawaddy.com/news/burma/advance-voters-cry-foul.html.

[42] "Remarks in Burma," US Department of State, March 15, 2012, https://2009-2017.state.gov/p/eap/rls/rm/2012/185928.htm.

[43] "1 April 2012 By-Election results," *The New Light of Myanmar* via Burma Library, April 4, 2012, https://www.burmalibrary.org/en/1-april-2012-by-election-results.

[44] Campbell, Charlie, "Webb Calls for Speedy End to Sanctions," *The Irrawaddy*, April 12, 2012, https://www.irrawaddy.com/news/urma/webb-calls-for-speedy-end-to-sanctions.html.

[45] Lalit K Jha, "McCain Calls for Lifting of Sanctions," *The Irrawaddy*, April 4, 2012, https://www.irrawaddy.com/news/burma/mccain-calls-for-lifting-of-sanctions.html.

[46] "Myanmar to invite Western observers for general election," *Reuters*, March 24, 2015, https://www.reuters.com/article/us-myanmar-election/myanmar-to-invite-western-observers-for-general-election-idUSKBN0MK0CL20150324.

[47] Transnational Institute, Myanmar Policy Briefing, "Ethnic Politics and the 2015 Elections in Myanmar," September 16, 2015.

[48] "Concerns About Burma's Candidate Disqualification," US Embassy Rangoon, September 17, 2015, https://mm.usembassy.gov/concerns-about-burmas-candidate-disqualificationseptember-17-2015/.

[49] Long, Kayleigh, "Embassies concerned at religion being used to create 'division,'" *Myanmar Times*, September 16, 2015, https://www.mmtimes.com/national-news/16493-embassies-concerned-at-religion-being-used-to-create-division.html.

[50] Campbell, Charlie, "Burmese President Removes Party Chief in Major Purge Before Landmark Elections," *Time*, August 13, 2015, https://time.com/3995708/burma-myanmar-shwe-mann-thein-sein-purge-elections-southeast-asia/.

[51] Wai Moe, "Aung San Suu Kyi Calls Ex-Leader of Myanmar Governing Party an 'Ally,'" *New York Times*, August 18, 2015, https://www.nytimes.com/2015/08/19/world/asia/myanmar-aung-san-suu-kyi-calls-shwe-mann-an-ally.html.

[52] "Suu Kyi Concerned by Shwe Mann Ouster," Voice of America, August 18, 2015, https://www.voanews.com/east-asia/suu-kyi-concerned-shwe-mann-ouster.

[53] "Shwe Mann Emerges with Facebook Post Addressed 'To The People,'" *Coconuts Yangon*, August 14, 2015, https://coconuts.co/yangon/news/shwe-mann-emerges-facebook-post-addressed-people/.

[54] Wroughton, Lesley, "Ousting of USDP Chairman Had 'Chilling Effect': US Official," *Reuters* via *The Irrawaddy*, September 12, 2015, https://www.irrawaddy.com/election/news/ousting-of-usdpchairmanhad-chilling-effect-us-official.

[55] Hindstrom, Hanna, "NLD Blocked Muslim Candidates to Appease Ma Ba Tha," *The Irrawaddy*, August 31, 2015, https://www.irrawaddy.com/election/news/nld-blocked-muslim-candidates-to-appease-ma-ba-tha-party-member.

[56] Hnin Yadana Zaw, "NLD Shuns Key Players in Election Candidates Roster," *The Irrawaddy*, August 2, 2015, https://www.irrawaddy.com/election/news/nld-shuns-key-players-in-election-candidates-roster.

[57] Aung Hla Tun, "88 Generation's Ko Ko Gyi Joins Suu Kyi's Party to Run in Polls," *The Irrawaddy*, July 19, 2015, https://www.irrawaddy.com/news/burma/88-generations-ko-ko-gyi-joins-suu-kyis-party-to-run-in-polls.html.

[58] Aung Hla Tun, "Cracks emerge in Myanmar opposition ahead of November election," *Reuters*, August 12, 2015, https://cn.reuters.com/article/uk-myanmar-opposition/cracks-emerge-in-myanmar-opposition-ahead-of-november-election-idUKKCN0QH1TU20150812.

[59] Interview with Ben Rhodes.

[60] Solomon, Feliz, "Obama Aide Wraps Burma Visit Airing Election Hopes, Conceding Flaws," *The Irrawaddy*, October 20, 2015, https://www.irrawaddy.com/election/news/obama-aide-wraps-burma-visit-airing-election-hopes-conceding-flaws.

[61] "Assistant Secretary Daniel Russel's Statement Before the House Foreign Affairs Committee Subcommittee on East Asian and Pacific Affairs," US Department of State, October 2, 2015, https://mm.usembassy.gov/assistant-secretary-daniel-russels-statement-before-the-house-foreign-affairs-committee-subcommittee-on-east-asian-and-pacific-affairs-washington-dc/.

[62] Martin, Michael, "Burma's 2015 Parliamentary Elections: Issues for Congress," Congressional Research Service, March 28, 2016, https://fas.org/sgp/crs/row/R44436.pdf.

[63] Fuller, Thomas and Wai Moe, "Victory by Aung San Suu Kyi's Party Catches One Group Off Guard: The Government," *New York Times*, November 13, 2015, https://www.nytimes.com/2015/11/14/world/asia/aung-san-suu-kyi-myanmar-election.html?searchResultPosition=16.

[64] Fuller, Thomas, "Military Concedes Election to Aung San Suu Kyi in Myanmar," *New York Times*, November 11, 2015, https://www.nytimes.com/2015/11/12/world/asia/aung-san-suu-kyi-myanmar-elections-military.html?searchResultPosition=2.

[65] "Obama commends Myanmar president, Suu Kyi for historic election," *The Nation* via *Reuters*, November 12, 2015, https://www.nationnews.com/2015/11/12/obama-commends-myanmar-president-suu-kyi-for-historic-election/.

[66] Brunnstrom, David and Doina Chiacu, "U.S. welcomes Myanmar election, watching military to honor results," *Reuters*, November 9, 2015, https://www.reuters.com/article/uk-myanmar-election-usa-idAFKCN0SY1W420151109.

[67] "Burma's Parliamentary Election," US Department of State, November 8, 2015, https://2009-2017.state.gov/secretary/remarks/2015/11/249297.htm.

[68] Collinson, Stephen, "Hillary Clinton celebrates Myanmar vote and her role in it," CNN, November 12, 2015, https://www.cnn.com/2015/11/12/politics/hillary-clinton-myanmar-election-role/index.html.

[69] 2015 meeting with Senator McConnell's staff.

[70] McLaughlin, Timothy and Simon Webb, "Amid transition, Myanmar's Senior General emerges from the shadow," *Reuters*, February 24, 2016, https://www.reuters.com/article/us-myanmar-politics-army/amid-transition-myanmars-senior-general-emerges-from-the-shadows-idUSKCN0VX2ZO.

[71] "Former Myanmar dictator backs Aung San Suu Kyi 'with all of my efforts'—report," *The Guardian* via *Reuters*, December 5, 2015, https://www.theguardian.com/world/2015/dec/06/former-myanmar-dictator-backs-aung-san-suu-kyi-with-all-of-my-efforts-report.

[72] Wa Lone, "NLD to ram through state counsellor law," *Myanmar Times*, April 4, 2016, https://www.mmtimes.com/national-news/nay-pyi-taw/19807-nld-to-ram-through-state-counsellor-law.html.

Chapter 5

[1] "President Barack Obama's Inaugural Address," The White House, January 21, 2009, https://obamawhitehouse.archives.gov/blog/2009/01/21/president-barack-obamas-inaugural-address.

[2] Interview with Ambassador Larry Dinger.

[3] Interview with Ben Rhodes.

[4] Cheak, Paul Seck Fai, Maj. "ASEAN's Constructive Engagement Policy Toward Myanmar (Burma)," US Army Command and General Staff College, 2008, https://apps.dtic.mil/dtic/tr/fulltext/u2/a483273.pdf.

[5] "Burma: Sanctions," US Department of State, May 19, 2009, https://2009-2017.state.gov/r/pa/prs/ps/2009/05/123623.htm.

[6] Interview with Secretary Hillary Clinton.

[7] Ibid.

[8] Interview with Dr. Kurt Campbell.

[9] "American: God asked me to protect Suu Kyi," CNN, May 27, 2009, http://www.cnn.com/2009/WORLD/asiapcf/05/27/myanmar.suu.kyi.trial/index.html.

[10] Kyaw Phyo Tha, "Housekeeper Recalls Swimmer who Surprised Suu Kyi's House," *The Irrawaddy*, January 28, 2017, https://www.irrawaddy.com/features/housekeeper-recalls-swimmer-who-surprised-suu-kyis-house%C2%AD.html.

[11] "American Leaves Myanmar After Release," CBS News, August 16, 2009, https://www.cbsnews.com/news/american-leaves-myanmar-after-release/.

[12] Interview with US Embassy officials.

[13] http://www.jameswebb.com/about/about-jim.

[14] Interview with Senator Jim Webb.

[15] Webb, Jim, *A Time to Fight: Reclaiming a Fair and Just America*, Broadway Books, 2008, p. 141–43.

[16] Interview with Senator Jim Webb.

[17] McCurry, Justin, "Senator Jim Webb's Burma visit raises speculation of new US policy," *The Guardian*, August 19, 2009, https://www.theguardian.com/world/2009/aug/14/us-senator-jim-webb-burma.

[18] Interview with Senator Jim Webb.

[19] Interview with Ambassador Larry Dinger.

[20] Webb, Jim, "We Can't Afford to Ignore Myanmar," *New York Times*, August 25, 2009, https://www.nytimes.com/2009/08/26/opinion/26webb.html.

[21] *New Light of Myanmar*, Volume XVII, Number 122, August 16, 2009, http://www.burmalibrary.org/docs07/NLM2009-08-16.pdf.

[22] "Burma: Senator Webb's Meeting with Prime Minister Thein Sein" US Department of State, Case No. F-2014-22125, Doc No. C05762089, Date: 08/11/2016.

[23] "Burma" Senator Webb Meets Than Shwe," US Department of State, Case No. F-2014-221125, Doc No. C05761990, Date: 08/11/2016.

[24] "Fw: (SBU) Yettaw to be Deported on 8/16," US Department of State, Case No. F-2014-20439, Doc No. C05763718, Date: 07/31/2015.

[25] "National League for Democracy Cautiously Optimistic After Webb Visit," US Department of State, Case No. F-2014-22125, Doc No C05761996, Date: 8/11/2016.

[26] Webb, Jim, "We Can't Afford to Ignore Myanmar," *New York Times*, August 25, 2009, https://www.nytimes.com/2009/08/26/opinion/26webb.html.

[27] Interview with Senator Jim Webb.

[28] Interview with David Pressman.

[29] Aroon, Preeti, "Clinton announces plan to engage Burma," *Foreign Policy*, September 24, 2009, https://foreignpolicy.com/2009/09/24/clinton-announces-plan-to-engage-burma/.

[30] Interview with Ambassador Scot Marciel.

[31] "U.S. Policy Toward Burma," US Department of State, September 28, 2009, https://2009-2017.state.gov/p/eap/rls/rm/2009/09/129698.htm.

[32] "U.S. Policy Toward Burma: Its Impact and Effectiveness," Hearing for the Senate Committee on Foreign Relations, September 30, 2009, https://www.foreign.senate.gov/hearings/us-policy-toward-burma-its-impact-and-effectiveness.

[33] "U.S. Policy Toward Burma," Hearing before the House Committee on Foreign Affairs, October 21, 2009, https://2009-2017.state.gov/p/eap/rls/rm/2009/10/130769.htm.

[34] Interview with Ambassador Scot Marciel.

[35] Interview with Ambassador Larry Dinger.

[36] Interview with Dr. Kurt Campbell.

[37] "Comments on meetings in Burma," UN Office for the Coordination of Humanitarian Affairs," November 4, 2009, https://reliefweb.int/report/myanmar/comments-meetings-burma.

[38] US Department of State, Case Number F-2014-20439, Doc No. C05766316, Date:07/31/2015.

[39] Interview with Ambassador Larry Dinger.

[40] Interview with Ambassador Joe Yun.

[41] "Purposes and Principles of U.S. Engagement in Burma," US Department of State, May 10, 2010, https://2009-2017.state.gov/p/eap/rls/rm/2010/05/141669.htm.

[42] Interview with Ambassador Scot Marciel.

[43] "Myanmar's Saffron Revolution: 10 Years Later," Radio Free Asia, https://www.rfa.org/english/news/special/saffron/.

[44] Larkin, Emma, *No Bad News for the King*, Penguin, 2011, p. 120

[45] Tom Lantos Block Burmese JADE (Junta's Anti-democratic efforts) Act of 2008, Public Law 110–286, July 29, 2008, https://www.congress.gov/110/plaws/publ286/PLAW-110publ286.pdf.

[46] Interview with Ambassador Derek Mitchell.

[47] "Burma: Appointment of Michael Green as Special Envoy," US Department of State, November 12, 2008, https://2001-2009.state.gov/r/pa/prs/ps/2008/nov/111795.htm.

[48] Green, Michael and Derek Mitchell, "Asia's Forgotten Crisis: A New Approach to Burma," *Foreign Affairs*, November/December 2007, https://www.foreignaffairs.com/articles/asia/2007-11-01/asias-forgotten-crisis.

[49] Interview with Ambassador Derek Mitchell.

[50] Interview with Ben Rhodes.

[51] Interview with Kate Nanavatty and Ambassador Patrick Murphy.

[52] "President U Thein Sein delivers inaugural address to Pyidaungsu Hluttaw," March 30, 2011, https://www.burmalibrary.org/docs12/2011-03-30-TS_inaugural_speech_to_Pyidaungsu_Hluttaw.pdf.

[53] Wai Moe, "Suu Kyi, Thein Sein Hold First Talks," *The Irrawaddy*, August 19, 2011, http://www2.irrawaddy.com/article.php?art_id=21927.

[54] US Department of State, "Burma: Some signs—though inconsistent—of a Changing Media Environment," FOIA Case No. F-2014-22713, Doc. No. C05740789, 2/23/2017.

[55] Interview with Priscilla Clapp.

[56] "Burma's President-Elect: A Clever Puppet," *The Irrawaddy*, February 25, 2011, http://www2.irrawaddy.com/article.php?art_id=20824.

[57] Fuller, Thomas, "A Most Unlikely Liberator in Myanmar," *New York Times*, March 14, 2012, https://www.nytimes.com/2012/03/15/world/asia/a-most-unlikely-liberator-in-myanmar.html

[58] Osnos, Evan, "The Burmese Spring," *New Yorker*, July 30, 2012, https://www.newyorker.com/magazine/2012/08/06/the-burmese-spring.

[59] Interview with Thant Myint-U.

[60] Interview with Priscilla Clapp.

[61] Ibid.

[62] Interview with Ambassador Derek Mitchell.

[63] Lalit K Jha, "US Special Envoy Makes First Trip to Burma," *The Irrawaddy*, September 7, 2011, http://www2.irrawaddy.com/article.php?art_id=22030.

[64] US Department of State, "Burma: Ambassador Mitchell Hears Two Visions of Democracy from Two Parliamentary Speakers," FOIA Case No. F-2014-22713, Doc No. C05740818, 2/23/2017.

[65] Interview with Ambassador Derek Mitchell.

[66] US Department of State, "Burma: Who's Who in the Regime," FOIA Case No. F-2014-22125, Doc No. C05762040, 8/11/2016.

[67] Aung Zaw, "For U Shwe Mann, Enemies Lurk Everywhere," *The Irrawaddy*, March 5, 2019, https://www.irrawaddy.com/opinion/commentary/u-shwe-mann-enemies-lurk-everywhere.html.

[68] US Department of State, "Burma: Ambassador Mitchell Hears Two Visions of Democracy from Two Parliamentary Speakers," FOIA Case No. F-2014-22713, Doc No. C05740818, 2/23/2017.

[69] Interview with Ambassador Derek Mitchell.

[70] Interview with Ambassador Derek Mitchell.

[71] "Something's Happening in Burma," *The Irrawaddy*, September 16, 2011, http://www2.irrawaddy.com/article.php?art_id=22085&page=1.

[72] Interview with Ambassador Joe Yun.

[73] Interview with Ambassador Derek Mitchell and Kate Nanavatty.

[74] Interview with Mike Posner.

[75] Interview with Kate Nanavatty.

[76] Sai Zom Hseng, "Burma to Free 6,359 Prisoners," *The Irrawaddy*, October 11, 2011, http://www2.irrawaddy.com/article.php?art_id=22240.

[77] Sai Zom Hseng, "Around 100 Political Prisoners Released," *The Irrawaddy*, October 12, 2011, http://www2.irrawaddy.com/article.php?art_id=22248.

[78] US Department of State, "Burma: Government Announces Release of 6,359 Prisoners; Does not Specify Who," FOIA Case No. F-2014-22713, Doc No. C05740800, 2/23/2017

[79] Wai Moe, "Myitsone Controversy Sparks Discord in Naypyidaw," *The Irrawaddy*, September 19, 2011, http://www2.irrawaddy.com/article.php?art_id=22103.

[80] Fawthrop, Tom, "Myanmar's Myitsone Dam Dilemma," *The Diplomat*, March 11, 2019, https://thediplomat.com/2019/03/myanmars-myitsone-dam-dilemma/.

[81] Wade, Frances, "Have protests succeeded in Myanmar?" *Al Jazeera*, October 8, 2011, https://www.aljazeera.com/indepth/opinion/2011/10/201110391126493167.html.

[82] Fuller, Thomas, "Myanmar Backs Down, Suspending Dam Project," *New York Times*, September 30, 2011, https://www.nytimes.com/2011/10/01/world/asia/myanmar-suspends-construction-of-controversial-dam.html.

[83] Interview with Danny Russel.

[84] Interview with Ben Rhodes.

[85] Interview with Jake Sullivan.

[86] Interview with Minister Wunna Maung Lwin.

[87] Interview with Ambassador W. Patrick Murphy.

[88] Interview with Ambassador Derek Mitchell.

[89] "From Foes to Friends: Military Trip Rekindles Burma-North Korean Relations," *The Irrawaddy*, April 19, 2017, https://www.irrawaddy.com/from-the-archive/foes-friends-military-trip-rekindles-burma-north-korean-relations.html.

[90] Interview with Derek Ambassador Mitchell.

[91] Interview with Secretary Hillary Clinton.

[92] Clinton, Hillary, *Hard Choices*, Simon and Schuster, 2014, p. 104–05.

[93] Interview with Secretary Hillary Clinton.

[94] Interview with Danny Russel.

[95] "Nov. 17, 2011—A Call From Air Force One," November 17, 2011, The White House, https://obamawhitehouse.archives.gov/photos-and-video/photo/2011/12/nov-17-2011-call-air-force-one.

[96] Schwandt, Kimberly, "Obama Announces Secretary Clinton to Travel to Burma," Fox News, November 18, 2011, https://www.foxnews.com/politics/obama-announces-secretary-clinton-to-travel-to-burma.

[97] "John Kerry stayed at US-blacklisted Myanmar hotel," *AP News*, August 12, 2014, https://www.apnews.com/1f7f899cd51b4d3487346c85fda30a6e.

[98] "Myanmar: Clinton's Visit Should be Measured in Human Rights Improvement," Amnesty International, November 29, 2011, https://www.amnesty.org/en/press-releases/2011/11/myanmar-clinton-s-visit-should-be-measured-human-rights-improvement-2011-11/.

[99] Clinton, Hillary, *Hard Choices*, Simon and Schuster, 2014, p. 104–05.

[100] Interview with Senator Mitch McConnell.

[101] US Department of State, "Fw: The Lady," Case No. F-2014-20439, Doc No. C05785207, Date: 10/30/2015.

[102] Interview with State Department staffer with knowledge of the event.

[103] Interview with Dr. Kurt Campbell.

[104] "Secretary Hillary Clinton's Historic Visit to Burma in 2011," US Department of State East Asia and Pacific Media Hub, January 12, 2012, https://www.youtube.com/watch?v=Uq1VFXHXL-g.

[105] Interview with Secretary Hillary Clinton.

[106] Ibid.

[107] Interview with Wunna Maung Lwin.

[108] US Department of State, "Schedule for Secretary Hillary Rodham Clinton, Thursday, December 1, 2011," FOIA Case No. F-2010-01376, Doc No. C06110839, 8/31/2016.

[109] Interview with Secretary Hillary Clinton.

[110] "Additional Protocol," IAEA, https://www.iaea.org/topics/additional-protocol

[111] Interview with Mike Posner.

[112] "Press Availability in Nay Pyi Taw, Burma," US Department of State, December 1, 2011, https://2009-2017.state.gov/secretary/20092013clinton/rm/2011/12/177994.htm.

[113] Interview with Secretary Hillary Clinton.

[114] "Background Briefing on Secretary Clinton's Meeting With Burmese President," US Department of State, December 1, 2011 https://2009-2017.state.gov/r/pa/prs/ps/2011/12/178025.htm.

[115] Interview with Ambassador Derek Mitchell.

[116] Interview with Secretary Hillary Clinton.

[117] Interview with Toe Naing Mann.

[118] Ibid.

[119] Interview with Secretary Hillary Clinton.

[120] "Lower Mekong Initiative," Mekong-US Partnership, January 1, 2014, https://www.lowermekong.org/about/lower-mekong-initiative-lmi.

[121] "Press Availability in Nay Pyi Taw, Burma," US Department of State, December 1, 2011, https://2009-2017.state.gov/secretary/20092013clinton/rm/2011/12/177994.htm.

[122] Kipling, Rudyard, *From Sea to Sea and Other Sketches: Letters of Travel, Volume I*, 1914.

[123] Quinn, Andrew, "Hillary Clinton barefoot in (Burma) Myanmar," *The Christian Science Monitor*, December 1, 2011, https://www.csmonitor.com/World/Latest-News-Wires/2011/1201/Hillary-Clinton-barefoot-in-Burma-Myanmar.

[124] Clinton, Hillary, *Hard Choices*, Simon and Schuster, 2014, p. 61, 101–102.

[125] Interview with Secretary Hillary Clinton.

[126] Interview with Danny Russel.

[127] "Background Briefing on Secretary Clinton's Meetings in Burma," US Department of State, December 2, 2011, https://2009-2017.state.gov/r/pa/prs/ps/2011/12/178125.htm.

[128] US Department of State, "Schedule for Secretary Hillary Rodham Clinton, Friday, December 2, 2011," FOIA Case No. F-2010-01376, Doc No. C06110840, 8/31/2016.

[129] Burke, Jason, "Clinton and Aung San Suu Kyi pledge to work together for Burma democracy," *The Guardian*, December 2, 2011, https://www.theguardian.com/world/2011/dec/02/hillary-clinton-aung-san-suu-kyi-burma-democracy.

[130] "Background Briefing on Secretary Clinton's Meetings in Burma," US Department of State, December 2, 2011, https://2009-2017.state.gov/r/pa/prs/ps/2011/12/178125.htm.

[131] Ibid.

[132] Clinton, Hillary, *Hard Choices*, Simon and Schuster, 2014, p. 52, 121–22.

[133] Interview with Senator Mitch McConnell.

[134] "Transcript of Senator McConnell's remarks to the Press in Naypyitaw, Burma," January 12, 2012, US Department of State, Case No. F-2014-20439, Doc No. C05788979.

[135] Interview with Congressman Joe Crowley.

[136] Ibid.

[137] Ibid.

[138] Interview with Ambassador Derek Mitchell.

[139] Ibid.

[140] Ibid.

[141] The Czechs were more hesitant in opening based on their experiences of national reconciliation and welcoming back diaspora populations. They wanted the EU to think through the long-term issues ahead, especially land rights and returning refugees and IDPs. Sanctions wer less about keeping businesses out and more about buying time for us to look at the landscape and figure out what to clean up first.

[142] "Ambassador-Designate to Burma," US Department of State, June 27, 2012, https://2009-2017.state.gov/p/eap/rls/rm/2012/06/194131.htm.

[143] Good, Allison, "Senators push for investing in Burmese Fossil Fuels," *Foreign Policy*, June 27, 2012, https://foreignpolicy.com/2012/06/27/senators-push-for-investing-in-burmese-fossil-fuels/.

[144] "Nominations of the 112th Congress-Second Session: Hearing before the Committee on Foreign Relations United States Senate," February 7–November 28, 2012, p. 429, https://books.google.com/books?id=GuVEAQAAMAAJ&pg=PA429&lpg=PA429&dq =marco+rubio+derek+mitchell+hearing+2012&source=bl&ots=Axp-vtHd_j&sig=AC fU3U2O3kFBR2EhuO8vr170pvqqWUMJJw&hl=en&sa=X&ved=2ahUKEwi2xt7T5-XoAhUymHIEHVPyCZoQ6AEwAnoECAsQKQ#v=onepage&q=marco%20rubio%20 derek%20mitchell%20hearing%202012&f=false.

[145] Interview with Patrick Murphy.

[146] "Aung San Suu Kyi," *Vanity Fair*, November 16, 2012, https://www.vanityfair.com/news/ politics/2012/12/burma-aung-san-suu-kyi.

[147] "Secretary Clinton Honors Daw Aung San Suu Kyi," US Department of State, September 18, 2012, https://2009-2017.state.gov/secretary/20092013clinton/rm/2012/09/197852.htm.

[148] "FW: ASSK- mission accomplished" October 4, 2012, US Department of State, Case No. F-2014-20439, Doc No. C05796226, Date: 11/30/2015

[149] Interview with Rena Pederson.

[150] "US fetes Daw Aung San Suu Kyi," *Myanmar Times* via *AFP*, September 24, 2012, https://www.mmtimes.com/national-news/1776-us-fetes-daw-aung-san-suu-kyi.html.

[151] "Congressional Gold Medal Ceremony for Aung San Suu Kyi," C-SPAN, September 19, 2012, https://www.c-span.org/video/?308271-1/congressional-gold-medal-ceremony-aung-san-suu-kyi.

[152] Interview with Senator Jim Webb.

[153] Harris, Elizabeth A. "In New York, Reverence for Myanmar's Opposition Leader," *New York Times*, September 22, 2012, https://www.nytimes.com/2012/09/23/nyregion/daw-aung-san-suu-kyi-draws-reverent-crowd-in-new-york.html.

[154] Nichols, Michelle, "Myanmar says not worried Suu Kyi upstaging president on U.S. visit," *Reuters*, September 21, 2012, https://uk.reuters.com/article/uk-myanmar-un/myanmar-says-not-worried-suu-kyi- upstaging-president-on-u-s-visit-idUKBRE88K1BQ20120922.

[155] "Treasury Department Lifts Sanctions Against Burma's President and Lower House Speaker," US Department of the Treasury, September 19, 2012, https://www.treasury.gov/ press-center/press-releases/Pages/tg1715.aspx.

[156] Interview with Ambassador W. Patrick Murphy.

[157] Zaccone, Janene, "Suu Kyi speaks about freedom, democracy at UofL," University of Louisville, McConnell Center, September 24, 2012, https://louisville.edu/mcconnellcenter/ news/archived/suu-kyi-speaks-about-freedom-democracy-at-uofl.

[158] Interview with Senator Mitch McConnell.

[159] "Suu Kyi Ends US Trip," Radio Free Asia, October 3, 2012, https://www.rfa.org/english/ news/myanmar/trip-10032012180512.html.

[160] May, Patrick, "Bay Area Burmese community gives Aung San Suu Kyi a rock-star welcome in San Francisco," *The Mercury News*, September 29, 2012, https://www. mercurynews.com/2012/09/29/bay-area-burmese-community-gives-aung-san-suu-kyi-a-rock-star-welcome-in-san-francisco/.

[161] Interview with Congressman Joe Crowley.

[162] Interview with Ambassador W. Patrick Murphy.

[163] "Obama's Trip to Burma an Opportunity to Press for Substantial Reforms," Physicians for Human Rights, November 1, 2012.

[164] Power, Samantha, *The Education of an Idealist*, Dey Street Books, 2019, p. 313–320

[165] "Supporting Human Rights in Burma," The White House, November 9, 2021, https://obamawhitehouse.archives.gov/blog/2012/11/09/supporting-human-rights-burma.

[166] Interview with Mike Posner.

[167] Interview with Colin Willet.

[168] Interview with Ben Rhodes.

[169] Rhodes, Ben, *The World as It Is: A Memoir of the Obama White House*, Random House, 2018, p. 192.

[170] Interview with Dr. Kurt Campbell.

[171] Rhodes, Ben, *The World as It Is: A Memoir of the Obama White House*, Random House, 2018, p. 192–193.

[172] Interview with Colin Willet.

[173] "Barack Obama meets Aung San Suu Kyi in Burma," November 19, 2012, https://www.youtube.com/watch?v=av6Iu78wGL0.

[174] "Remarks by President Obama at the University of Yangon," The White House, November 19, 2012, https://obamawhitehouse.archives.gov/the-press-office/2012/11/19/remarks-president-obama-university-yangon.

[175] Schearf, Daniel, "Obama's Historic Burma Speech Mostly Well Received," Voice of America, November 19, 2012, https://www.voanews.com/east-asia/obamas-historic-burma-speech-mostly-well-received.

[176] "Remarks by President Obama and President Thein Sein of Burma After Bilateral Meeting," The White House, November 19, 2012, https://obamawhitehouse.archives.gov/the-press-office/2012/11/19/remarks-president-obama-and-president-thein-sein-burma-after-bilateral-m.

[177] Interview with government official with knowledge of policy.

[178] Australia, Japan, the Philippines, South Korea, and Thailand.

[179] "A Free and Open Indo-Pacific: Advancing a Share Vision," US Department of State, November 4, 2019, https://www.state.gov/wp-content/uploads/2019/11/Free-and-Open-Indo-Pacific-4Nov2019.pdf.

[180] Interview with Francisco Bencosme.

[181] "White House National Security Council Senior Director for Asian Affairs Travels to Myanmar," US Indo-Pacific Command, June 15, 2018, https://www.pacom.mil/Media/News/News-Article-View/Article/1551999/white-house-national-security-council-senior-director-for-asian-affairs-travels/.

[182] Interview with official with knowledge of the meetings.

[183] Interview with official with knowledge of the meetings and policy.

[184] "Bangladesh Is Not My Country: The Plight of Rohingya Refugees from Myanmar," Human Rights Watch, August 5, 2018, https://www.hrw.org/report/2018/08/05/bangladesh-not-my-country/plight-rohingya-refugees-myanmar.

Chapter 6

[1] The World Bank Group Boards of Directors refers to four separate boards of directors, namely the Board of the International Bank for Reconstruction and Development (IBRD), the International Development Agency (IDA), the International Finance Corporation (IFC), and the Multilateral Investment Guarantee Agency (MIGA). Each board is responsible for the general operations of their respective organization. The executive directors as individuals cannot exercise any power nor commit or represent the bank unless specifically authorized by the board of directors to do so. Executive directors are appointed or elected by the governors. Generally, the governors are member countries' ministers of finance or ministers of development.

[2] Martin, Michael, "US Sanctions on Burma," Congressional Research Service, October 19, 2012, https://fas.org/sgp/crs/row/R41336.pdf.

[3] An Executive Order (EO) is a directive issued by the president of the United States. An EO becomes an enforceable law by a variety of measures, including acts of Congress or the International Emergency Economic Powers Act (IEEPA), which allows the president to regulate commerce by declaring a national emergency.

[4] Kucik, Peter, "Difficulties in Easing Sanctions on Myanmar," Columbia, SIPA, Center of Global Energy Policy, April 2016, https://energypolicy.columbia.edu/sites/default/files/CGEP_Difficulties%20in%20Easing%20Sanctions%20on%20Myanmar_April%202016.pdf.

[5] "Administration of George W. Burma, 2003/July 28," US Government Information (GPO), https://www.govinfo.gov/content/pkg/WCPD-2003-08-04/pdf/WCPD-2003-08-04-Pg991.pdf.

[6] Kucik, Peter, "Difficulties in Easing Sanctions on Myanmar," Columbia, SIPA, Center of Global Energy Policy, April 2016, https://energypolicy.columbia.edu/sites/default/files/CGEP_Difficulties%20in%20Easing%20Sanctions%20on%20Myanmar_April%202016.pdf.

[7] "Sanctions Actions Pursuant to Executive Order 13448, Executive Order 13310, and Executive Order 13464," Federal Register, May 23, 2016, https://www.federalregister.gov/documents/2016/05/23/2016-12011/sanctions-actions-pursuant-to-executive-order-13448-executive-order-13310-and-executive-order-13464.

[8] "Tom Lantos Block Burmese JADE (Junta's Anti-Democratic Efforts) Act of 2008, Public Law 110–286, July 29, 2008, https://www.congress.gov/110/plaws/publ286/PLAW-110publ286.pdf.

[9] Campbell, Charlie, "UK PM Cameron in Historic Burma Visit," The Irrawaddy, April 12, 2012, https://www.irrawaddy.com/news/burma/uk-pm-cameron-in-historic-burma-visit.html.

[10] "EU agrees to suspend most Burma sanctions," BBC, April 23, 2012, https://www.gov.uk/government/news/eu-foreign-ministers-discuss-suspension-of- sanctions-on-burma.

[11] Campbell, Charlie, "Webb Calls for Speedy End to Sanctions," The Irrawaddy, April 12, 2012, https://www.irrawaddy.com/news/burma/webb-calls-for-speedy-end-to-sanctions.html.

[12] Lalit K Jha, "McCain Calls for Lifting of Sanctions," The Irrawaddy, April 4, 2012, https://www.irrawaddy.com/news/burma/mccain-calls-for-lifting-of-sanctions.html.

[13] Interview with Peter Kucik.

[14] Interview with Congressman Tom Malinowski.

[15] "Recognizing and Supporting Burma's Democratic Reforms," US Department of State, April 4, 2012, https://2009-2017.state.gov/secretary/20092013clinton/rm/2012/04/187439. htm.

[16] Frank, Marc, "Explainer: The state of Raul Castro's economic reforms in Cuba," *Reuters*, April 17, 2018, https://www.reuters.com/article/us-cuba-politics-castro-changes-explaine/ explainer-the-state-of-raul-castros-economic-reforms-in-cuba-idUSKBN1HO0CL.

[17] Rhodes, Ben, *The World as It Is: A Memoir of the Obama White House*, Random House, 2018, p. 209–211.

[18] "Remarks With Foreign Minister of Burma U Wunna Maung Lwin After Their Meeting," US Department of State, May 17, 2012.

[19] "Burma Responsible Investment Reporting Requirements," US Department of State, May 23, 2013, https://2009-2017.state.gov/r/pa/prs/ps/2013/05/209869.htm.

[20] Kucik, Peter, "Difficulties in Easing Sanctions on Myanmar," Columbia, SIPA, Center of Global Energy Policy, April 2016, https://energypolicy.columbia.edu/sites/default/files/ CGEP_Difficulties%20in%20Easing%20Sanctions%20on%20Myanmar_April%202016. pdf.

[21] OFAC revised the rule to make it more complicated by expanding the 50 percent rule's impact by applying this bar to entities owned 50 percent or more in the aggregate by one or more blocked persons. In the parlance of OFAC, "if Blocked Person X owns 25 percent of Entity A, and Blocked Person Y owns another 25 percent of Entity A, Entity A is considered to be blocked . . . because Entity A is owned 50 percent or more in the aggregate by one or more blocked persons." Another example, "if Blocked Person X owns 50 percent of Entity A and 10 percent of Entity B. Entity A also owns 40 percent of Entity B. Entity B is considered to be blocked. This is so because, through its 50 percent ownership of Entity A, Blocked Person X is considered to indirectly own 40 percent of Entity B. When added to Blocked Person X's direct 10 percent ownership of Entity B, Blocked Person X's total ownership (direct and indirect) of Entity B is 50 percent."

[22] Kyaw Lin Htoon, "The return of Tay Za," *Frontier Magazine*, October 20, 2017, https://frontiermyanmar.net/en/the-return-of-tay-za.

[23] Szep, Jason and Andrew R.C. Marshall, "Special Report: An image makeover for Myanmar Inc," *Reuters*, April 13, 2012, https://www.reuters.com/article/us-myanmar-cronies-image/special-report-an-image-makeover-for-myanmar-inc-idUSBRE83B0YU20120413.

[24] Thit Nay Moe, "Burmese Tycoon Tay Za Claims Uranium Unearthed in Burma," *The Irrawaddy*, January 20, 2015, https://www.irrawaddy.com/business/burmese-tycoon-tay-za-claims-uranium-unearthed-burma.html.

[25] Ferrie, Jared, "Myanmar's log export ban to hurt businessmen but help forest," *Reuters*, March 20, 2014, https://www.reuters.com/article/us-myanmar-forests/myanmars-log-export-ban-to- hurt-businessmen-but-help-forests-idUSBREA2J27K20140320.

[26] Htet Aung, "Cronyism: A Legacy of Military Rule in Burma," *The Irrawaddy*, July 6, 2011, https://www2.irrawaddy.com/article.php?art_id=21635&page=1.

[27] Ferrie, Jared, "Burmese Tycoon Tay Za Under Scrutiny," *Forbes*, August 17, 2014, https://www.forbes.com/sites/forbesasia/2014/07/23/burmese-tycoon-tay-za-under-scrutiny/?sh=5ad418eb6a7a.

[28] Ibid.

[29] Bultrini, Raimondo, "Tay Za talks sanctions, business and politics," *Le Republica*, June 6, 2011, https://www.slideshare.net/myanmarbusiness/tay-za-interview-for-la-republica.

[30] Mullins, Jeremy and Ei Thant Sin, "Air Bagan settles crash as U Tay Za mulls its future," *Myanmar Times*, August 9, 2014, https://www.mmtimes.com/business/11299-air-bagan-settles-crash-as-u-tay-za-mulls- its-future.html.

[31] "Tracking the Tycoons," *The Irrawaddy*, Volume 16, No.9, September 2008, https://www2.irrawaddy.com/article.php?art_id=14151&page=2.

[32] "John Kerry stayed at US-blacklisted Myanmar hotel," *AP*, August 12, 2014, https://apnews.com/1f7f899cd51b4d3487346c85fda30a6e.

[33] Aliases are quite common in Myanmar. For example, a person could have an ethnic name, a Burmese name, and/or a nom de guerre. Aliases do not necessarily suggest illicit behavior.

[34] "Tracking the Tycoons," *The Irrawaddy*, Volume 16, No.9, September 2008, https://www2.irrawaddy.com/article.php?art_id=14151&page=2.

[35] Szep, Jason and Andrew R. C. Marshall "Special Report: An image makeover for Myanmar Inc," *Reuters*, April 13, 2012, https://www.reuters.com/article/us-myanmar-cronies-image/special-report-an-image-makeover-for-myanmar-inc-idUSBRE83B0YU20120413.

[36] "Issuance of Burma General License 20," US Department of State, December 7, 2015, https://2009-2017.state.gov/r/pa/prs/ps/2015/12/250427.htm.

[37] Pennington, Matthew, "US Lifts Sanctions on Prominent Burmese Businessman," *The Irrawaddy*, April 24, 2015, https://www.irrawaddy.com/news/burma/us-lifts-sanctions-on-prominent-burmese-businessman.html.

[38] Interview with John Goyer.

[39] "Suu Kyi Attends Football Match," *The Irrawaddy*, September 14, 2011, https://www2.irrawaddy.com/article.php?art_id=22073.

[40] Aung Hla Tun, "Suu Kyi's party accepts crony donations in reform-era Myanmar," *Reuters*, January 17, 2013, https://www.reuters.com/article/us-myanmar-suukyi/suu-kyis-party-accepts-crony-donations-in-reform-era-myanmar-idUSBRE90G0C820130117.

[41] O'Connor, Brennan, "The last prince of Hsipaw," *Frontier*, April 25, 2016, https://frontiermyanmar.net/en/the-last-prince-of-hsipaw.

[42] Interview with Tom Malinowski.

[43] Kucik, Peter, "Difficulties in Easing Sanctions on Myanmar," Columbia SIPA, Center on Global Energy Policy, April 2016, https://energypolicy.columbia.edu/sites/default/files/CGEP_Difficulties%20in%20Easing%20Sanctions%20on%20Myanmar_April%202016.pdf.

[44] "Press Release on Assistant Secretary Malinowski's Visit to Burma," US Indo-Pacific Command, July 3, 2014, https://www.pacom.mil/Media/News/News-Article-View/Article/564323/press-release-on-assistant-secretary-malinowskis-visit-to-burma/.

[45] Ferrie, Jared, "Burmese Tycoon Tay Za Under Scrutiny," *Forbes*, August 17, 2014, https://www.forbes.com/sites/forbesasia/2014/07/23/burmese-tycoon-tay-za-under-scrutiny/#121504736a7a.

[46] "Economic interests of the Myanmar military," UN Human Rights Council, September 16, 2019, https://www.ohchr.org/EN/HRBodies/HRC/MyanmarFFM/Pages/EconomicInterestsMyanmarMilitary.aspx.

[47] "Delisting of SDN Win Aung," US Department of State, April 23, 2015, https://2009-2017.state.gov/r/pa/prs/ps/2015/04/241034.htm.

[48] "Dead Generals, Crony's Wife Removed From US Blacklist," July 10, 2015, *The Irrawaddy*, https://www.irrawaddy.com/news/burma/dead-generals-cronys-wife-removed-from-us-blacklist.html.

[49] 2015 Meeting with HFAC Staffers.

[50] "Publication of Burma General Licenses, Burma Removals, and Burma Designations," US Department of the Treasury, May 17, 2016, https://home.treasury.gov/policy-issues/financial-sanctions/recent-actions/20160517.

[51] Samuels, David, "The Aspiring Novelist Who Became Obama's Foreign-Policy Guru," *The New York Times Magazine*, May 6, 2016, https://www.nytimes.com/2016/05/08/magazine/the-aspiring-novelist-who-became-obamas-foreign-policy-guru.html.

[52] "Remarks by Deputy National Security Advisor Ben Rhodes on Burma Policy at the Center for New American Security," The White House, May 17, 2016, https://obamawhitehouse.archives.gov/the-press-office/2016/05/18/remarks-deputy-national-security-advisor-ben-rhodes-burma-policy-center.

[53] Interview with Francisco Bencosme.

[54] "Cardin, McCain Introduce Legislation To Support Burma During Historic Political, Economic Transition, Remain Focused on Human Rights Issues," United State Senate Committee on Foreign Relations. September 13, 2016, https://www.foreign.senate.gov/press/ranking/release/cardin-mccain-introduce-legislation-to-support-burma-during-historic-political-economic-transition-remain-focused-on-human-rights-issues.

[55] Interview with Francisco Bencosme.

[56] Meeting with congressional staffer.

[57] Burma: 2009 Investment Climate Statement, FOIA Case Number: F-2014-22125, https://www.foia.state.gov/searchapp/DOCUMENTS/OctNov2016/F-2014-22125/DOC_0C05761930/C05761930.pdf.

[58] Interview with Francisco Bencosme.

[59] Interview with a congressional staffer.

[60] Interview with Francisco Bencosme.

[61] "Joint Statement between the Republic of the Union of Myanmar and the United States of America," The White House, September 14, 2016, https://obamawhitehouse.archives.gov/the-press-office/2016/09/14/joint-statement-between-republic-union-myanmar-and-united-states-america.

[62] The GSP program is intended to provide opportunities for developing countries to grow their economies through trade with the US by eliminating duties on nearly 5,000 types of products. To qualify for GSP benefits, a country must meet statutory requirements, including taking steps to ensure internationally recognized worker rights and provide adequate and effective protection of intellectual property rights.

[63] "Remarks by President Obama and State Counselor Aung San Suu Kyi of Burma," The White House, September 14, 2016, https://obamawhitehouse.archives.gov/the-press-office/2016/09/14/remarks-president-obama-and-state-counselor-aung-san-suu-kyi-burma.

[64] Interview with Congressman Tom Malinowski.

[65] Interview with Steve Pomper.

[66] Interview with Ambassador Scot Marciel.

[67] Interview with congressional staffers.

[68] Toosi, Nahal, "The Genocide the U.S. Didn't See Coming," *Politico Magazine*, March/April 2018, https://www.politico.com/magazine/story/2018/03/04/obama-rohingya-genocide-myanmar-burma-muslim-syu-kii-217214/.

[69] Interview with Ambassador W. Patrick Murphy.

Chapter 7

[1] Trindle, Jamila, "Former U.S. Officials Cash In on Myanmar," *Foreign Policy*, July 29, 2014, https://foreignpolicy.com/2014/07/29/former-u-s-officials-cash-in-on-myanmar/.

[2] Loewenstein, Antony, "It's time we stopped drinking the thinktank kool-aid," *The Guardian*, October 18, 2013, https://www.theguardian.com/commentisfree/2013/oct/18/thinktanks-kurt-campbell-lowy-institute.

[3] Hammer, Joshua, "Visiting Myanmar: It's Complicated," *New York Times*, August 3, 2012, https://www.nytimes.com/2012/08/05/travel/visiting-myanmar-its-complicated.html.

[4] Ibid.

[5] Aung Hla Tun and Jared Ferrie, "Foreign investment in Myanmar surges, office rents sizzle," *Reuters*, September 20, 2013, https://www.reuters.com/article/myanmar-investment/foreign-investment-in-myanmar-surges-office-rents-sizzle-idUSL3N0HG0L420130920.

[6] "Unicef Confirms $87,000-a-Month Rent for Rangoon Office," *The Irrawaddy*, May 22, 2014, https://www.irrawaddy.com/news/burma/unicef-confirms-87000-month-rent-rangoon-office.html.

[7] Mahtani, Shibani, "Property Prices Keep the Locks on Myanmar," *Wall Street Journal*, September 17, 2013, https://www.nytimes.com/2012/04/13/business/global/in-myanmar-stumbling-blocks- in-a-booming-economy.html.

[8] Mahtani, Shibani, "An Expat's Adventure Apartment-Hunting in Yangon, Myanmar," *Wall Street Journal*, December 18, 2014, https://blogs.wsj.com/expat/2014/12/18/an-expats-adventure-apartment-hunting-in-yangon-myanmar/.

[9] Shoon Naing and Yimou Lee, "Myanmar to double electricity capacity by 2021 to fill power shortages," *Reuters*, January 31, 2018, https://www.reuters.com/article/myanmar-electricity/myanmar-to-double-electricity-capacity-by-2021-to-fill-power-shortages-idUSL4N1PQ2UM.

[10] Nam, Kee-Yung, Maria Rowena Cham, and Paulo Rodelio Halili, "Power Sector Development in Myanmar," Asian Development Bank, October 2015, https://www.adb.org/sites/default/files/publication/175801/ewp-460.pdf.

[11] Greene, Will, "Myanmar's Promising Experiment With Internet Freedom," *Forbes*, November 5, 2013, https://www.forbes.com/sites/techonomy/2013/11/05/myanmars-promising- experiment-with-internet-freedom/#112dc07cf435.

[12] Heijmans, Philip, "The Unprecedented Explosion of Smartphones in Myanmar," *Bloomberg*, July 10, 2017, https://www.bloomberg.com/news/features/2017-07-10/the-unprecedented-explosion-of-smartphones-in-myanmar.

[13] Belford, Aubrey and Min Zayar Oo, "Insight: Myanmar's aviation industry booms despite grim safety record," *Reuters*, October 21, 2013, https://www.reuters.com/article/us-myanmar-aviation-insight/insight-myanmars- aviation-industry-booms-despite-grim-safety-record-idUSBRE99K11920131021.

[14] "Out with the old as Myanmar restricts used car imports," *Frontier* via *AFP*, January 18, 2017, https://frontiermyanmar.net/en/out-with-the-old-as-myanmar-restricts-used-car-imports.

[15] Steinberg, David, *Burma/Myanmar: What Everyone Needs to Know*, Oxford University Press, 2010, p. 96–97.

[16] "Corruption Perceptions Index 2013," Transparency International, 2013, https://www.transparency.org/cpi2013/results#myAnchor1.

[17] https://www.worldbank.org/en/news/press-release/2013/10/28/for-the-first-time-this-years-doing-business-report-measures-regulations-in-myanmar.

[18] Launched in 2002, the EITI is a multi-stakeholder organization that improves corporate governance and transparency in the extractives industry by requiring signatory countries to disclose information throughout the value chain, including from licensing to extraction, to how revenue makes its way through to government, and to how it contributes to the economy and wider society. More than fifty countries have signed on, and the initiative is supported by well-known companies (including all the major oil and gas companies), civil society organizations (like Transparency International, Global Witness, and Open Society Institute), international banks and multilateral financial institutions, and some of the wealthiest countries, including the US.

[19] Ko Ko Aung and Htin Linn Aung, "Eight companies set to begin operations in Thilawa SEZ," *Myanmar Times*, April 29, 2015, https://www.mmtimes.com/business/14178-eight-companies-set-to-begin-operations-in-thilawa-sez.html.

[20] Bouckley, Ben, "Heineken follows Carlsberg into Burma with $60m brewery build," *Beverage Daily*, May 13, 2013, https://www.beveragedaily.com/Article/2013/05/13/Heineken-follows-Carlsberg-into-Burma-with-60m-brewery-build.

[21] Ferrie, Jared, "Unilever plans second plant in Myanmar with first barely open," *Reuters*, June 6, 2013, https://www.reuters.com/article/myanmar-forum-unilever/unilever-plans-second- plant-in-myanmar-with-first-barely-open-idUSL3N0EI1TM20130606.

[22] "Rowe and Co. Department Store," Yangon Time Machine, https://yangontimemachine.com/2018/03/20/rowe-co-dept-store-aya-bank/.

[23] "Sofaer Building," Gekko Yangon, https://gekkoyangon.com/the-building/.

[24] Interview with John Goyer.

[25] Ibid.

[26] Chan Mya Htwe, "GE eyes expansion in Myanmar energy, healthcare sectors," *Myanmar Times*, October 30, 2019, https://www.mmtimes.com/news/ge-eyes-expansion-myanmar-energy-healthcare-sectors.html.

[27] Petty, Martin, "GE lands first deal as US firms descend on Myanmar," *Reuters*, July 14, 2012, https://www.reuters.com/article/us-usa-myanmar-ge/ge-lands-first-deal-as-us-firms-descend-on-myanmar-idUSBRE86D03Z20120714.

[28] "Pepsi to re-enter Burma with new distribution agreement," BBC, August 10, 2012, https://www.bbc.com/news/business-19204614.

[29] "Burma's Economic Opening (Part 2): Garments Lead Manufacturing, Construction is Booming," US Department of State, Case No. F-2015-12128, Doc No. C05875046, Date: 04/12/2016.

[30] Toppa, Sabrina, "Inside Burma's First Kentucky Fried Chicken," *Vice*, March 29, 2016, https://www.vice.com/en_us/article/53q43b/inside-burmas-first-kentucky-fried-chicken.

[31] "Burma's Economic Opening (Part 3): Surging Tourism and Trade" US Department of State, Case No. F-2015-12128, Doc No. C05875052, Date: 04/12/2016.

[32] Schatz, Joseph J. "White House visit by Burma's Thein Sein a sign of changing times," *Washington Post*, May 17, 2013, https://www.washingtonpost.com/world/asia_pacific/white-house-visit-by-burmas-thein-sein-a-sign-of-changing-times/2013/05/16/e00ba568-bc9c-11e2-97d4-a479289a31f9_story.html.

[33] Weng, Lawi, "Burma Police Say Karen Businessmen Plotted Bombings," *The Irrawaddy*, October 18, 2013, https://www.irrawaddy.com/news/burma/burma-police-say-karen-businessmen-plotted-bombings.html.

[34] "Myanmar man convicted for 2013 hotel blast," *The Straits Times*, July 5, 2015, https://www.straitstimes.com/asia/se-asia/myanmar-man-convicted-for-2013-hotel-blast.

[35] The OECD is an intergovernmental economic organization comprised of thirty-seven member countries to stimulate economic progress, development, and world trade.

[36] Not her real name.

[37] Not his real name.

Chapter 8

[1] "Ko Ni: Gunman gets death penalty in murder of Myanmar lawyer," BBC, February 15, 2019, https://www.bbc.com/news/world-asia-47234999.

[2] San Yamin Aung, "Two Sentenced to Death for Killing NLD Lawyer U Ko Ni," *The Irrawaddy*, February 15, 2019, https://www.irrawaddy.com/news/burma/two-sentenced-death-killing-nld-lawyer-u-ko-ni.html.

[3] Lasseter, Tom, "Gunned Down: The death of a reformer in Myanmar," *Reuters*, December 13, 2018, https://www.reuters.com/investigates/special-report/myanmar-murder-politics/.

[4] Ibid.

[5] Thant Myint-U, *The Hidden History of Burma*, W. W. Norton, 2019, p. 26–27, 35–36.

[6] "II. Historical Background," Human Rights Watch, https://www.hrw.org/reports/2000/burma/burm005-01.htm.

[7] "1978 Repatriation Agreement," Annexure III, July 9, 1978.

[8] "Perilous Plight: Burma's Rohingya Take to the Seas," Human Rights Watch, May 25, 2009, https://www.hrw.org/report/2009/05/26/perilous-plight/burmas-rohingya-take-seas.

[9] "Burma: Policy Review," US Department of State, November 5, 2009, https://2009-2017.state.gov/p/eap/rls/rm/2009/11/131536.htm.

[10] "Correction copy—Burma: USAID/OFDA Follow-up Assessment of Rakhine State," August 22, 2012, US Department of State, Case No. F-2014-22713, Doc No C05740994, Date: 02/23/2017.

[11] "Burma: 'Great concern' over Rakhine," Radio Free Asia, September 10, 2012, https://www.refworld.org/docid/506040548.html.

[12] Interview with Ambassador Joe Yun.

[13] Nyein Nein, "President Yields to Protesters, Says No to OIC Office," *The Irrawaddy*, October 18, 2012, https://www.irrawaddy.com/news/burma/president-yields-to-protesters-says-no-to-oic-office.html.

[14] "Full transcript: My farewell message for my husband was too late, says Aung San Suu Kyi," NDTV, November 15, 2012, https://www.ndtv.com/india-news/full-transcript-my-farewell-message-for-my-husband-was-too-late-says-aung-san-suu-kyi-to-ndtv-504680.

[15] Beech, Hannah, "The Face of Buddhist Terror," *Time*, July 1, 2013, http://content.time.com/time/subscriber/article/0,33009,2146000-1,00.html.

[16] Palatino, Mong, "The Politics of Numerology: Burma's 969 vs. 786 and Malaysia's 505," *The Diplomat*, May 16, 2013, https://thediplomat.com/2013/05/the-politics-of-numerology-burmas-969-vs-786-and-malaysias-505/.

[17] DeHart, Jonathan, "Ashin Wirathu: The Monk Behind Burma's 'Buddhist Terror,'" *The Diplomat*, June 25, 2013, https://thediplomat.com/2013/06/ashin-wirathu-the-monk-behind-burmas-buddhist- terror.

[18] Moe Moe, "Ma Ba Tha Changes Name, Still Officially Illegal," *The Irrawaddy*, September 2018, https://www.irrawaddy.com/news/ma-ba-tha-changes-name-still-officially-illegal.html.

[19] "Myanmar: Scrap 'race and religion laws' that could fuel discrimination and violence," Amnesty International, March 3, 2015, https://www.amnesty.org/en/latest/news/2015/03/myanmar-race-and-religion-laws/.

[20] Nyein Nyein and San Yamin Aung, "Nationalist Monk Criticized After Inflammatory Speech," *The Irrawaddy*, January 19, 2015, https://www.irrawaddy.com/news/burma/nationalist-monk-criticized-inflammatory-speech.html.

[21] Salai Thant Zin and Zarni Mann, "Ma Ba Tha: NLD is the Party of 'Islamists,'" *The Irrawaddy*, September 21, 2015, https://www.irrawaddy.com/election/news/ma-ba-tha-nld-is-the-party-of-islamists.

[22] Lefevre, Amy Sawitta, "Over 2,500 Migrants Still Adrift, UN Says Ahead of SE Asia meeting," *The Irrawaddy*, May 28, 2015, https://www.irrawaddy.com/news/asia/over-2500-migrants-still-adrift-un-says-ahead-of-se-asia-meeting.html.

[23] McLaughlin, Timothy, "'Boat People' Likely Posing as Rohingya for Aid, Says Burma General," *The Irrawaddy*, May 22, 2015, https://www.irrawaddy.com/news/burma/boat-people-likely-posing-as-rohingya-for-aid-says-burma-general.html.

[24] "Myanmar: Kofi Annan to head Commission on Rakhine State," Amnesty International, August 24, 2016, https://www.amnesty.org/en/latest/news/2016/08/kofi-annan-to-head-commission-on-rakhine-state/.

25 "Myanmar: A New Muslim Insurgency in Rakhine State," International Crisis Group, December 15, 2016, https://www.crisisgroup.org/asia/south-east-asia/myanmar/283-myanmar-new-muslim-insurgency-rakhine-state.

26 "Towards a Peaceful, Fair and Prosperous Future for the People of Rakhine: Final Report of the Advisory Commission on Rakhine State," Advisory Commission on Rakhine State, August 2017, http://www.rakhinecommission.org/the-final-report/.

27 British Embassy Rangoon, Southeast Asia Department, "Burmese Citizenship Law, " November 25, 1982, 340/1.

28 "Towards a Peaceful, Fair and Prosperous Future for the People of Rakhine: Final Report of the Advisory Commission on Rakhine State," Advisory Commission on Rakhine State, August 2017, http://www.rakhinecommission.org/the-final-report/.

29 Wa Lone and Shoon Naing, "At least 71 killed in Myanmar as Rohingya insurgents stage major attack," Reuters, August 24, 2017, https://www.reuters.com/article/us-myanmar-rohingya/at-least-71-killed-in-myanmar-as-rohingya-insurgents-stage-major-attack-idUSKCN1B507K.

30 "Report of Independent International Fact-Finding Mission on Myanmar," Office of the High Commission on Human Rights, August 27, 2018, https://www.ohchr.org/EN/HRBodies/HRC/MyanmarFFM/Pages/ReportoftheMyanmarFFM.aspx.

31 Wa Lone, Kyaw She Oo, Simon Lewis, and Antoni Slodkowski, "Massacre in Myanmar," Reuters, February 8, 2018, https://www.reuters.com/investigates/special-report/myanmar-rakhine-events/.

32 "Rohingya crisis: Myanmar to try Reuters journalists who reported on massacre," BBC, July 9, 2018, https://www.bbc.com/news/world-asia-44762425.

33 An interagency meeting at the assistant secretary-level and below to formulate initial policy plans to be run up the chain to the next level of command or to be implemented at the working level. In some administrations, PCCs have been called interagency policy committees (IPCs). Deputy committees are at the deputy secretary-level, and principals committees are at the cabinet level.

34 Interview with policymakers with knowledge of these meetings.

35 Ibid.

36 Ibid.

37 "Acting Assistant Secretary of State for Population, Refugees, and Migration Simon Henshaw Leads a Delegation to Burma and Bangladesh," USAID, October 29, 2017, https://reliefweb.int/report/myanmar/acting-assistant-secretary-state-population-refugees-and-migration-simon-henshaw.

38 "U.S. Diplomatic Team Witnesses Tough Conditions For Rohingya Refugees," NPR, November 10, 2017, https://www.npr.org/2017/11/10/563224309/u-s-diplomatic-team-witnesses-tough-conditions-for-rohingya-refugees.

39 https://www.state.gov/background-briefing-on-secretary-tillersons-trip-to-burma/.

40 https://www.reuters.com/article/us-myanmar-rohingya/tillerson-in-myanmar-calls-for-credible-probe-of-atrocities-idUSKBN1DF0GM.

41 Interview with official familiar with the policy.

[42] Gramer, Robbie, "Tillerson Finally Brands Myanmar Crisis 'Ethnic Cleansing,'" *Foreign Policy*, November 22, 2017, https://foreignpolicy.com/2017/11/22/tillerson-finally-brands-myanmar-crisis-ethnic-cleansing-rohingya-muslims-war-crimes-genocide-state-department-asia-refugees/.

[43] "United States Sanctions Human Rights Abusers and Corrupt Actors Across the Globe," US Department of the Treasury, December 21, 2017, https://home.treasury.gov/news/press-releases/sm0243.

[44] "The Global Magnitsky Human Rights Accountability Act," Congressional Research Service, October 28, 2020, https://crsreports.congress.gov/product/pdf/IF/IF10576.

[45] "Treasury Sanctions Commanders and Units of the Burmese Security Forces for Serious Human Rights Abuses," US Department of the Treasury, August 17, 2018, https://home.treasury.gov/news/press-releases/sm460.

[46] "Treasury Sanctions Individuals for Roles in Atrocities and Other Abuses," US Department of the Treasury, December 10, 2019, https://www.treasury.gov/resource-center/sanctions/OFAC-Enforcement/Pages/20191210.aspx.

[47] "H.Res.1091—Expressing the sense of the House of Representatives that atrocities committed against the Rohingya by the Burmese military and security forces since August 2017 constitute crimes against humanity and genocide and calling on the Government of Burma to release Burmese journalists Wa Lone and Kyaw Soe Oo sentenced to seven years imprisonment after investigating attacks against civilians by the Burmese military and security forces, and for other purposes," House Foreign Affairs Committee, September 27, 2018, https://www.congress.gov/bill/115th-congress/house-resolution/1091/text.

[48] "S.2736—Asia Reassurance Initiative Act of 2018," https://www.congress.gov/bill/115th-congress/senate-bill/2736/text.

[49] Interview with Senator McConnell.

[50] Interview with Paul Grove.

[51] "Statement by Governor Bill Richardson—A Reluctant Resignation from the Advisory Board on Rakhine State," The Richardson Center, January 24, 2018, https://www.richardsondiplomacy.org/news/statement-by-governor-bill-richardson-a-reluctant-resignation-from-the-advisory-board-on-rakhine-state/.

[52] Beech, Hannah and Rick Gladstone, "Citing 'Whitewash,' Bill Richardson Quits Rohingya Post," *New York Times*, January 24, 2018, https://www.nytimes.com/2018/01/24/world/asia/bill-richardson-myanmar-rohingya.html.

[53] "'Bangladesh Is Not My Country:' The Plight of Rohingya Refugees from Myanmar," Human Rights Watch, August 5, 2018, https://www.hrw.org/report/2018/08/05/bangladesh-not-my-country/plight-rohingya-refugees-myanmar.

[54] "Report of the independent international fact-finding mission on Myanmar," Human Rights Council, September 18, 2018, https://www.ohchr.org/Documents/HRBodies/HRCouncil/FFM-Myanmar/A_HRC_39_64.pdf.

[55] Toosi, Nahal, "Leaked Pompeo statement shows debate over 'genocide' label for Myanmar," *Politico*, August 13, 2018, https://www.politico.com/story/2018/08/13/mike-pompeo-state-department-genocide-myanmar-775270.

[56] "Pompeo decries 'abhorrent ethnic cleansing' in Myanmar on anniversary," *Reuters*, August 28, 2018, https://www.reuters.com/article/us-myanmar-rohingya-anniversary-usa/pompeo-decries-abhorrent-ethnic-cleansing-in-myanmar-on-anniversary-idUSKCN1LB06V.

[57] "Documentation of Atrocities in Northern Rakhine State," US Department of State, August 2018, https://www.state.gov/wp-content/uploads/2019/01/Documentation-of-Atrocities-in-Northern-Rakhine-State.pdf.

[58] Interview with Francisco Bencosme.

[59] "Mike Pence tells Aung San Suu Kyi that her country's persecution of Rohingya is inexcusable," CNBC via *Reuters*, November 14, 2018, https://www.cnbc.com/2018/11/14/us-vice-president-mike-pence-meets-with-aung-san-suu-kyi.html.

[60] Disis, Jill and Brian Stelter, "Time Person of the Year: 'The Guardians and the War on Truth,'" CNN, December 11, 2018, https://www.cnn.com/2018/12/11/media/time-person-of-the-year-2018/index.html.

[61] Nakamura, David, "As his aides pressure foreign regimes on press freedoms, Trump focuses on punishing reporters," *The Washington Post*, November 14, 2018, https://www.washingtonpost.com/politics/as-his-aides-pressure-foreign-regimes-on-press-freedoms-trump-focuses-on-punishing-reporters/2018/11/14/9c347cba-e839-11e8-a939-9469f1166f9d_story.html.

[62] Wamsley, Laura, "Trump Administration Sanctions ICC Prosecutor Investigating Alleged US War Crimes," NPR, September 2, 2020, https://www.npr.org/2020/09/02/908896108/trump-administration-sanctions-icc-prosecutor-investigating-alleged-u-s-war-crim.

[63] Safi, Michael, "ICC says it can prosecute Myanmar for alleged Rohingya crimes," *The Guardian*, September 6, 2018, https://www.theguardian.com/world/2018/sep/06/icc-says-it-can-prosecute-myanmar-for-alleged-rohingya-crimes.

[64] Aung San Suu Kyi, " Give Myanmar time to deliver justice on war crimes," *Financial Times*, January 23, 2020, https://www.ft.com/content/dcc9bee6-3d03-11ea-b84f-a62c46f39bc2.

[65] "World Court Rules Against Myanmar on Rohingya," Human Rights Watch, January 23, 2020, https://www.hrw.org/news/2020/01/23/world-court-rules-against-myanmar-rohingya.

[66] "Myanmar submits first report to ICJ on Rohingya measures," *The Straits Times*, May 26, 2020, https://www.straitstimes.com/world/europe/myanmar-submits-first-report-to-icj-on-rohingya-measures.

[67] "Rohingya genocide: Argentine court moves closer to opening case against Myanmar," *The Daily Star*, June 2, 2020, https://www.thedailystar.net/rohingya-crisis/news/rohingya-genocide-argentine-court-moves-closer-opening-case-against-myanmar-1907933.

[68] Hume, Tim, "Curfew imposed after deadly clashes between Buddhist, Muslims in Myanmar," CNN, July 6, 2014, https://www.cnn.com/2014/07/04/world/asia/myanmar-mandalay-religious-violence/index.html.

[69] Thant Myint-U, *The Hidden History of Burma*, W. W. Norton, 2019, p. 206–07.

[70] NGO letter to Mark Zuckerberg, April 5, 2018, https://progressivevoicemyanmar.org/wp-content/uploads/2018/04/Burmese-NGOs-to-Facebook-April-2018.pdf.

[71] McLaughlin, Tim, "How Facebook's Rise Fueled Chaos and Confusion in Myanmar," *Wired*, July 6, 2018, https://www.wired.com/story/how-facebooks-rise-fueled-chaos-and-confusion-in-myanmar/.

[72] "Transcript of Mark Zuckerberg's Senate Hearing," *The Washington Post*, April 10, 2018, https://www.washingtonpost.com/news/the-switch/wp/2018/04/10/transcript-of-mark-zuckerbergs-senate-hearing/.

[73] "Kalar" is a Burmese slur for foreigners, particularly those of Indian or Bangladeshi origin.

[74] Stecklow, Steve, "Inside Facebook's Myanmar operation: Hatebook," *Reuters*, August 15, 2018, https://www.reuters.com/investigates/special-report/myanmar-facebook-hate/.

[75] Slodkowski, Antoni, "Facebook bans Myanmar Army chief, others in unprecedented move," *Reuters*, August 27, 2018, https://www.reuters.com/article/us-myanmar-facebook/facebook-bans-myanmar-army-chief-others-in-unprecedented-move-idUSKCN1LC0R7.

[76] Allison-Hope, Dunstan, "Our Human Rights Impact Assessment of Facebook in Myanmar," BSR, November 5, 2018 https://www.bsr.org/en/our-insights/blog-view/facebook-in-myanmar-human-rights-impact-assessment.

[77] McPherson, Poppy, "Facebook rejects request to release Myanmar officials' data for genocide case," *Reuters*, August 6, 2020, https://www.reuters.com/article/us-myanmar-facebook/facebook-rejects-request-to-release-myanmar-officials-data-for-genocide-case-idUSKCN2521PI.

[78] Interview with Ambassador Derek Mitchell.

[79] Interview with Ambassador Scot Marciel.

[80] Interview with Ben Rhodes.

[81] Interview with Steve Pomper.

[82] Ibid.

[83] Interview with Tom Malinowski.

[84] Interview with Senator Mitch McConnell.

[85] Interview with Secretary Hillary Clinton.

Epilogue

[1] Goodman, Jack. "Myanmar coup: Does the army have evidence of voter fraud?", BBC, February 5, 2021, https://www.bbc.com/news/55918746.

[2] Daily Briefing in Relation to the Military Coup, July 13 2021, Assistance Association for Political Prisoners, https://aappb.org/?p=16487.

[3] Strangio, Sebastian, "Myanmar Shadow Government Pledges Citizenship for Rohingya," *The Diplomat*, June 4, 2021, https://thediplomat.com/2021/06/myanmar-shadow-government-pledges-citizenship-for-rohingya/.

[4] "Chairman's Statement on the ASEAN Leader's Meeting," April 24, 2021, ASEAN Secretariat, https://asean.org/storage/Chairmans-Statement-on-ALM-Five-Point-Consensus-24-April-2021-FINAL-a-1.pdf.

[5] Allard, Tom and Michelle Nichols, "SE Asia states want to drop proposed U.N. call for Myanmar arms embargo," *Reuters*, May 28, 2021.

[6] Tani, Shotaro, "ASEAN meets with China as progress on Myanmar consensus stalls," *Nikkei Asia Review*, June 7, 2021, https://asia.nikkei.com/Spotlight/Myanmar-Coup/ASEAN-meets-with-China-as-progress-on-Myanmar-consensus-stalls.

[7] "Statement by President Joseph R. Biden, Jr. on the Situation in Burma," The White House, February 1, 2021, https://www.whitehouse.gov/briefing-room/statements-releases/2021/02/01/statement-by-president-joseph-r-biden-jr-on-the-situation-in-burma/.

[8] "US Relations With Burma: Bilateral Relations Fact Sheet," US Department of State, June 3, 2021, https://www.state.gov/u-s-relations-with-burma/.

[9] "House passes bill to create commission to investigate Jan. 6 attack on Capitol, but its chances in the Senate are dim." May 19, 2021, https://www.washingtonpost.com/politics/mcconnell-comes-out-against-jan-6-commission-imperiling-its-chances-of-becoming-law/2021/05/19/60de1f52-b8b3-11eb-a5fe-bb49dc89a248_story.html.

[10] Vlamis, Kelsey, "Former Trump Advisor Michael Flynn said the US should have a coup like Myanmar, where the military overthrew the democratically elected government," *Business Insider*, May 30, 2021, https://www.businessinsider.com/michael-flynn-said-us-should-have-a-coup-like-myanmar-2021-5?fbclid=IwAR1-hVsU_T6lq5HhoyD7BuPgLnNQDEChNwYE0pYtY8mZI1MLYSX1H1P4Xx8.

ACKNOWLEDGMENTS

This is the most stressful part of the book because I know I'm going to forget someone. It is certainly the most important part for me as I would not have been able to do this without the help of so many.

Thank you to Dylan Colligan and the Javelin team for taking a risk on an unknown author and a very niche topic to support this book. I appreciated trading Kipling quotes and felt encouraged by your belief in me as a writer. Your work on this has been incredible.

A major thanks to Jon Wilson and Dr. Bill Tsutsui at the Association for Asian Studies for enthusiastically agreeing to publish this book. This could not have happened without AAS. You have been so encouraging, good humored, and helpful throughout the process.

Thank you to Michael Hsieh, my fellow CFR fellow, for giving me the idea to do this.

I also want to give a major thanks to my research assistant. Mo, you are a star in every sense. Your work was critical, timely, and so well done. I could not have done this without you.

Khine also helped enormously, tracking down archived documents, translating key articles, and providing perspective on historical developments. Thank you so much.

Thank you to those who took the time to speak with me at length about the project (for most, reliving bad memories), and providing me with additional resources and direction to help with my research. A huge thanks to Secretary Hillary Clinton, Senator Mitch McConnell, Senator Jim Webb, Congressman Joe Crowley, Congressman Tom Malinowski, Admiral Timothy Keating, Jake Sullivan, Ben Rhodes, Ambassador Joe Yun, Ambassador Shari Villarosa, Ambassador Paula Dobriansky, Danny Russel, Priscilla Clapp, Ambassador Larry Dinger, John Whalen, Ambassador Kelley Currie, Linnea Beatty, Eric Schwartz, David Pressman, Stephen Pomper, Mike Posner, Colin Willett, Samantha Carl-Yoder, Kate Nanavatty, Tom Hawkins, Chris Brose, Don Stewart, Tom Vallely, Paul Grove,

Marta McLellan-Ross, Jennifer Hendrixon-White, Francisco Bencosme, Philippe Reines, Josh Cartin, Brenan Richards, Murray Hiebert, Dr. Michael Green, Bill Wise, David Steinberg, Vikram Nehru, Thant Myint-U, Moe Thuzar, John Goyer, and Rena Pederson.

There were many people who pulled double duty as an interviewee and peer reviewer. A big thank you to Dr. Kurt Campbell, Ambassador Derek Mitchell, Ambassador Scot Marciel, Ambassador Patrick Murphy, Gwen Robinson, and Peter Kucik.

Prior to the coup, I met with now-SAC Foreign Minister Wunna Maung Lwin, Vice Admiral (ret) Soe Thane, and Toe Naing Mann. It was a different time when we spoke and when we worked together. I hope you remember what was achieved and the impact that had on the people of your country. Myanmar is going down a dark path; you can be in a position to change that. I can't say that I'm shocked by what happened, but this is beyond the pale.

I also had friends take what little time they had to read through chapters and provide honest feedback (which shows why we're friends). Thank you so much to Kate Charlet, Kristie Canegallo, Mirentxu Meyer, Sandra Sitar, and Alex Pascal.

I also want to use this space to give my thanks to my research assistants over the years that helped me navigate Myanmar: Nihal Chauhan, Martin House, Aundrea Montano, Jack Myint, Nathan Ives, Jonathan Tai, Zach Harris, Aaron Filous, and Chris Blood. Also a big thanks to Inle's former board of advisors, who encouraged this project and were my biggest cheerleaders: Sandee Pyne, Tom Platts, Bertrand Laurent, and Pete Gaudet.

To my family who I tortured when I was younger by reading stories I wrote during the holidays, thank you. I always wanted to become an author and here I am thanks to your encouragement and pretending to be interested in my stories about haunted houses, killer peaches, and other nonsense. To the Vernile, Murphy, and Carelli clans, thank you for your patience and support. I won't read this book during the holidays.

And finally, to my parents, Bill and Carol, who not only had to read and listen to my stories year round, but put up with a lifetime of crazy ideas and global adventures. Thank you for your love and support, continued patience, taking care of Monty when I travel, and for reading the book and giving me feedback. I'm sure there were a few stories in there you were glad to hear about after the fact. Thank you.

ABOUT THE AUTHOR

Erin Murphy has worked on Asia issues since 2001. She has spent her career in several public and private sector roles, including as an analyst on Asian political, foreign policy, and leadership issues at the Central Intelligence Agency, a director for Indo-Pacific with a development finance agency, leading her boutique advisory firm focused on Myanmar, and as an English teacher with the Japan Exchange and Teaching (JET) Program in Saga ken, Japan.

Erin received her master's degree in Japan Studies and International Economics from Johns Hopkins' School of Advanced International Studies, and her bachelor's degree in International Relations and Spanish from Tufts University. She was also a 2017–2018 Hitachi International Affairs Fellow-Japan with the Council on Foreign Relations.

CPSIA information can be obtained
at www.ICGtesting.com
Printed in the USA
JSHW042312240322
24247JS00001B/28

9 781952 636257